Front cover:
A pre-war audience at the Union Theater, Berlin, 1913.

This Issue:

AUDIENCES and FANS

Edited by John Belton

Editorial office:

Richard Koszarski
American Museum of the Moving Image
36–01 35th Avenue
Astoria, NY 11106
USA

Publishing office:

John Libbey & Company Ltd
13 Smiths Yard
Summerley Street
London SW18 4HR
UK
Telephone: +44 (0)181–947 2777
Fax: +44 (0)181–947 2664

© 1994 John Libbey & Company Ltd

Other offices:

John Libbey Eurotext Ltd,
92120 Montrouge, France
John Libbey – CIC s.r.l.,
00161, Rome, Italy

Printed in Great Britain by
Biddles Ltd, Guildford, UK

FI HI

An International Journal

Volume 6, Number 4, 1994

Film History, Volume 6, pp. 419–421, 1994. Copyright © John Libbey & Company
ISSN: 0892-2160. Printed in Great Britain

Audiences

Who goes to the movies? No one really knows. Several books have been written about the subject, ranging from Leo Handel's *Hollywood Looks at its Audience* (1950) to Bruce Austin's *Current Research in Film: Audiences, Economics, and Law* (1985) and his more recent *Immediate Seating: A Look at Movie Audiences* (1989). For years, George Gallup has polled audiences for the American motion picture industry and the Opinion Research Corporation conducted surveys of domestic audiences for the Motion Picture Association of America.

Handel estimated that an equal number of men and women went to the movies, refuting previous suggestions that the audience was 70 per cent female. His studies also revealed that post-war audiences were affluent and better educated. A 1957 survey by the Opinion Research Corporation concluded that the typical motion picture audience was young – 72 per cent were under the age of 30. Studies in the early 1970s noted that 25 per cent of the moviegoing audience in the USA was black. But statistics tell us very little about what audiences expected when they went to the movies, how they behaved at the movies, or how their moviegoing activity related to their other, leisure time pursuits.

This issue of *Film History* provides a special focus on the audience, while also featuring additional essays on other topics. The section on audiences looks at moviegoers not so much as statistics but as consumers of different varieties of motion picture experiences. The character or nature of this audience – or, more properly, these audiences – is defined by the larger cultural context within which they encounter the cinema. Tom Gunning considers the ways in which various non-film attractions at the 1904 St. Louis Exposition and the physical layout of exhibits at the fair addressed audiences. The spectacle of visual display, dependent in part upon modern technologies such as electricity, looks forward to the ways in which early cinema engages with its audience. Not only do the genres of early cinema derive from the sorts of things on display at the fair but so does the nature of the film experience. Thus the films later featured in the Hale's Tours mimic the sense of movement through attractions at the fair itself in which the audience plays the role of passenger or voyager looking at the sights on the Pike or Midway.

Scott Curtis analyses the effect of motion pictures on the bodies of their audiences – in particular, the reaction of children to early cinema in Germany. More specifically, he looks at the attempts of reformers to control those effects and to regulate the sorts of physical and psychological stimulation provided by the cinema. The cinema's assault on the eye, symbolized by the flicker effect, was deemed responsible for eyestrain, fatigue and neurasthenia, which, in turn, resulted in inattentiveness and lack of concentration on the part of the nation's youth. Through its own film programmes, the reform movement sought to protect – and to control – German children, women, and the masses. Reformers attempted to educate the senses of motion picture audiences, to train their vision, to exercise 'the will against the excessive stimuli of modernity'.

Mary Morley Cohen writes about the audiences at American drive-ins in the post-war period. She finds that drive-in audiences differ dramatically from the homogeneous, general audience associated with classical Hollywood cinema of the pre-war era, marking an important site where the transition to the more heterogeneous audience of today began to make itself more and more apparent. Drive-ins serviced a mass audience but also provided a way in which different groups or units within the mass could establish their own, separate space. The public space of the theatre as a whole gave way to the private space of individual cars. Drive-ins catered to the 'forgotten audience', that is, to the audience ignored by traditional, hardtop theatres. They attracted 'the physically handicapped, invalids, convalescents, the aged, deaf people, expectant mothers, [and] parents with infants and small children'. As Cohen notes, drive-ins were also the first theatres in the South to desegregate, effectively observing racial barriers (blacks and whites remained in separate cars) within a larger, desegregated space.

William Paul provides a portrait of contemporary moviegoing, viewing current production, distribution, and exhibition practices within the larger context of consumer culture. The kinds of films Hollywood produces are seen to be integrally linked to the way in which they are marketed and consumed. The advent of multiplexes and mall cinemas accompanied the mass marketing of a new cinematic commodity – the big-budget exploitation film. Beginning with *Jaws* (1975), which opened in over 500 theatres on its first day of release, audiences have begun to regard movies in much the same way they regard other mass produced products featured at K-Mart and other mall outlets. Audiences no longer search for a theatre that is playing the film they want to see; they merely go to the nearest mall, where it is most likely playing on one of the four, six, eight or ten screens of the local multiplex. Much as consumers count on their mall supermarket to carry their favourite, brand name product, they now expect their neighbourhood multiplex to be featuring that week's biggest hits. If audiences have always been consumers of sorts, today's moviegoers consume films in a mode that is significantly different from that of previous generations. Movies exist as merely one commodity within a sea of others; less and less separates them from their related co/by-products. For audiences of the 1980s and 1990s, they share an increasingly incestuous, commercial life with video games, videotapes, soundtrack albums, and other products.

Audiences go to the movies, in part, to see their favourite movie stars. The public reception of these stars in the media reveals something of how a star's identity is constructed off the screen. Charlene Regester researches the response of the African American press to one of the first black stars, Stepin Fetchit. She documents his attempts to promote himself in the black media as a columnist and his subsequent attempts at damage control, when his off-screen escapades prompted the press to question the negative image he had created for black performers. Regester's extensive use of primary research paints a portrait of Fetchit and his relation to the black press that sheds light on one of the most controversial figures in American film history and that helps to explain Fetchit's decline in popularity.

A star's persona is the product of a negotiation between the star and the public. It combines the star's physical characteristics, the various roles the star has played, publicity surrounding the star, and the audience's perception of the star. Lucy Fischer explores the screen identity of Erich von Stroheim, a star whose principal public persona is that of 'The Man You Love to Hate'. Laura Mulvey's seminal article on 'Visual Pleasure and Narrative Cinema' (1975) viewed the cinema's way of seeing, epitomized by classical Hollywood cinema, as an objectification of patriarchal vision. Mulvey's primary examples of this 'vision' consisted of the work of two directors, Josef von Sternberg and Alfred Hitchcock. Since then, feminists have sought to expand her argument, in part by giving it an historical dimension and by considering audience reactions to performers rather than directors. Thus, in *Babel & Babylon: Spectatorship in American Silent Film*, Miriam Hansen has taken up the figure of Rudolph Valentino and studied his reception among female spectators. Gaylyn Studlar is currently conducting similar research into the reception of other stars of the silent screen, including Douglas Fairbanks, John Barrymore, Valentino and Lon Chaney. Here, Fischer looks at issues of voyeurism, fetishism, rape and romance as they figure in the silent films of actor/-director von Stroheim. She situates his growing popularity as a male villain within the cultural context of feminist social advances during the 1920s, ranging from the advent of the middle class 'New Woman', the influx of women into the workplace, and 'the decline of Victorian sexual mores' to the roles women played during the first World War. Von Stroheim's popularity as a villain emerges as a complex reaction to the increasing empowerment of women during this period, a phenomenon which Fischer effectively explores. The fact that audiences 'loved to hate' von Stroheim epitomizes the dilemma he presents. Von Stroheim was loved because his character articulated the resistance of patriarchy to the advances women were making in the post-war era. He was hated because his resistance needed to be disavowed.

Special thanks to Tom Gunning, Malcolm Keele, Richard Koszarski, Paul Rayton and Steve Wurtzler for their help in the preparation of this issue.✳

John Belton
Associate Editor

**UPCOMING ISSUES/
CALL FOR PAPERS**

Asian Cinema
   edited by Kristin Thompson
   (in press)

**Early Cinema: An Outline
Chronology**
   edited by Deac Rossell
   (in press)

Film Preservation vs Scholarship
   edited by Paolo Cherchi Usai
   (deadline for submissions 1 March 1995)

Auteurism Revisited
   edited by Richard Koszarski
   (deadline for submissions 1 June 1995)

Cinema and Nation
   edited by Mark Langer
   (deadline for submissions
   1 September 1995)

Films of the 1950s
   edited by John Belton
   (deadline for submissions
   1 December 1995)

FILM HISTORY encourage the submission of manuscripts within the overall scope of the journal. These may correspond to the an-nounced themes of future issues above, but may equally be on any topic relevant to film history. It is the journal's policy to publish non-thematic contributions in future issues.

Film History, Volume 6, pp. 422–444, 1994. Copyright © John Libbey & Company
ISSN: 0892-2160. Printed in Great Britain

The world as object lesson: Cinema audiences, visual culture and the St. Louis world's fair, 1904

Tom Gunning

Evanescent monuments and dazzling world pictures: object lessons in modernity

As the study of early cinema broadens, it reveals itself less as a narrow, specialized field than as a dynamic site of cultural interaction. Cinema's first two decades provide a vantage point from which we can examine not only the earliest period of cinema, but also the current modern age that may be drawing to a close (and the possibly 'post-modern' future that awaits us) by allowing us to explore the experience of modernity when it was taking shape. The history of the beginning of cinema previously provided an origin and infancy for the development of the newest art form. Seeing early cinema as a site of complex cultural intersections makes the marking of this origin more problematic and the metaphor of biologic immaturity nearly untenable. As we move away from a naive teleology we must not only abandon conceiving of early cinema as the ur-form of later practices, but also avoid valorizing it as the climax and culmination of a series of inventions and cultural practices understood simply as stages in the invention of 'the movies'. New approaches to early cinema must place it carefully within the visual and

technological culture which marks the turn of the century and must resist situating cinema as the apex of that culture. Cinema emerges, not as a pinnacle, but as an occasionally marginal player upon a contested terrain.

Emmanuelle Toulet in her masterful study of the role cinema played in the 1900 Paris Universal Exposition has summed up film's status at the Exposition as 'both glorious and marginal'[1].

Its glory came from an unprecedented public recognition and a number of highly visual uses of cinema, such as the massive (70' × 53') screen of the Lumière Giant Cinématographe. But among the triumphs of technology and the elaborate attractions of the Fair, film remained a sideshow rather than the main event. As Toulet puts it, 'It was not felt in this

Tom Gunning is a Founding Member of Domitor, author of *D.W. Griffith and the Origins of American Narrative Film: The Early Years at Biograph* (University of Illinois Press), and of numerous articles on early cinema. He teaches Film History in the Department of Radio, Television and Film at Northwestern University. Address correspondence c/o Radio, TV, Film, Annie Mae Swift Hall, Northwestern University, Evanston, IL 60208, USA.

context to be a revolutionary attraction, but formed part of a tradition of technical reproduction and of spectacles of illusion of which it seemed to be the industrial forerunner rather than the perfected replacement'[2].

Initial research into The Louisiana Purchase Exposition held in St. Louis, Missouri in 1904 reveals that four years later and on another continent the role of cinema was, if anything, more marginal. Cinema had no official recognition or high profile presence at the St. Louis Fair. Its main role was that of a backstage technology for other attractions which offered mechanical illusions more vivid and sensational than the rather feeble experience offered by motion pictures alone. And yet a close examination of this fair (particularly in relation to the fair it sought to rival, The Columbian Exposition in Chicago in 1893) highlights the context in which cinema appeared, the celebration of modernity and technology through an emerging visual culture, both official and popular. The new forms of mechanical illusions so popular at the St. Louis Exposition also ultimately influenced the way that cinema was popularly launched – after the Fair – as an attraction in its own right.

The World's Fair provides one of the richest instances of the visual and technological culture that emerged in industrialized countries from the middle of the nineteenth century into the twentieth. Cinema moves within this culture less as its culmination than as a parasite, drawing upon both its forms and its themes but initially remaining relatively neglected, seeming like a pale shadow of richer, more vivid, forms. But as such it has a great deal to tell us about the visual practices which cinema sought to emulate and from which it emerged.

The World Fair of the nineteenth and twentieth century revealed its modernity through a seemingly paradoxical combination of grandeur and transience. The form of all the Universal Expositions was monumental and often explicitly recalled the image of an imperial city, as neo-classical architectural motifs expressed its universal ambitions in terms of world domination. Yet, at the same time, from the Crystal Place (the ur-form of the modern exposition) of 1851 on, these grand structures were also transient, made to be constructed quickly and designed to be impermanent[3]. As Neil Harris has said of the White City of the Columbian Exposition:

Fairgoers had a sense of evanescence even during the height of the exposition. The dream metaphors so easily applied to the White City suggested not only its magical and illusionistic qualities, but also an awareness that it would all soon vanish, that its pomp and beauty were the things of just a day. Everyone knew that the fairgrounds would not be maintained, that Jackson Park would be returned to the South Park system with the exposition palaces taken down after the closing date[4].

The creation of a disposable imperial city, expressing the power of man's dominance over the earth, but designed to be ultimately discarded, is more than an amusing oxymoron, however. The Universal Exhibition was intended as the showplace for a commodity culture based on a worldwide network of production, distribution and consumption which derived its impetus from novelty, a market driven by the desire for the new. This spectacle of an ever renewing and changing universal market place sketched both the form and content of the World Exposition. As Walter Benjamin observed:

> The world exhibitions glorified the exchange values of commodities. They created a framework in which their use value receded into the background. They opened up a phantasmagoria in which people entered in order to be distracted[5].

In this respect the very evanescence of the fair reflected the nature of the commodity it showcased, especially their transient novelty and the rapidity of their worldwide circulation. The World's Fair Exhibitions in which the ability to purchase goods was replaced by their purely optical consumption, imaged the commodity as spectacle[6]. As such it served as one of the great training grounds and laboratories for a new commodity-based visual culture. It raised the act of spectating to a civic duty and a technological art. These spectacles, designed to be both entertaining and educational, served several semiotic functions: they provided an image of the world wide power of capitalism; they transformed a market place into a symbolic landscape that not only celebrated but exemplified modernity; and they formed a spectacle in which commodity provided the entertainment, and the commodity form of entertainment itself was raised to a new technical perfection. As Alan Tractenberg has described the effect of the Columbian Exposition:

> Visitors to the Fair found themselves as *spectators*, witnesses to an unanswerable performance which they had no hand in producing or maintaining. The fair was delivered to them, made available to them. And delivered, moreover, not as an actual place, a real city, but as a frank illusion, a picture of what a city, a real city, might look like. White City represented itself *as a representation*, an admitted sham[7].

The World Exposition, then, served as a site where not only the products of modernity were displayed but the protocols of modern spectating were rehearsed within the context of a new consumer culture. In this site Capitalism, Industrialism and Imperialism stagemanaged a complex interaction among technology, commodity, spectacle and, ultimately, new forms of popular culture, all of which shaped the emergence of cinema.

The World Exposition was designed, then, not simply as a site of display but as a carefully laid out text, whose mode of organization served an educational and ideological function. This effort in planning and arrangement marked the cultural pretension of the Expositions which

Figs. 1a, 1b, 1c. The St. Louis World's Fair as an imperial city of new technology: 1a The Palace of Transportation, 1b The Palace of Electricity, and 1c The Palace of Machinery. From *Louisiana Purchase Exposition* (St. Louis: Official Photographic Co., 1904). [Courtesy of Special Collections, Deering Library, Northwestern University.]

sought not simply to gather the marvels of the world but to sort them into a schema which would demonstrate man's technological progress and the world wide dimensions of modern production. Such organization was already evident at the Crystal Palace where Prince Albert proposed dividing the displays into four categories: Raw Materials; Machinery and Mechanical Inventions; Manufactures; Sculpture and Plastic Arts Generally[8]. Most of the World Expositions followed a similar plan, by which visitors could trace the logic of civilization from the potential of raw natural material (including the display of colonial peoples, or the beauties of nature), through the mechanical means of technological transformation, to the exhibition of final products, accompanied by a display of the Fine Arts as the final form of cultural sublimation.

Planners of World Expositions explicitly designed the events as educational texts. The Exposition was most often compared to an encyclopaedia which not only gathered but also classified and organized the diverse knowledge of a culture. The Director of Exhibitions for the St. Louis Fair, Frederick V. Skiff described his Fair as:

> an encyclopaedia of society ... a classified, compact, indexed compendium available for ready reference − of the achievements and ideas of society in all phases of its activity, extending to the most material as well as the most refined[9].

But this was a peculiarly modern text, one embodied less in verbal signifiers than in visual ones, exemplifying a new conception of education which made use of things themselves rather than conventional signs. By the turn of the century the World Exposition served as the demonstration of the latest theory in education, the 'object lesson', an approach pioneered in schools and museums which depended less on language to convey knowledge than on pictures and, when possible, scrutinized actual objects for the lessons they contained[10]. George Brown Goode of the Smithsonian Institute, who arranged exhibits for a large number of World Expositions (beginning with the 1876 Philadelphia Centennial Exposition), was a strong advocate of the object lesson which he traced back to the Crystal Palace. Goode proclaimed the dictum, 'to see is to

know', and his theory of education valorized visual methods of conveying information:

> The eye is used more and more, the ear less and less, and in the use of the eye, descriptive writing is set aside for pictures, and pictures in their turn are replaced by actual objects. In the schoolroom, the diagram, the blackboard and the object lesson unknown thirty years ago are universally employed[11].

For Goode, an Exposition should be 'an illustrated Encyclopaedia of Civilization'[12]. The term 'object lesson' became the buzz word which justified the World Exposition as an educational experience. (The guide prepared by the Boston and Maine Railroad to lure visitors on their tour of the St. Louis Fair urged them not to miss 'This marvellous object lesson of Twentieth Century Progress'[13]). The object lesson's scientific pretentions could also cloak its ideological role. For instance, Director General Buchanan of the Buffalo Pan-American Exposition of 1901 (the largest American International Fair between the Chicago Exposition and the St. Louis Fair and the first after the United States fulfilled its imperial ambitions by obtaining colonial possessions) used the concept to explain its Philippine exhibition. 'This is the first and best opportunity we have had', he declared, 'to justify, by means of the most available object lesson we can produce, the acquisition of new territory'[14]. In this case the 'objects' included not only raw material and artifacts from the Philippines, but also native peoples.

The object lesson with its direct and visual evidence, seemed to short circuit the act of signification and to bring the things themselves before the spectating public. However, the discourse surrounding the expositions continued to describe the experience as a mediated one, organized as knowledge and demonstration, and experienced as a picture. Director Skiff of the St. Louis Fair described its effect as a 'living picture' (a term which, of course, was also applied to the nascent cinema, although with a somewhat different meaning). The grounds of the Expositions in the United States from Chicago through Buffalo to St. Louis were laid out not only as demonstrations of the relations between nature and technology, but with a strong concern for the unifying effects of the picturesque, with the axial boulevards providing predetermined view points and

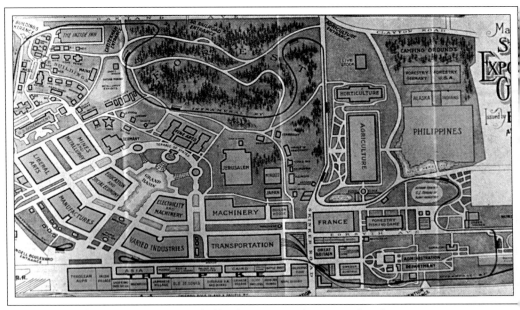

Fig. 2. A map of the St. Louis Fair provided by the Boston and Maine Railroad (1904).
[Courtesy of Special Collections, Deering Library, Northwestern University.]

compositional centres, visual effects underscored by reflecting pools and nocturnal electrical illumination. The Boston and Maine Railroad guide to the St. Louis Fair described it as a 'matchless picture'. The official proclamation of the St. Louis Exposition indicated that visual effects and liveliness could serve educational and ideological purposes when it announced, 'Life, colour, motion and demonstration [will be] the chief feature of all departments[15].

Of course, the total effect of a World Exposition rested on its attempt to produce a *world* picture, an *imago mundi* organized around the demands of commerce and the methods of technology. As the Exposition celebrated the triumphs of technology in the 'annihilation of space and time'[16], the image it offered of the world contained within its bounded grounds sought to provide a miniature compendium of all the world had to offer, brought together at great expense and effort. One official history of the St. Louis Fair described it as the 'latest attempt to bring what is practically the whole world into an enclosure of 1240 acres'[17]. The Fair itself was a world in which space and time had been, if not annihilated, significantly reduced. The World's Fair was a microcosm whose miniaturization not only affirmed the new unity of the globe but also made possible its consumption as a single, though diverse,

spectacle. A trip around the fairgrounds was seen as the substitute for a trip around the world, a compressed and timesaving educational experience. As the Boston and Maine Railroad guide to the St. Louis Fair put it:

> Taking it all altogether, the domestic and foreign exhibits combined represent the concrete expression of modern civilization and impress upon the eye and the mind of the beholder that which would require years of time and thousands of dollars to learn by personal travel[18].

But if the compression and variety of the World Exposition was designed to educate and enrich the spectator, the modernity of this experience is also revealed by its excessive nature. While a profound and extensive understanding of the modern world and man's progress provided the purpose for a visit to the Fair, the initial effect (at least) often produced neither knowledge nor insight, but dazzlement and sensory overload. This response of complete astonishment in the face of the spectacle is vividly expressed by a postcard preserved from the Philadelphia Centennial Exposition in which words give way to sheer play of phonemes:

Dear Mother, Oh. Oh. o-o-o-o-o-o-o-o !!!!!![19]

Observers more articulate (if no more expressive) describe similar experiences. Owen Wister, the author of the novel *The Virginian*, described his entry into the Columbian Exposition: 'before I had walked for two minutes, a bewilderment at the gloriousness of everything seized me ... until my mind was dazzled to a standstill'[20]. And a journalist for *Harpers Weekly* covering the Trans-Mississippi and International Exposition held in Omaha in 1898 reported, 'I have seen men and women stand stupified at the entrance of the Grand Court, blinded as they would have been by a flash of lighting'[21]. Occasionally this dazzlement was literal, caused by the bright white scheme of most American World Expositions from the White City on, a key aspect of the visual experience devised by Fair planners. But more often the dazzlement was the product not of a single visual stimulus but of their accumulation. The special Exposition Number of the magazine *The World's Work* covering the St. Louis Fair warned would-be visitors about the Fair's 'endless variety of things to see – these at first produce an impression of bewilderment'[22]. In fact, Dr. Charles Hughes a professor of neurology at Barnes Medical College in St. Louis urged his colleagues to prevent any patients diagnosed with nervous disorders from visiting the St. Louis Fair for fear its very massiveness might occasion a total collapse[23].

The most poignant account of the overwhelming effect of a World's fair comes from author Hamlin Garland's memoirs of bringing his aged parents from their midwest homestead to visit Chicago's White City. Garland described his mother's reaction as they watched the nightly spectacle of the electrical illumination of the fairgrounds:

Stunned by the majesty of the vision, my mother sat in her chair, visioning it all yet comprehending little of its meanings ... At last utterly overcome she leaned her head against my arm, closed her eyes and said, 'Take me home. I can't stand any more of it'. ... In truth they were surfeited with the alien, sick of the picturesque. Their ears suffered from the clamour of strange sounds as their eyes ached with the clash of unaccustomed color'[24].

The visual effect of the World Exposition, then, teeters between the rational and classifying knowledge of the object lesson and an experience of bewilderment before the intensity of technology and cultural and sensual variety. Rather than visual mastery and understanding, the spectacle could produce an excessive experience which risked leaving no impression at all other than that of the limits of perception and no lesson other than Dorothy Gale's plaintive, 'There's no place like home'.

Dazzlement played an essential role in the visual attraction of the fair, even if its place was rarely explicitly theorized. Most descriptions limit this dazzlement to an initial experience on first beholding the Fair, a suitably awed entry which would then give way to the more rational object lessons of the exhibition. However, the somewhat uneasy relation between dazzlement and knowledge marks the complex experience of this exemplar of modern visuality, as it also marked the contemporary cinema of attractions[25]. A journalist covering the St. Louis Fair described the exposition's educational method in terms of the modern experience of 'shock', proclaiming: 'The fair is a succession of mental shocks, cumulative and educational'[26]. It is no wonder that doctors might advise their neurasthenic patients to avoid this rather jolting educational experience.

Why would shock and dazzlement play a central role in a supposedly educational experience? While the answers for this are undoubtedly multiple (e.g. the political uses of awesome spectacle in a society demanding new disciplines for its work force and building support for military involvement in the struggle for colonial possessions), it is possible to consider the World Exposition as the monumental form of a visual processing of modern life through the medium of spectacular attractions. While the experience of dazzlement came largely from the effect of the fairgrounds itself – their immensity, variety and intense visuality, it also served as the proper framework in which to experience the wonders of new technology which promised bewildering transformations in daily life.

Modern technology played an increasingly central role in World Expositions as they moved towards the twentieth century. Machinery, Electricity and Transportation exhibitions seem to elbow their way into the ideological and spatial centre of the symbolic geography of the fairgrounds. Electricity especially commanded an increasingly central position, gaining its own building at the Columbian Exposition, represented by the massive Electrical

Fig. 3. The Palace of Electricity at night. From *The Greatest of Expositions Completely Illustrated* (St. Louis: Official Photographic Co., 1904).
[Courtesy of Special Collections, Deering Library, Northwestern University.]

Tower at the Buffalo Exposition (meant to 'suggest the triumph of man's achievement' according to the Fair's planners)[28], and occupying the true centre at the St. Louis Exposition. The *World's Work* read the symbolic layout of the St. Louis Fair in a manner that underlined the role of electricity: 'The larger meaning of the whole scheme is this: First Power and Electricity and Machinery. The machines that run and light the Fair mark a new era in the use of electricity. ... For the first time electricity is the dominant power. It may well turn out that the new age of Electricity will date from the Fair. The public will, for the first time, be made aware of the extent to which such a new era has already come'[28].

As had been true of World Fairs from The Chicago Exposition on, the illumination of the fairgrounds by electric light – the spectacle that produced Mrs. Garland's desire to return home – served as the principal demonstration of the power of the new energy. With its transfiguration of night, this scientific demonstration in the form of a spectacle overcame the order of nature. A history of the St. Louis Fair describes the deep audience absorption in the technological spectacle of the first official lighting of the fairgrounds:

In whispering silence the great throng watched the first faint glow of the lights in the various buildings, and as the splendour grew, animated expressions produced a humming noise which gave way to deafening cheers as the full

effect of the glorious spectacle was realized .. The myriads of electric lights, glimmering and twinkling from every nook and corner of the big World s Fair building, transformed the grounds into an enchanted city filled with fairy palaces of light and gold[29].

The new scientific era of electricity was presented as a strange and otherworldly spectacle a fairyland attraction more than an object lesson. O rather its effectiveness as a lesson was founded upon its uncanny power. The *World's Work* described the dazzling sensual effect of entering the electrical exhibit:

As you enter the Palace of Electricity you hea uncanny whirrings and snappings; you se electrical lights of hues and intensities that yo never saw before; strange machines begin t glide or whirr or glow or click. The meaning c all these things is that electricity is put to mor varied uses ... than ever before[30].

But if this description moves effortlessly fror dazzlement to meaning, the cumulative effect of th display of the new uses of electricity could st deliver a shock as these magical technologie caused a revolution in the experience of space, tim and human presence. The St. Louis Fair in particula abounded in technological inventions which cou send messages instantaneously across distance Among these were the 'telautograph' which 'throug

Fig. 4. The De Forest Wireless
Telegraph Tower.
[From *The Greatest of
Expositions Completely
Illustrated.*]

the medium of but two wires connecting distant
points, is used to transmit with exactness a message
written at a sending point to a receiving station. The
person writing the message writes with a stylus much
like an ordinary pencil, and at the distant receiving
station a second stylus accurately reproduces each
stroke of the point in the hand of the sender'[31]. The
telegraphone, an early form of answering machine
using wire recording, was capable of receiving
messages 'during one's absence'[32]. These inventions not only maximized the ability of previous technologies to overcome distance, but could transport
the traditional sign of one's presence, the signature,
or could receive messages during one's absence.
Technology was increasingly problematizing the nature of bodily presence and experience.

The Machinery and Transportation Exhibits at
the St. Louis Fair also pictured a world in which
distance was collapsing. The Louisiana Purchase
Exposition presented the first large automobile display at an American Fair[33], and announced a
grand competition in aeronautic achievement, although due to stiff regulations no aircraft was able to
qualify for a prize[34]. But the dominant technological
marvel at St. Louis was certainly the De Forest Wireless Telegraph Tower. One history of the Fair
claimed that as the Philadelphia Centennial Exposition was remembered for the introduction of the
telephone and the Chicago Exposition had popularized the incandescent light bulb, the St. Louis Fair
would be recalled for the De Forest Tower[35]. The De

Forest Tower stood hundreds of feet high, a major
structure of the Fair. It could transmit radio messages
a distance of 1500 miles, with receiving stations in
Kansas City and Springfield, Illinois.

The encroaching domain of popular amusements: exoticism, technology and virtual voyages

I paid a visit to the Fair, the wondrous sights to
see;
I really felt bewildered, I confess
Such marvellous inventions of ingenuity
'Twas strange to see the different styles of dress.
On the Midway, the Midway, the Midway
Plaisance
Where the naughty girls from Algiers do the
Kouta Kouta dance,
Married men when with their wives give a
longing glance,
At the naughty doings on the Midway Plais-
ance.

– song by W.C. Robey, 1893 (my thanks to
Richard Crangle)

The World Exposition, then, offered object lessons in
technology through the medium of visual spectacle
which presented the astounding transformations of
modern life within a form designed to dazzle as well
as instruct. But it is possible that the enduring legacy
that the World Exposition left modern visual culture

lies precisely in its dazzling effects which may convey as much about the transformations of modern experience as the lessons they were supposed to communicate. Visual spectacle pervades the World Exposition but finds its purest demonstration in what was known as the Concessions Section, the commercial amusement areas of the Fair which progressively invaded American Expositions, looming as their dark shadow or evil twin. It is in this area that the Exposition's links to early cinema are the strongest.

The attitude of the American Expositions towards commercial amusements moved from exclusion through grudging inclusion and containment to a somewhat cautious embrace, charting a change in official culture's relation to popular entertainment as well as a technical transformation of popular culture itself. At the Philadelphia Centennial in 1876 commercial amusements had been excluded. However, outside the perimeter of the fairgrounds an unregulated commercial 'Centennial City' had grown up down Elm Street, thronged with visual entertainments such as dioramas, displays of 'Wild Men of Borneo' and freak shows, as well as food stands. These flimsily constructed attractions drew crowds and caused concerns about fire, safety, crime, and propriety[36]. The Columbian Exposition in Chicago in 1893 decided to include a commercial entertainment section primarily in order to exert control over it. The Midway, originally designed as an area for the overflow of crowds waiting to get into the Fair, became a thoroughfare of commercial attractions leading away from the orderly space of the Exposition proper.

The Exposition's ambivalent attitude toward this form of popular commercial entertainment can be seen through its marginal placement within the Fair's symbolic geography, a rectangular section leading perpendicularly away from the grounds proper. The Exposition's president, Harlow Higginbotham, justified the inclusion of commercial entertainments on the Midway Plaisance through their spatial positioning:

> ... located as it was, separate from the Exposition proper, so that those who were not disposed to visit the sights to be seen there did not have them forced upon them, the Plaisance was a feature from the absence of which the Exposition would have suffered greatly[37].

Like the eccentric placement of this area, Higginbotham's elaborate use of litotes expresses the literal and cultural distance the Exposition maintained from the commercial amusements. The orderly facades of the main exhibition buildings, the neo-classical palaces, the Grand Basin and the Court of Honor, which formed, as Neil Harris puts it 'the visible centre, the ordered heart, the source of control'[38] of the Fair occupied a carefully designed central area from which the Fair radiated outward. The Midway dangled like an appendage pointing toward the dispersal of unordered urban space along the risky pathways of pleasure. The actual attractions offered there often played on the disorientation that visual distortion offered, rather than the centered and orderly space of the main Exposition which guaranteed cultural solidity and enriched personal identity. In contrast the amusement areas of the Exposition's displayed a carnivalesque confusion of identity, as in this description of 'The Temple of Mirth', an attraction from the 'Pike', the St. Louis Exposition s amusement area: 'Mirrors that distort the human body confront the visitor, turn which way he will; looking one direction you seem to weigh 300 pounds, another less than 100; or a tall man is made short and a short man tall'[39].

But like the bodies of water included in nearly all American Expositions which mirrored an etherealized reflection of Fairground buildings, the Midway actually served a vital role in the Chicago Exposition's symbolic geography, providing a bit of shadow for the dazzling White City, a ballast for it. idealism. Fair designer Daniel Burnham saw the trajectory from the central Court of Honor to the Midway as a journey from order to chaos[40]. The Rand McNally Guide to the Columbian Exposition organized the fair according to three distinct architectural styles: the dignified neoclassicism of the buildings around the Grand Basin, the less formal architecture of the outlying buildings and state and foreign pavilions and finally the Midway Plaisance where 'no distinct order is followed, it being instead a most unusual collection of almost every type of architecture known to man – oriental villages, Chinese bazaars, tropical settlements, ice railways, the ponderous Ferris Wheel and reproductions of ancient cities. All these are combined to form the lighter and more fantastic side of the Fair'[41].

The Midway Plaisance served not only as the

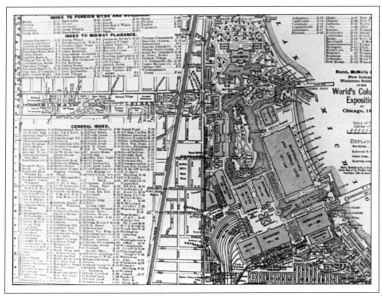

Fig. 5. The Rand McNally
Guide to the Columbian
Exposition.
[From *Grand Illusion: The
World Columbian
Exposition* (Chicago:
Chicago Historical Society,
1993).]

fantastic aspect of the fair, but as a literal counter-image to the civilization emblazoned in the monumental architecture of the official buildings. The strong presence of exotic oriental (Bedouins, Egyptians, Tunisians, Sudanese, Turks, Chinese, Japanese and Javanese) and 'primitive' cultures (American Indians, Dahomeans and South Sea Islanders) related the Midway to the non-white majority of the world, positioned on the outskirts of civilization. The *Chicago Tribune* described a trip along the Midway as an 'opportunity to descend the spiral of evolution', viewing these peoples from the racist perspective that historian Robert Rydell demonstrates was embodied by the Fair's popularization of Darwinian principles[42]. Similarly a character in a contemporary novel describing a trip to the Exposition fitted the Midway back into the object lesson classifications of the larger schema by claiming, 'Midway is just a representation of matter and the great White City is an emblem of Mind'[43].

But if the layout of the symbolic space of the Columbian exposition encouraged a contrast between the White City and the Midway, one could also find a number of similarities between the two areas. The Midway with its exotic international attractions could claim as justifiably as the White City to be a microcosm, an *imago mundi*. And while the Midway (and the other concession sections found in later American Expositions) certainly encouraged mocking racist attitudes in many visitors, it was also possible to invert the implied value structure of the fairground and prefer the colour and cultural diversity of the Midway to the solemn and sterile ideal City Beautiful proposed by the White City. The young Jewish entrepreneur placed in charge of the Midway, Sol Bloom, indicated in his memoirs that this was his own experience, claiming that 'the spiritual intensity of the performance presented by a troupe of Bedouin acrobats exceeded the emotional power of a pre-Renaissance tapestry'[44]. The Midway carried other object lessons for Bloom than the official one:

> I came to realize that a tall skinny chap from Arabia with a talent for swallowing swords expressed a culture which to me was on a higher plane than the one demonstrated by a group of earnest Swiss peasants who passed their day making cheese and milk chocolate … And I could not pretend to deny that God's handiwork seemed more clearly shown in the music of even a second rate band than in all the products of the world's mills and factories here on display[45].

On the other hand, the relation between the Midway and the White City might best be characterized as neither contrast nor identity, but as demystification, as the Midway with its overt commercialism and open courting of visual fascination tended to desublimate the pretensions of the official Exposition and bare its devices. On the Midway, The White City's capitalism and imperialism cloaked in universal idealism became a commercial carnivalesque Tower of Babel, where the powers of visual dazzle provided their own justification.

As if acknowledging the secret identity between the methods of official exhibits and the concession area, eleven years later at the St. Louis Fair the amusement centre, known as the Pike, had switched positions. As the *St. Louis World* noted, for

the first time 'a street of concessions becomes the earliest impression of the visitors'[46]. The official attitude toward the amusements area still expressed reservations about its popularity. An official history of the Fair expressed this tentative acceptance of the Pike as an undeniable, if not entirely felicitous, reality: 'Indeed it must be admitted with however much regret that the side shows probably draw as many people as the main exhibit'[47].

Although the Pike still holds something of a liminal place within the Fair, its position parallel to the entrance seems to proclaim it as an alternative centre to the Exposition, another way to conceive its image of the world. The St. Louis Fair seemed determined to stress the Pike's similarities to the fair rather than its opposition.

And, indeed, the terms used to describe the Pike clearly reflect those used to describe World Expositions generally. The press agent for the Pike described it in terms that recall Goode's description of the Fair as object lesson: 'The Pike is a living colour page of the world, and pictures speak louder than words'[48]. The *St. Louis World* declared in a headline 'To See The Pike Is to See the Entire World'[49], a sentiment seconded by the Boston and Maine Railroad Guide which claimed, 'a journey up and down the 'the Pike' practically amounts to a tour of the world'[50]. Similarly *Jackson's Famous Photographs of the St. Louis Exposition and 'the Pike'* saw the Pike as the most international area of the Fair, describing it as 'the most cosmopolitan thoroughfare in the world. Denizens from all quarters of the globe come and go, attracting the visitor's attention by their quaint customs, peculiar speech and strange garb'[51].

Once again this world picture consisted primarily of exotic native peoples on display, including attractions inhabited by natives of Persia, Ceylon, Burma, Hindustan, Japan, Palestine, Turkey; Spanish gypsies, Hairy Ainus from Japan, Patagonian Indians,

Fig. 6. Two views of 'the Pike'.
Fig. 6a (upper). Looking down the Pike, from *The Greatest of Expositions Completely Illustrated*. Fig. 6b (lower). The Pike, looking east, from *Louisiana Purchase Exposition*.

African pygmies, Kwakiutl and Zuni Native Americans (as well as visits by such great war chiefs as Geronimo, Chief Joseph and Quantah Parker). This assembly of non-western peoples was climaxed by the largest 'anthropological' exhibit, displaying the inhabitants of the United States recent colonial possession, the Philippines, including a variety of cultural groups: Visayans, Moros, Bagobos, Negritos and Igorots.

As the Pike's image of the world was not only more colourful and exotic than the non-commercial exhibits, it was also less unified and thrived on the unexpected juxtapositions that the bringing together of diverse attractions allowed. A guide to the Fair published by the Pennsylvania Railroad emphasized the contrasts along the Pike: 'The spectacular sights range from The Creation to The Hereafter. The Cliffdwellers are neighbours to the Southsea Islanders and Old St. Louis to Cairo'[52]. A feature in the Boston and Maine guide entitled 'Odd Things on the Pike' listed in intentionally random order attractions to be found along the amusement thoroughfare, clearly delighting in their incongruity. These included:

A flood of fifty thousand gallons of water every minute ...
Man who carves images on a single grain of rice ...
Relics from Golden temple in Rangoon ...
Zuni Indians dance the mask, flute and snake dance
Eleven sections of arcaded bazaars of Stamboul ...
Devil dancers – the strange medicine men of Burmah ...
Gypsy lane of Barcelona with genuine Romanys, ...
Geishas dance sing and serve tea in native kiosk.
World recreated in shell 150 feet in diameter; 115 feet high ...
Transparent mirrors; you dissolve into a masterpiece ...
Café Chantants the elixir of Parisian fever ...
Burmese village with houses of straw and strange people.
The Maine will be blown up in Havana harbour ...
Church of Holy Sepulchre, size of original in Jerusalem ...
Whole streets transplanted from Asakusa in tight Japan.
Flight over the ocean by airship ...
Discovery of the North Pole in twenty minutes...[53]

While the tone of this list certainly situates the visitor as a privileged western voyeur of the world of 'strange' events and customs which are often displayed in a condescending and exploitative manner, nonetheless it is in the polyglot chaos of the Pike that a more diverse *imago mundi* was available.

The range of attractions along the Pike was enormous, and its sense of variety and contrast did not come exclusively from the display of exotic culture. In fact the Pike served as a compendium of popular culture as much as the Exposition proper served as an encyclopaedia of official culture. The Boston and Maine guide to the St. Louis Fair compared the variety of attractions offered along the Pike to a vaudeville show[54]. Most of the exotic peoples were, in fact, performers, offering dances, acrobatic feats or demonstrations of craftsmanship for the curious crowds, and were joined by performers from Europe and the United States as well. But beyond its actual vaudeville component, the Pike offered a range of visual entertainments consisting of attractions which entrepreneurs felt could separate gawkers from their coins. This range of attractions directly corresponds to the subjects of early cinema.

Running down the list of Pike attractions, a historian of early cinema becomes overcome with *déjà vu*. The attractions directly parallel the genres of early film, both staged films and actualities. Clearly the exotic locales reproduced on the Pike court the same curiosity about foreign lands that early travel films do. These exhibits consisted not only of native performers and crafts, but also of recreations of their environment. The Pike included recreations of Philippine villages, the streets of Cairo, the Taj Mahal, Constantinople, an Irish village, the streets of Seville, The Holy City of Jerusalem, St. Louis in 1804, and an astonishingly realistic mock up of the Tyrolean Alps. Railway journeys, so important to the early travel genre, also abounded on the Pike, from the three mile long Scenic Railway, to a forty-five minute trip over the Trans-Siberian Railway. Historic and recent events that served as the subjects of films were re-enacted as well, with the Galveston Flood recurring on the hour; major battles of the Boer War restaged in an arena with several of the original participants; the Battle of Santiago and the explosion of the Battleship Maine were enacted with a 22-foot model battleship in a huge tank at the Naval Exhibit; and a series of battles were presented in cycloramas in Battle Abbey (including Philippoteaux's famous circular panorama of Gettysburg).

A dramatic re-enactment of the dangers in the life of American firemen was staged in George C. Hale's spectacle 'A Midnight Fire in Greater New York'. Visual tricks were offered in the Temple of Mirth, with a labyrinth of distorting mirrors and transformation effects. The Tyrolean Alps even offered a recreation of Oberamergau Passion Play 'seen and approved by 1000s of ministers'[55]. Of course, this extraordinary parallel in themes between early films and the Pike attractions does not indicate imitation on the part of the Fairway amusements, but the contrary. These were the range of visual amusements that early cinema sought to emulate and reproduce.

One of the contrasts between the Pike and the Chicago Midway about a decade before lies in the enormous increase in mechanical attractions which vied with the exotic exhibitions as the main attractions of the amusement section. The director of the St. Louis Fair stressed that the Pike amusements embodied the sort of technological progress that the main exhibits celebrated, claiming that 'advances in the theory of presenting such attractions made the scientific mechanical and spectacular features far superior to those of preceeding expositions'[56]. Entertaining scientific attractions offered a common ground between the amusement sections and the Exposition proper. The placement of a scientific demonstration in one area or the other seems often arbitrary (at the Columbian Exposition, for instance, the Edison kinetoscope was slated to appear in the Electricity Building while Muybridge's zoopraxoscope demonstrating the laws of animal locomotion was placed on the Midway). Many of the Pike's attractions demonstrated scientific technology, such as the pavilion of baby incubators in which spectators could observe premature infants in their transparent warmers, 'a unique testimony of the power of modern science'[57].

Technology in these mechanical attractions

played a complex role similar to that of new technological devices appearing during these same decades in the magical theatre of illusions of Maskelyne or Méliès or in the fascination offered by the first projections of cinema[58]. On the one hand they sought a vivid sensual intensity and verisimilitude that moved the attractions toward an illusion of reality. On the other hand, this effect of verisimilitude also displayed a triumph of technology. Such masterful illusions demonstrated an openly acknowledged stagecraft rather than seamlessly creating a naturalistic illusion aimed at an effect of realism. Thus mechanical attractions delivered to their spectators not simply a simulacrum of real events, but marvels of technology. The criteria of realism served more as a measure of the effectivity of the technology rather than simply as the final aim of the representation.

The elaborate technical effects of two attractions, The Galveston Flood and Hale's Midnight Fire, show how verisimilitude and a *tour de force* of 'scientific, mechanical and spectacular features' both supplied spectators with astonishment and satisfaction:

> The Galveston Flood was a living picture of remarkable effects obtained by the use of plastic art combined with mechanics and electricity. The immediate foreground was real and the still life was full size. Real grass, real trees, fences and houses appeared around the spectator. As the picture receded, objects gradually flattened out, yet with their angles so constructed that each retained its true perspective. They became flatter and flatter until they merged into silhouettes. In the view of Galveston the foreground was real water carried back into the picture, so that practically all the water lapping the beach and stretching away into the middle distance was real. A new invention kept the water in continual motion. The illusion was carried out all the way to the horizon so that the eye could follow a wave as it flowed from under the feet of the spectator far away into the picture, until its individuality was lost in the wide ocean distance[59].

Firefighting was something new under the guise of entertainment. A corps of wonderfully trained firemen who were almost circus performers in

Fig. 7. The Galveston Flood,
from *The Greatest of
Expositions Completely
Illustrated.*

agility and acrobatic skill kept the thrills working for nearly an hour. Seated in a vast auditorium the audience watched the alarm turned in
to a modern fire station five hundred feet from
the grandstand. The firemen were seen to leave
their beds, slide down the brass poles, hitch the
horses and respond by dashing through a moving panorama of the New York streets. Just in
front of the audience a six storey block was
ablaze. People appeared at the windows
screaming for help. As the firemen rescued the
unfortunates by aerial hooks, the whole scene
was enveloped in a fiery glare. No fire was
used but the effect was produced by electricity,
steam, stained glass, celluloid, silk and other
mechanical appliances. The effect was startling
especially as the building collapsed after the
victims were removed[60].

The 'special effects' of these mechanical illusions did more than reproduce reality. Like the spectacular electrical effects witnessed as visitors entered
the Palace of Electricity, they demonstrated in a
stunning manner the possibilities of the new technology. It is no wonder that projected motion pictures
on a flat screen might seem a rather tepid attraction
next to these extravanganzas, a poor man's illusion.
At the same time such illusions undoubtedly used

projections and possibly some form of motion pictures as part of their backstage technology.

Perhaps the most seamless blending of technology and entertainment on the Pike came with its rich
offering of technological 'virtual' voyages[61]. Some
of these imaginary modes of world travel likely
employed cinematic devices, but even those which
were pre-cinematic in technology had a determinant
influence on the way cinema became popularized
as an attraction after the Fair. These virtual voyages
also literalize the basic trope of the World Exposition itself, the world tour compressed in space and
time and rendered effortless for the tourist, in which
the role of tourist and spectator are truly collapsed.

The effortless spectator voyage had played a
major role in the rise of visual entertainments earlier
in the century (especially the Diorama and panorama which frequently portrayed distant tourist sites).
It motivated not only the World Exposition as a
whole, but also the recreation of foreign lands which
thronged the Midway and the Pike. But the technological virtual spectator voyage forms a particular
sub-genre of great consequence for early cinema.
The origin of the spectator voyage comes as well
from transformations within tourist travel itself. Wolfgang Schivelbusch describes the growing comfort of
train travel in which the upholstered seat insulated
the traveller from the discomforts of the journey, as
the railroad itself had delivered them from the physi-

Fig. 8. New York to the
North Pole from *The
Greatest of Expositions
Completely Illustrated.*

cal effort of travel[62]. Schivelbusch locates a new visual perception arising with train travel, 'panoramic perception' in which 'the traveller sees the objects, landscapes, etc. *through* the apparatus that moves him through the world'. The ideal of a 'frictionless'[63] voyage around the world had been pushed to the point of parody in 1873 by Jules Verne in his *Around the World in Eighty Days* whose impassive hero Phileas Fogg was described as 'not travelling, but only describing a circumference ... he was a solid body traversing an orbit around the terrestrial globe, according to the laws of rational mechanics'[64].

The virtual technological voyages offered along the Pike reproduced the Exposition's dominant trope of the collapse of space, time and distance. One attraction was called 'New York to the North Pole in Twenty Minutes' and publicity emphasized that the trip over the the entire route of the Trans-Siberian railway took only forty-five minutes. But just as important as diminished space and time was the seduction of effortless travel, consumed primarily through the eyes. The movement through space required no effort on the part of the spectator who sat impassively transported, like Phileas Fogg, by the power of technology. The descriptions of these attractions stress repeatedly that the passive visitor is 'carried' or 'taken'. Even the announcements of the Edisonia (a concession area holding hundreds of coin-operated vending machines and amusements)

hawked its travel attractions as effortless (though not gratuitous) visual voyages. Describing what most likely are peepshow devices of the kinetoscope or mutoscope sort, the Edisonia's publicity invited visitors to:

> ... enter the world of travel, imagine yourself at the top of Telegraph Hill in San Francisco, looking through the Golden Gate upon the broad expanse of water where the light of day reflects its departing rays of brilliant splendour upon the placid Pacific, until you are reminded that another coin will take you to the snow clad peaks of the Alps, the boulevards of fascinating Paris, or among the palm trees of the tropics[65]

The voyage attractions stressed magical transformations of landscape with their relatively short travel time as well as providing simulacra of new technological modes of travel (including ones not yet invented, introducing an utopian aspect to their travel illusions). 'New York to the North Pole' took place on an elaborate and detailed mock up of an Atlantic steamer (two hundred by fifty feet) which moved from panoramas of the teeming metropolis to arctic landscapes, with 'great fields of snow and ice and huge icebergs 100s of feet high'[66], accompanied by 'an electrical effect giving a startling illustration of the Northern Aurora'[67]. 'Over and Under the Sea' provided 'a mechanical and electrical illusion which supported the sensation of a trip in a submarine'[68] to Paris with 'an aerial return via London, New York and Washington'[69] during which the 'visitor first entered an airship and seemingly sailed away' and later landed on the Eiffel Tower. 'This illusion was reported to 'have a strong suggestion of reality'[70], and may have involved some use of motion pictures (although other devices may be just as likely).

Although the St. Louis Fair might be considered the climax of these entertainments (which had remained in a rudimentary stage of development at the Chicago Exposition), they had been developing steadily in the eleven years between fairs. The Paris Exposition had probably served as their first great triumph. There 21 of the 33 major attractions involved some illusion of a voyage, including the Mareorama sea voyage so well described by Toulet, a Trans-Siberian panorama (which was most probably the same one exhibited on the Pike) and Grimoin-Sansom's ill-fated Cineorama which planned to use motion pictures to convey the illusion of a balloon voyage[71]. A number of such attractions also appeared at the smaller intermediary fairs such as the Scenic Railway at the 1898 Omaha Trans-Mississippi Exposition, or the Pan-American Exposition in Buffalo in 1901, which included a voyage to the realms of Satan in 'Darkness and Dawn Underworld' and an attraction (which also seems to have been displayed at the Paris Exposition) which offered a Trip to the Moon. The extra-terrestrial nature of this last attraction prompted one journalist to comment, 'There you see, not satisfied with exhausting the earth [showmen] have already begun on the universe. Behold the world is a sucked orange'[72].

In addition, between the two fairs the United States had experienced a rapid proliferation of new amusement parks located on the outskirts of large urban areas, such as Coney Island or Riverside Park near Chicago. As John F. Kasson has shown, the development of these parks was directly indebted to the popularity of the Midway at the Chicago Exposition[73]. The new amusement parks were in many respects patterned on the Midway, both in their layout and in the attractions they offered, which had been either imported directly from Chicago or were modelled on its most popular offerings. Mechanical illusions such as The Trip to the Moon, the Galveston Flood, or Twenty Thousand Leagues Under the Sea proliferated at these amusement centres, particularly

at Luna Park which opened in 1903, just before the St. Louis Exposition and at Dreamland which opened a year later. As Kasson demonstrates, these amusement parks both drew upon the World Expositions and inverted their values, as had the Midway. While amusement park architecture adopted the technological possibilities of visual spectacle premiered at the Chicago Exposition – such as the elaborate use of electric light[74] – it used them to its own ends. As Kasson puts it, contrasting Luna Park and the Chicago Exposition:

> In its neoclassical formalism, the Exposition represented an architecture of responsibility; here, however, was an architecture of pleasure. The Columbian Exposition preached discipline; Luna Park invited release. Constructed out of the same impermanent plaster materials as the White City, Luna's buildings achieved monumentality without oppressiveness, grandeur without solemnity[75].

The rise of these amusement parks and their overtly technological attractions may have affected the change in attitude (and position within the fairground) of the concessions area at the St. Louis Fair.

As the journalist at the Pan-American Exposition quoted earlier noted, the technological virtual journey illusion, untrammelled by the confines of realistic representation or actual geography, could easily slide into fantastic voyages. A number of travel attractions on the Pike left the real world behind entirely and launched spectators into the realms of metaphysics. 'The Hereafter' offered a voyage in which, 'the visitor was taken through the underground domain of Satan and thence through Daphne's Grove to the Gates of Paradise'[76]. 'Creation', one of the most popular attractions on the Pike, was even more ambitious in its metaphysical itinerary, taking visitors back through millenia. This attraction combined a boat ride in which time travel was experienced as another virtual voyage. This upstream trip against the flow of time deposited its passengers at the moment of creation itself, followed by a display of demiurgic power made palpable through a visual spectacle combining all the devices of visual transformation available in the contemporary technology of manipulated light and stage craft.

Fig. 9. Creation, from *The Greatest of Expositions Completely Illustrated.*

The visitor glided backwards through twenty centuries in a grotesque craft along a water canal encircling the dome for a distance of one thousand feet. A moving panorama of the centuries in plastic and real life was passed en route to the master mechanical denouement. At the first century the passengers left the boats and entered a temple of that period. The walls of the temple melted away and a feeling of vast void surrounded the Piker. It was chaos. The spectator was in the midst of the dome and completely enveloped in a cloud wrack. A loud voice uttered the words: 'The Lord made the heaven and earth in six days'. Intense darkness surrounded the waiting audience. The voice continued the story of creation. 'Let there be light' was obeyed as the soft glow of dawn pervaded the hollow dome. It increased until the glare of the day revealed the void of clouds about the spectators. The light faded into the evening of the sixth day. 'Let there be a firmament', proclaimed the voice. It appeared, separating from the waters. 'Let the dry land appear'. The limitless ocean rolled back revealing the land. Trees, flowers and shrubs gradually resolved themselves into the Garden of Eden. 'And the Lord made two great lights'. The sun and moon came forth making a day and night effect. 'Let the waters bring forth living creatures'. Fantastic shapes moved through the

waters while the birds were seen and heard overhead. Reptiles and beasts of long ago crept and walked through the forest. 'Let us make man after our image', said the voice. A spectral form of Adam seen approaching from the invisible reached the foreground in full light. Adam and Eve discovered one another and the story of the creation was complete[77].

The mode of representation here is syncretistic, seemingly using a wide series of means, ranging from projected images to full three-dimensional actors. Motion pictures may have played some role in these illusions, but only as one component in a carefully managed spectacle. 'Creation' outlasted the St. Louis Fair and became the central attraction of the last of the great Coney Island amusement parks, Dreamland, where its massive nude female flanked the entranceway to the park[78].

Coda: the world's exposition and the film spectator

The place of motion pictures at the St. Louis Exposition seems to have been resolutely secondary. Animated pictures were no longer sufficiently novel to be accorded attention as an important scientific innovation (if they ever truly had that status). Beyond their likely role as backstage devices for the more spectacular illusions, films were also used in the educational exhibits outside the Pike as illustrative material. The reproduction of the Holy City of Jerusalem, for instance, included within Solomon's Temple 'dissolving views, moving picture and lectures illustrated the various customs of the Israelites'[79]. The American Biograph and Mutoscope company produced several series of such illustrative films which were shown in at least two venues, public and private, at the St. Louis Fair.

First, Biograph films were shown daily in the United States Government Exhibits. The Department of the Navy supplemented their displays with film showings. The Department of the Interior showed a series of films of American Indians and of views of Yellowstone and Yosemite National Parks[80]. These films showed both Native American rituals (such as Kachina dances by Pueblo Indians from Walpi and Orabi, Arizona, and Crow Indian dances on a Government reservation), Navaho women weaving baskets, and Native Americans engaging in a variety of sports (wrestling, basket ball, racing, tug of war). Scenes on reservations and at Government Indian Schools contrasted with the ritual dance films by showing 'well educated and civilized Indians'[81] undertaking such tasks as performing a firedrill, taking classes in carpentry, and raking hay. These films of Native Americans conformed to the central enthographic view of the Exposition, displaying the exotic while simultaneously celebrating the civilizing influence of White domination. The Interior Department's tourist views offered vicarious tours of the recently established National Parks in Yellowstone and Yosemite, including views of famous sights (e.g. Bridal Veil Falls and Artist's Point at Yosemite; Fountain Geyser, Old Faithful and the Mammoth Paint Pots at Yellowstone), and included films in colour (most likely tinted or stencil coloured)[82]. The United States Post Office Exhibition also used motion pictures to display contemporary mail handling techniques. The device used here seems to have been a mutoscope machine outfitted for several viewers:

> ... a half dozen or more biographs were placed in the Post-office Division, and fitted with several stereoscopic eye-pieces so that four or five persons might use one instrument at the same time. These were kept constantly running and being free to visitors were enthusiastically patronized. The motion pictures showed operations in every department of the postal service, collecting, delivering, assorting, distributing and depositing[83].

Besides the Government sponsored films, Biograph motion pictures also displayed the achievements of private enterprise in some of the earliest film 'industrials'. The extraordinary series of Biograph films shot by Billy Bitzer in Westinghouse factories in Pennsylvania in April and May of 1904 were shown as part of the Westinghouse Exhibit in the Hall of Machinery[84]. The auditorium in which these films were shown had a seating capacity of 350 and the three daily film shows were 'nearly always given to standing room only audiences'. The exterior of the theatre was described as resembling 'a fairy land, contrasting strangely with the cold commonplaces of the surrounding machinery exhibits'[85]. An official history of the Fair described even these industrial films as virtual voyages:

> The novelty of sitting in a comfortable seat and literally taking a stroll through the different Westinghouse plants and seeing them in full operation was one that will be remembered with pleasure as long as memory lasts with those who saw the highest development of the photographer's art[86].

There are undoubtedly other examples of films shown within exhibits. From sources not directly publicizing the Fair there is evidence that foreign motion picture showmen presented films either at the Fair or somewhere in St. Louis at the same time. Oskar Messter apparently showed examples of his talking films at the Louisiana Purchase Exposition[87], although I have not discovered in what context. The early travelling exhibitor from Quebec, the vicomte Henry d'Hauterives, indicated in his publicity for showings in Quebec in November, 1904, that he had 'arrived directly from St. Louis where he had spent twenty weeks at the Exposition'[88]. I have not found him listed as a concessionaire, however. The famous Hale's Tours, the novel form of film exhibition which had an enormous impact on future film exhibition, is often claimed to have premiered at the St. Louis Fair, but my research does not indicate that it actually appeared at the Exposition.

Hale's Tours is worth discussing in some detail, since it clearly shows the strong relation early film shows maintained with the tradition of virtual voyages so well displayed on the Pike. This novel attraction reveals early film's vital relation to the visual culture pioneered at the World's Fairs. To an important degree, Hale's Tours represents an attempt to bring these virtual voyages to a broader section of the population, making them geographically more accessible and economically more affordable. This attraction housed its audience in a screening room designed to resemble a railway car. Motion pictures shot from the front of trains and trolleys were projected at the front of this railway mock-up. Combined with a lecturer conductor and the noise of click-clacking wheels, the exhibition produced the sensation of train travel[89].

The relation of the Hale's Tours to the St. Louis Exposition is a vexed issue, much like the presence or absence of Edison's kinetoscope at the Columbian Exposition. No guide book or account of the Pike that I have read mentions a Hale's Tours attraction and it is not listed in the official list of 40 concessionaires[90]. Although he concedes this lack of evidence, Raymond Fielding in his carefully researched pioneering article on Hale's Tours maintains that the attraction did premiere at the 1904 Fair, basing himself on Terry Ramsaye and on the childhood memories of two witnesses[91]. Part of the confusion may be due to the fact that the description Fielding gives of Hale's original patent (which involved a mobile train car open at the side running on a track through an underground tunnel on which projected images were shown) could well correspond to other Pike attractions, such as the Scenic Railway. Or memories recalled from childhood might confuse the elaborate moving panoramas of the Trans-Siberian Railway (which involved five different moving canvases at different distances from the observation car and running at different rates of speed)[92] with projected motion pictures. Barring further evidence, I doubt that Hale's Tours premiered at the St. Louis Fair, at least under that name or in its later form.

However, the relation between Hale's Tours and the St. Louis Fair remains significant. The entrepreneur from whom it takes its name was the ex-fire-chief of Kansas City, George C. Hale whose exhibition of firefighting did provide one of the chief attractions on the Pike. Although the patent application for the attraction was filed in March 1904[93] (shortly before the opening of the St. Louis Fair), it

seems likely that his experience on the Pike where so many attractions offered virtual voyages must have convinced Hale of the viability of his motion picture attraction. The first Hale's Tours (other than the putative opening at the Fair) opened at the Electric Park amusement centre in Hale's native Kansas City in May of 1905[94]. For the next three years Hale's Tours spread through the United States, opening a new venue for motion pictures. Besides providing an opportunity for many investors who later became prominent in the nickelodeon era, Hale's Tours liberated motion pictures from the vaudeville theatre, providing the first large-scale network of exhibition outlets which offered motion pictures as their main attraction. Hale's Tours served as the shock troops for the imminent nickelodeon invasion which transformed motion pictures from a mechanical invention whose novelty was fading (and an amusement whose status had become increasingly marginal) to the harbinger of a technical and social revolution in international show business and the creation of a mass audience.

Motion pictures conveying the experience of travel through a camera mounted on some means of transportation are as old as Promio's cinematographic gondola trip down the Venetian Grand Canal in 1896, and exhibition situations which imitated means of transportation certainly predate Hale's Tours. Yet the significance of this new form of cinematic entertainment as a successful commercial enterprise cannot be denied. Located initially in amusement parks, they undoubtedly provided a low-budget version of the elaborate virtual voyages offered at World Expositions and large scale amusement parks. Less overwhelming than these attractions and of a stature probably beneath the notice of such prestigious events as World Fairs, their nickel or dime admission was also less than the 50 cents charged for 'Creation'. Their initial popularity undoubtedly derived not only from the fact that they offered a substitute for expensive world tours, but also for the more elaborate mixed media technological illusions familiar from World Expositions and their publicity.

But the Hale's Tours also borrowed from these forms a newly-defined spectator accustomed to virtual illusions of travel. What Charles Musser calls the 'viewer-as-passenger' convention[95] drew its inspiration from a newly formulated modern visual culture that had been exemplified by, and to a large degree created for, the World Expositions. This essay has attempted to outline the key aspects of this new visual culture: a new faith in the power of visual knowledge; a conception of the world itself as a consumable picture, imaged through the collapse of space and time; and an aggressive visual address aimed at dazzling the viewer with a new control over the gaze. The World Exposition embodied and proselytized this new visual culture, serving as a new form of visual presentation whose dialectic teetered between object lesson and sensual dazzlement, whose 'first goal' was (as Catholic journalist Maurice Talmeyr observed of the Paris Exposition) 'to attract, to hold'[96]. The complex methods for attracting and holding attention formed the basis of a visual culture from which the cinema issued. After its initial run as a vaudeville novelty, it was in the form of Hale's Tours, that film emerged independently to wedge a first fragile beachhead in the competitive world of popular entertainments. Leaving this beachhead behind, the cinema then moved into the urban landscape, launching an invasion destined to radically transform modern culture.

The difference in price between a fairground attraction like 'Creation' and the Hale's Tours or the nickelodeon must also indicate a change in the economic status of the projected audience for each amusement. Clearly the movement of motion pictures out of the vaudeville houses and the extension of virtual voyages to a larger public reflects a broadening of the class address of the visual culture nurtured by the World Expositions[97]. While the localities in which Expositions were given offered special days in which working class patrons could attend at reduced admissions, they met with mixed success[98]. The admission prices for the World Expositions, their cultural pretentions and locations signalled them as middle or upper class events. As Alan Tractenberg indicates about the Columbian Exposition, they were largely celebrations of:

> ... the victory of élites in business, politics and culture over dissident but divided voices of labour, farmers, immigrants, blacks and women. Elite culture installed itself as the official doctrine of the Court, claiming dominion over the 'low' confined to the outskirts of the Midway[99].

However, as we have seen, the exile of low culture had become problematic by 1904 and the carefully defined differences between low and high culture were in peril of confusion in the polyglot carnival of the Pike. The inner consanguinity of official exhibits and the Pike (which flowed beneath their still maintained spatial segregation) sprang from their common exemplification of a visual culture, offering an object lesson instructing viewers about new technology and the shrinking distances of exotic lands, paradoxically brought closer by the impulses of imperialism. As nineteenth century socialists had recognized a powerful lesson of internationalism running parallel with the Crystal Palace's celebration of capitalism[100], so the new visual popular culture found along the Pike offered both visions of racist imperialism and of a new multicultural world.

The World Expositions discovered more than technology and world wide markets; they also formulated new visual modes for understanding this new world. The growing accommodation of popular culture evident in the changing place accorded to the amusement concessions in World Expositions certainly charts a re-negotiation of American culture. Did the cultural élite who backed the Expositions simply discover a way to manage the fascination of the fairground attractions, or did a different view of pleasure and visual excitement begin to overwhelm the monuments of official culture? Undoubtedly elements of both transformations took place. Whether this new visual culture simply dazzled viewers with the blindingly white surfaces of evanescent monuments to élite culture or began to provide a new basis for international and cross class experience remains perhaps the most vital enigma the Expositions bequeathed to the new phenomenon of the movies. Need we point out that it is still unresolved and its history remains to be fully researched and written?✳

Notes

This essay was originally delivered in a somewhat different form at the third Domitor Conference, 'Cinema Turns One Hundred' 13–18 June 1994 held at New York University and the Museum of Modern Art. I would like to thank the organizers of the conference and its participants for valuable discussions, with special thanks due to Andre Gaudreault, Germaine Lacasse, Gregory Waller, Paul Spehr, Martin Loiperdinger, Richard Crangle and John Belton. I would also like to thank the Deering Library Special Collections, Northwestern University, the Chicago Historical Society and Rick Wojick.

1. Emmanuelle Toulet, 'Cinema at the Universal Exposition, Paris, 1900' *Persistence of Vision* No. 9, 1991, 10–36.

2. *Ibid.*, 33

3. On the Crystal Palace of the Great Exhibition of 1851 in London, see Thomas Richards, *The Commodity Culture of Victorian England: Advertising and Spectacle, 1851–1914* (Stanford: Stanford University Press, 1991), 17–72. And for a different view, see Marshall Berman in *All that is Solid Melts into Air: The Experience of Modernity* (New York and London: Penguin Books, 1988), 235–248. Berman also stresses the transience of the Crystal Palace, 237.

4. Neil Harris, 'Memory and the White City' in Harris, de Wit, Gilbert and Rydell, *Grand Illusions: Chicago's World's Fair of 1893* (Chicago: Chicago Historical Society, 1993), 3.

5. Walter Benjamin, *Charles Baudelaire: A Lyric Poet in the Era of High Capitalism* (London: Verso, 1985), 165.

6. The commodity as spectacle forms a central theme of Richards' treatment of the Crystal Palace and its effect on Victorian commodity culture. See note 3.

7. Alan Trachtenberg, *The Incorporation of America: Culture and Society In the Gilded Age* (New York: Hill and Wang, 1982), 231.

8. Richards, 32.

9. David R. Francis, *The Universal Exposition of 1904* (St. Louis: St. Louis Purchase Exposition Co., 1913), 371.

10. Simon J. Bronner, 'Object Lessons: The Work of Ethnological Museums and Collections', in Bronner, ed. *Consuming Visions: Accumulation and Display of Goods In America 1880–1920* (New York: W.W. Norton and Co., 1989), 217. Rosalind H. Williams also discusses the object lesson in a French context, in *Dream Worlds: Mass Consumption in Late Nineteenth Century France* (Berkeley: University of California Press, 1982), 58–59.

11. Quoted in Bronner, 222.

12. Quoted in Wim de Wit, 'Building an Illusion: The Design of the World Columbian Exposition' in Harris, de Wit, Gilbert and Rydell, *Grand Illusions*.

13. St. Louis Exposition, 30 April to 1 December 1904 via Boston and Maine Railroad (Boston: Boston and Maine Railroad, 1904) 2.

14. Quoted in Robert W. Rydell, *All the World's a Fair: Visions of Empire at American International Expositions, 1876–1916* (Chicago: University of Chicago Press, 1984), 139.

15. Message from the President of the United States Transmitting a Statement Showing Receipts and Disbursements for the Louisiana Purchase Exposition, (Washington, D.C.: Goverment Printing Office, 1903) 42.

16. H.B. Wendell, *In a Nutshell: 1000 Facts about the World's Fair* (St. Louis, Publication Office 1903), 6.

17. J.W. Buel, ed. *Louisiana and the Fair: An Exposition of the World, its People and their Achievements* (St Louis: World's Progress Publishing Co., 1904) Vol IV, 1401–1402.

18. Boston and Maine Railroad, 5.

19. Quoted in Rydell, 13.

20. Quoted in Tractenberg, 213.

21. Quoted in Rydell, 107.

22. *The World's Work* Vol VIII No. 4 Aug. 1904 Special Double Exposition Number, 5053.

23. Rydell, 157.

24. Hamlin Garland, *Son of the Middle Border*, (New York: Macmillian Co, 1923) 460.

25. See my article 'The Cinema of Attractions: Early Film, its Spectator and Avant-Garde' in Thomas Elsaesser, ed. *Early Cinema: Space Frame Narrative* (London: British Film Institute, 1990), 56–62.

26. Quoted in Rydell, p. 159. On the concept of shock in modern culture see also Wolfgang Schivelbusch, *The Railway Journey: Trains and Travel In the Nineteenth Century* (New York: Urizen Books, 1977) 135–160, and Walter Benjamin, *Baudelaire*, 113–120. I have discussed shock in relation to the cinema of attractions in 'An Aesthetic of Astonishment: Early Film and the [In]credulous Spectator' *Art & Text* no 34, Spring, 1989, 31–45.

27. Quoted in Rydel 1, 134.

28. *World's Work*, 5057.

29. Buel, Vol IV, 1392.

30. *World's Work*, 5088.

31. Buel, Vol X, p . 3349.

32. *World's Work*, 5092.

33. Mark Bennitt, ed., *History of the Louisiana Purchase Exposition* (St. Louis: Universal Exposition Pub . Co., 1905), 576.

34. Buel, Vol IX, 3179.

35. Bennitt, 623.

36. On Philadelphia's 'Centennial City', see de Wit, 95 and Rydell, 34.

37. Quoted in James Gilbert, *Perfect Cities: Chicago's Utopias of 1893* (Chicago: University of Chicago Press, 1991), 94.

38. Neil Harris, *Cultural Excursions: Marketing Appetites and Cultural Tastes in Modern America* (Chicago: University of Chicago Press, 1990), 121.

39. *Jackson's Famous Photographs of the St. Louis Exposition and 'the Pike'.* (Chicago: Metropolitan Syndicate Press, 1904) (no page numbers).

40. Quoted in Gilbert, 88.

41. Quoted in Tractenberg, 213.

42. Quoted in Rydell, 65.

43. This passage from the novel *Sweet Clover* written by Clara Louisa Burnham, is quoted in Rydell, 67.

44. Quoted in Rydell, 62.

45. Quoted in Gilbert, 87.

46. Quoted in Rydell, 179.

47. Buel, Vol IV, 1388.

48. Thomas R. MacMechen quoted in Rydell, 178.

49. Quoted in Rydell, 179.

50. Boston and Maine Railroad, 31.

51. *Jackson's Famous Photographs* (no page numbers).

52. Pennsylvania Railroad to the World's Fair, St. Louis Mo. Descriptive notes, list of hotels, rates of fare, schedule of trains, and general information (Philadelphia: Allen, Lane and Scott, printers, 1904), 24.

53. Boston and Maine Railroad, 31.

54. *Ibid.*, 6.

55. *Jackson's Famous Photographs* (no page numbers).

56. Francis, 594.

57. *Ibid.*, 597.

58. See, 'My "Primitive" Cinema – a Frame-up? or The Trick's on US' *Cinema Journal* 28, no. 2 Winter, 1989, 3–12., as well as 'Aesthetic of Astonishment'.

59. Francis, 600.

60. *Ibid.*, 600.

61. Anne Friedberg s discussion of the 'mobilized and virtual gaze' in her book *Window Shopping: Cinema and the Postmodern* (Berkeley: University of California Press, 1993) introduces an important context for the virtual voyage of the fairground and the emergence of cinema. See, especially, 15–38.

62. Schivelbusch, 123–124.

63. The concept of the urge towards a 'frictionless' environment in contemporary life has been developed by Rick Wojick in an unpublished seminar paper at Northwestern University.

64. Jules Verne, *Around the World in Eighty Days* (New York: William Morrow and Company, 1988) trans. William Makepeace Towle, 52.

65. Bennitt, 726.

66. *Jackson's Famous Photographs* (no page numbers).

67. Francis, 600.

68. *Ibid.*, 595.

69. *Jackson's Famous Photographs* (no page numbers).

70. Bennitt, 721.

71. The best description of these attractions is provided by Toulet, 17–23. See also Williams, 73 A description with illustrations and diagrams of the panoramas from the 1900 Paris Exposition is given in Leonard de Vries, *Victorian Inventions* (London: John Murray, 1991), 124–25, reprinted from the Dutch magazine *De Natuur*.

72. Quoted in Rydell, p. 151. Although not mentioned by Toulet, Williams places the 'Trip to the Moon' attraction at the Paris Exposition, 75.

73. John F. Kasson, *Amusing the Million: Coney Island at the Turn of the Century* (New York: Hill and Wang, 1978), 17–28; 61–72. Kasson's slim volume has been a major inspiration for this essay. A detailed and insightful discussion of Riverside Park in relation to early cinema is given in Lauren Rabinovitz, 'Temptations of Pleasure: Nickelodeons, Amusement Parks, and the Sights of Female Sexuality' in *Camera Obscura* 23 May 1990, 71–90. I would also like to thank Prof. Rabinovitz for sharing with me her work and thoughts on the Chicago Columbian Exposition.

74. *Ibid.*, 65.

75. *Ibid.*, 63.

76. Bennitt, 717.

77. Francis, 567.

78. Kasson, 82–85.

79. Francis, 601.

80. Francis, 560–561 lists film showings for the Navy and Interior Department. The Interior Department screenings are given in detail. In 1905 the American Mutoscope and Biograph Company offered some of the films shown at the Interior Departments Exhibition to showmen. See, Kemp Niver, *Biograph Bulletins 1896–1908* (Los Angeles: Locare Research Group, 1971) 145, which reproduces 'Biograph Bulletin no. 40, 21 January 1905 *American Indians and Yellowstone Park Views*'. Comparing the titles offered here with those listed in Francis, it would seem Biograph offered the public only a partial selection. I would like to thank Paul Spehr of the Library of Congress for calling my attention to both the Dept. of the Interior films and the Westinghouse films at St. Louis.

81. Niver, 147.

82. Francis, 561.

83. Buel, Vol. IX, 3292.

84. Musser, 359–60.

85. Buel, Vol. IX, 3395.

86. *Ibid.*

87. Martin Loiperdinger informed me of Messter's presence at the St. Louis Fair.

88. Germaine Lacasse (avec la collaboration de Serge Duigou), *L'Historiographe (Les debuts du spectacle cinématographique au Quebec) Les Dossier de la Cinématheque*, no. 15 (Montreal: Cinématheque Québécoise, 1985), 38. I thank André Gaudreault and M. Lacasse for this reference.

89. Accounts of Hale's Tours can be found in Raymond Fielding, 'Hale's Tours: Ultrarealism in the Pre-1910 Motion Picture' in John Fell, ed., *Film Before Griffith* (Berkeley: University of California Press, 1983), 116–130 and in Charles Musser, *The Emergence of Cinema* (New York: Scribners, 1990), 429–430.

90. See List of Concessionaires, Francis, 584.

91. Fielding, 121.

92. See De Vries, 124–25.

93. Fielding, 120.

94. Musser, 429. Lauren Rabinovitz offers an interesting discussion of the role of Hale's Tours at the Riverside amusement park, 79–82.

95. *Ibid.*, 429.

96. Quoted in Williams, 64. William Leach in *Land of Desire: Merchants, Power, and the Rise of a New American Culture* (New York: Pantheon Books, 1993) provides a brilliant account of this new commercial culture of visual attraction.

97. Gregory Waller has sent me an ad appearing in the *Lexington [Kentucky] Leader* on 25 July 1906 which proclaims, in part:

> We are to have a World s Fair. This is unexpected and Startling news, but we hope it will be none the less welcome ... Prof. Forrest D. High, of St. Louis, the world-famous lecturer and entertainer, will give an exhibition of World's Fair scenes, showing the world at a glance, moving pictures, with startling effects ... combining in a brilliant display the latest inventions in the use of the Stereopticon ...
> ABSOLUTELY FREE OF COST TO YOU
> Prof. High comes here as the representative of The Brown Shoe Co. of St. Louis ... in order to afford the people an evening of unmixed pleasure and entertainment.
> REMEMBER BUSTER BROWN AND HIS DOG 'TIGE' will be shown in comic motion pictures.
> A large canvas will be stretched across the front of McElhone & Moloney's store.

This announcement shows the way the motion pictures served to disseminate the visual culture and fascination of the Expositions to a wider public both economically and geographically. The offering of World's Fair films as part of an evening of 'unmixed pleasure and entertainment' programmed with the comic Edison series of *Buster Brown* films is typical of the initial reception of motion pictures. I thank Prof. Waller for this valuable reference.

98. Rydell chronicles the mixed results (and often dubious motives) of these attempts to make the Fairs accessible to working class patrons, from the Centential Exhibition (32–33) to the Portland Lewis and Clark Centential in 1907 (188–191). The Crystal Palace had also offered 'Shilling Days' of reduced admission prices to encourage working class attendance with uncertain results (Richards, 37).

99. Tractenberg, 231.

100. A more ambivalent view of the Crystal Palace than Richards condemnation of it as the seedbeed of consumer capitalism is given by Marshall Berman in *All that Is Solid Melts into Air* He details Chernyshevsky's utopian reaction to the Crystal Palace on 243–245. Benjamin briefly discusses the influence of World Expositions on the International Workers movements of the nineteenth century, beginning with a delegation of French Workers to the Crystal Palace (*Baudelaire*, 166).

Film History, Volume 6, pp. 445–469, 1994. Copyright © John Libbey & Company
ISSN: 0892-2160. Printed in Great Britain

The taste of a nation: Training the senses and sensibility of cinema audiences in Imperial Germany

Scott Curtis

I step in; intermission has just begun. An oppressive, damp draft blows against me, even though the door is open. The entire room (500 capacity) is filled to the last seat with children. There is an indescribable din: running, yelling, shrieking, laughing, talking. Boys scuffle. Orange peels and empty bon-bon boxes fly through the air. The ground is studded with candy wrappers. Along the windowsill and radiator young toughs romp around. Girls and boys sit together, densely packed. Fourteen-year-old boys and girls with hot, excited faces tease each other in unchildlike ways. Children of all ages, even two- and three-year-olds, sit there with glistening cheeks. Young women walk among them selling sweets. Many children sneak candy and drink soda [Brause]; young boys smoke furtively.

Then the movie begins[1].

For the cinema reformers of Imperial Germany, this was a scene from hell. This is what German *Kultur* had come to, what modernity had wrought: children melting and spoiled like day-old candy on the floor of a movie theatre. Like Professor Rath of *Der Blaue Engel* (*The Blue Angel*, 1930), who follows his students into a seedy nightclub and is initially shocked by the sexuality and degeneracy within, this schoolteacher from Bremen walked into a matinée and was horrified by what she saw. Her emphasis on the corporeality of the scene, on the *body* of the audience, so to speak – fighting, eating, sweating and awaken-

Scott Curtis currently works at the Academy of Motion Picture Arts & Sciences Center for Motion Picture Study in Beverly Hills, CA. He is a Ph.D. candidate in film studies at the University of Iowa and his dissertation concerns the discourse on cinema in Germany before World War I. Please address correspondence to 6448 1/2 Orange Street, Los Angeles, CA 90048, USA.

ing sexuality — attests to the perception that cinema presented a grave danger to the children's emotional and moral fitness, and especially their physical health. Given the traditional bourgeois association of sensuality with the lowly 'masses', this scene also represented a threat to the well-being of the nation, of the body politic[2]. As I will later demonstrate, 'children' and 'the masses' were often interchangeable concepts. Indeed, while cinema was often depicted as a gaping Moloch devouring innocent children in some pagan ritual, the children here are far from sacrificial lambs. They present something of a veiled threat to the narrator, as if she had entered a strange, chaotic culture. In the contemporary literature on children and cinema, the anxieties produced by scenes like this one are manifested as twin, contradictory paternal urges: to protect and to control.

'Young women walk among them selling sweets'. Along with the concern for sensuality (and its tacit partner, capitalism), the numerous references to sweets stand out in this description. Implicit is the assumption that cinema is spoiling the 'taste' of the children for financial gain. Reformers complained constantly about the 'tastelessness' of both the theatre atmosphere and the films themselves. Figuratively speaking, the concession candy which ate at the children's teeth was also rotting their aesthetic sensibilities. Konrad Lange, a noted art historian of Imperial Germany and a ferocious cinema reformer, put it more bluntly: 'If one were to judge the artistic understanding of our good, middle-class citizens, one would have to say that their taste is rotten to the core. They have a morbid taste for the slick, the effeminate, the sentimental, and the sugary. They display a demoralizing aversion to the healthy dark bread of true art'[3].

Here the relation between taste, class, and the body is made as explicit as possible. Taste, as the simultaneous expression of individual judgement and social distinction, serves as a connection between the private and the public spheres. It is, as Pierre Bourdieu notes, 'a class culture turned into nature, that is, *embodied*'[4]. It therefore provides a link between individual consumption and a national agenda. Lange anxiously condemns the feminization of culture accompanying the onslaught of modernity. He was not alone with his fears; most middle-class males of the Western world seemed to

share his concerns[5]. Lange's solution, like that of many teachers and educators involved in cinema reform, stressed the education of children and adults. The abiding faith in the ability of education to overcome social ills and promote social progress was a fundamental plank in the platform of many *fin-de-siècle* movements, from the socialists to the progressives. But the tradition of *aesthetic* education, with its promise to harmonize the senses and sharpen judgement, offered a quintessentially German solution[6]. By pointing the way to a 'true' and 'pure' aesthetic experience, aesthetic education also pledged to counteract the corrupting influence of the cinema. While many reformers, such as Lange, steadfastly refused to be seduced by cinema's charms, some flirted with this particular 'Lola', courting her in hopes of making her an honest woman by giving her an aesthetic education (or an education in aesthetics). Even while cinema used the reformers for its own ends, it revealed the contradictions of their ideology. Just as Professor Rath's affair with Lola reveals the indefensibility of his position – a teacher who, ultimately, does not have the best interests of his students at heart – so, too, the reformers' involvement with cinema shows that there were larger issues at stake than the health of the children.

This essay will explore both the facts and fissures of Germany's cinema reform movement as it dealt with the relation between cinema, children and the masses, taste and nation, education and the body. After placing cinema reform in the context of other reform movements, this article will outline some of the concrete steps *Kinoreformers* took to protect child audiences from the hazards of cinema. Censorship, taxes, and child protection laws were accompanied by attempts to create an alternative film system by controlling means of production, distribution, and exhibition. It will also describe reformers' efforts to persuade production companies and theatre owners to support reform films and exhibition values, which led to the creation of reform theatres and community cinemas. The essay will also discuss the discourse on 'the child' and its relation to the concept of 'the masses'. The urge to protect children from the 'degeneracy' of mass entertainments went hand-in-hand with the desire to educate the general public. Both concerns drew life from child and crowd psychology popularized at the turn of the century.

Fig. 1. Children's matinée at the Nord-Kino, Berlin, 1910. In a poster [far right], two locomotives crash, promising a violence that is an affront to bourgeois taste.
[Photo courtesy of Uta Berg-Ganschow and Wolfgang Jacobsen.]

Finally, this article will focus on the work of one reformer, Hermann Häfker, and his attempts to use cinema as an instrument of ideological solidarity. Increasingly worried about the 'bad taste' of mass entertainments, Häfker enlisted cinema in a programme of aesthetic education designed to raise the sensibility of the people to a unified, national level. Taking his cue from a long tradition of aesthetic education dating back to Schiller, as well as the art education movement then taking place, Häfker wanted to use cinema to 'train' the tastes of the nation. His special exhibition projects best exemplify reformers' attempts to establish certain rules of spectatorship for their audiences. Furthermore, in trying to influence the way the audience actually viewed the films, the reformers' programme was, at bottom, one of bodily discipline.

The spirit of reform

In their desire to make a change for the better, the men and women involved in *Kinoreform* were part of a much larger set of movements sweeping the industrialized world around the turn of the century. As increased industrialization and urbanization brought on one social upheaval after another, 'reform' expressed the mood of the times in many ways throughout Europe and the United States. In Britain, constitutional reforms swept through Parliament as various groups demanded suffrage throughout the last third of the century. In the United States, the agrarian Populist movement of the 1890s and the Progressive movement of the 1900s reflected a broad impulse toward criticism and change. Progressivism, in particular, captured the spirit of reform through its outrage over the excesses of capitalism, its faith in progress, and its interventionist policies. During the 1880s, the pressures of industrialization and democracy prompted the French parliament to create the only state-run, compulsory, secular primary school system in the world. The growing confrontations between the forces of labour and capital also prodded republican politicians to campaign for social legislation, such as regulation of working conditions, in order to insure social peace[7].

Germany, in particular, was deluged by swelling transformations in the public sphere provoked by rapidly changing demographics. The industrial revolution and national unification came relatively late to Germany and accelerated very quickly. The resulting discord between the classes and between rural and urban lifestyles seemed especially acute[8]. During the high tide of these changes, which occurred from around 1890 to 1920, the concept of 'reform', as an expression of the sense of transition and as a plan for managing it, took on special significance for self-understanding. Germany's groundbreaking legislation providing for compulsory insurance for workers' sickness, workplace accidents, and retirement pension became an influential model for Great Britain, the United States and France. These measures, dealing in some form with physical conditions and consequences of the workplace, illustrate the strong connection between class and somatic issues in reform movements during the late nineteenth century. Reform manifested itself in everything from *Jugendstil* decor to a new, more 'natural' style in women's clothing (*Reformkleidung*), to nutrition reform (*Ernährungsreform*)[9]. 'Reform' implied a battle against tradition, against perceived cultural and social stagnation and as such, it provided a plan for the formation of new, more 'authentic' concepts for living. In fact, the connections between the reform movements and the more general tradition of *Kulturkritik* are very strong; from Rousseau and Pestalozzi in the eighteenth century to Nietzsche and Lagarde in the nineteenth, the critique of society paved the way for a general re-evaluation of values in the twentieth[10].

Very often, the critique of society focused on the educational system. Education reform was among the first movements to sweep across Germany. The Kaiser himself had set the agenda on a December morning in 1890 while addressing a congress of educators in Berlin; Wilhelm II claimed he grasped 'the spirit of an expiring century' with his calls for school reform. In answering the question of how the German schools of the nineteenth century could be reshaped to meet the needs of the twentieth, the Kaiser echoed sentiments that had been expressed throughout Europe during the often rocky transition from the Victorian age to the modern. Specifically, he voiced his fears that the *Gymnasium* failed to train its students adequately for the requirements of Germany's rapid industrialization. Secondly, he complained about the 'excess of mental work' in the schools, arguing that such 'overburdening' was threatening the physical health of Germany's youth.

Lastly, he insisted that German schools devote more time and energy to fostering specifically national values: 'We must make German the basis of the *Gymnasium*; we should raise young Germans, not young Greeks and Romans'[11].

The Kaiser's concerns about 'the modern', 'the healthy' and 'the national', reflected and reinforced similar fixations of the European élite. Like them, he found the educational system to be both the problem and the solution to the crises. By inadequately preparing the nation's children for the demands of the future, the system risked irrelevance. Swift reform promised both a brighter future and a greater measure of control over the rapid changes taking place. Among the different examples of education reform were the *Landerziehungsheime*, which were experimental schools located in the countryside as an explicit rejection of urban culture. Their emphasis on the 'physical education' of their students echoed the hopes of the youth movement for a spiritually renewing combination of countryside, fresh air and *Volk*. Likewise, the *Arbeitsschule* hoped to renew the creative (and ethical, hence political) spirit through manual labour, such as gardening and handicrafts, such as wood sculpting or leather crafts[12]. The art education movement (*Kunsterziehungsbewegung*) similarly stressed the creative capacities of children as well, advocating renewal through art and education of the aesthetic sensibility.

Cinema reformers shared the Kaiser's anxiety about 'the modern', 'the healthy' and 'the national'[13]. At the centre of their concerns lay cinema, which they also found to be both scourge and cure. The emblem of modernity, cinema represented a plague, especially toxic to children, and proper education of the public was the only hope to halt the epidemic. At the same time, cinema was the most powerful instrument of mass education, and therefore provided the surest treatment for whatever ills modernity had spread. Before treatment could begin, however, commercial interests had to be persuaded to participate in this remedy. Moreover, cinema needed a stamp of legitimacy in order to have any authority in this rescue mission. *Kinoreform* was the process by which these goals were attempted, if not completely achieved. It shared roots, objectives and ideology with other reform movements of the day, especially, and not surprisingly, educational reform.

It does seem rather unusual that the head of the German empire, almost by definition the representative of a conservative *status quo*, would come out so strongly in favour of reform. The mixture of progressive reforms and reactionary politics indicated the ambivalent attitude of the bourgeoisie toward the troubling issues of the day[14]. All reform movements revealed, in one way or another, the fundamental irony of the Kaiser's position. The calls for clothing reform in Germany exemplified this contradiction. In his 1901 book, *The Culture of the Female Body as a Foundation for Women's Clothing*, Paul Schultze-Naumberg made an extensive study of the debilitating physical effects resulting from methods of forcing the female form into an aesthetic ideal. In a graphic and impassioned plea to eliminate the corset, in particular, Schultze-Naumberg demonstrated how its use eventually caused deformation of the muscles, bones and internal organs. He called for a more functional clothing in keeping with 'a new concept of corporeality'[15]. While consistent with similar efforts by women's movements to liberate themselves from the pressures of social constraints, Schultze-Naumberg's 'new concept' of more 'natural' bodies included only those from healthy German stock. Carl Heinrich Stratz, another strong advocate of clothing reform, took a similar approach in his book *Women's Clothing and its Natural Development*, grounding his arguments for the elimination of the corset on the conclusion that it threatened the racial superiority of European women. Schultze-Naumberg and Stratz, whose concerns for the health of women were cloaked in worries about the integrity of the Fatherland, are excellent examples of the fusion of progressive goals of more liberal movements and reactionary, nationalist politics[16].

Schultze-Naumberg, Stratz and the Kaiser shared with their fellow guardians of culture a general anxiety about the decline in German cultural life[17]. This anxiety found voice in a cluster of complaints, ranging from protests about the lack of creativity in higher education to the decadence of mass entertainments, such as cinema or 'trashy novels' (*Schundliteratur*). In many cases, as Schultze-Naumberg and Stratz illustrate, the preoccupation with 'degeneracy' was often connected to an obsession with and fear of female sexuality. As the women's movement gained momentum, it represented an in-

creasing threat to male domination of the public sphere[18]. Although the motivations of a class of people can be difficult to ascertain, the mandarins' alarm over a 'crisis of culture' is usually attributed to this declining authority[19]. The women's movement only exemplified a menace that surrounded German intellectuals; actions such as the youth movements threatened to undermine paternal credibility even in the home. Faced with such massive structural changes, the cultural élite embraced reform as a way of coping with, and controlling, the assault of modernity. Education reform, in particular, flourished as only the most visible and dominant in a series of movements to which the bourgeoisie looked with both hope and apprehension.

The cinema reform movement

Cinema reform patterned itself after these movements, both in terms of ideology and practice. Because most of the reformers were teachers and educators, their close ties to the education reform groups of the period remained a formative aspect of their own efforts. Hermann Lemke, a *Gymnasium* professor from Hagen and one of the founders of *Kinoreform*, was well connected to the Society for the Dissemination of Adult Education (*Gesellschaft zur Verbreitung von Volksbildung*), the leading educational organization in Germany. Hermann Häfker, the most articulate representative of cinema reform and arguably Germany's first film theorist, was a journalist and writer who was also close to the leaders of the art education movement. Before he became the chief film censor in Berlin, Karl Brunner was also a *Gymnasium* professor and one of the most visible participants in the national movement against 'trashy novels'. Konrad Lange, one of the leading voices of the art education movement, taught art history at the University of Tübingen.

Despite their similar backgrounds, these reformers were not all of one mind. The disparate views and priorities of all involved, as well as the absence of a central organization or platform, make it difficult to even characterize *Kinoreform* as a movement. Scattered around mostly northern and small-town Germany, the representatives worked at the local level, trying to coordinate national efforts through the trade press, such as *Der Kinematograph* out of Düsseldorf. The birth of trade magazines devoted exclusively to cinema coincides with the birth of the reform movement in 1907; during its earliest years,

Fig. 2. A banner from *Der Kinematograph*, ca. 1913, a trade magazine that helped to coordinate reform efforts.

Der Kinematograph acted as a willing partner in *Kinoreform*[20]. The range of viewpoints in its pages, and in the other magazines that followed shortly thereafter, testifies to the difficulty the reformers had choosing the most effective course of action.

If they did not agree on methods, they did have a set of common objectives. First and foremost, they felt compelled to protect children from what they perceived to be the dangerous effects of cinema. This was first explicitly stated in 1907, when a teacher's group in Hamburg, the Society of Friends of the Schools and Instruction for the Fatherland (*Gesellschaft der Freunde des vaterländischen Schul- und Erziehungswesens*), formed a commission to study the effects of cinema on school children. Its conclusions were predictable: both the films themselves and the theatres produced physical and moral side effects in school-age children. The combination of the 'flicker effect' and the lack of adequate ventilation in theatres caused 'eyestrain, nausea and vomiting', according to the commission. Emphasizing the connection between the body and ethical judgement, the committee hinted that these physical symptoms were a sign of a deeper moral sickness, manifested in school by 'apathy for learning, carelessness, and a tendency to daydream'[21]. Jurist Albert Hellwig, certainly the most prolific reformer, echoed these concerns in 1914, when he argued that 'a promotion of a certain superficiality and inattentiveness, as well as a retardation of concen-

tration and aesthetic cultivation' could be counted among the psychological dangers to young movie-goers[22].

Second, the reformers made it clear from the very beginning that they hoped to use cinema for educational purposes. In this and many other ways, the German reformers were very similar to their American counterparts, who also took it upon themselves to 'uplift' both the theatres and the films for the good of the masses[23]. The Hamburg commission concluded its study with the recommendation that:

> Technically flawless cinematic presentations with suitable topics could be an outstanding medium for instruction and entertainment. Educators and artists should sit down with prominent members of the [motion picture] industry and come to an understanding. Encouraging the filmmakers to create good productions appropriate for children – to be shown in special children's shows – would be a step toward better and nobler use of the cinema particularly worth striving for[24].

This call to arms was answered independently by Hermann Lemke in the summer of 1907, when he persuaded a Friedenau cinema theatre owner to open Germany's first reform theatre. Lemke gave the opening address, making the goals of cinema reform clear to the mostly middle-class audience of teachers, press and community leaders. He charged that the current state of cinema had caused the aesthetic sensibilities of the people to regress. Calling on the combined power of educators and the press, he maintained that 'when the taste of the people is so backward, it's the duty of the intellectual [*geistigen*] leaders to influence them and put their aesthetic taste back on the right track'. Cleaning up the cinema theatres was the first order of business in this project. Lemke demanded that:

> This reformation should begin by giving the theatres a respectable appearance. Gone is the small, narrow room where everyone is crammed and squeezed together; in its place we find a larger, airier hall, so that the visitor no longer has the impression that he is in a second-rate establishment. Good ventilation has been provided in order to reduce health risks[25].

Lemke's concerns demonstrate how closely 'taste' and 'respectability' were tied to 'the body', and especially the body of 'the masses'. He was preaching to the converted, however. *Der Kinematograph* later reported, 'it seems that the middle class is more interested than the working class in the direction the reform theatre is taking. While the seats in the third section show hardly any patrons, the first section (50 cents admission) is mostly sold out'[26]. Still, Lemke was sufficiently encouraged to organize a 'Cinema Reform Party' the following autumn. Represented by teachers, members of the press, theatre owners, and production companies, the society was one of many throughout Germany that hoped to coordinate efforts from these quarters towards their educational goals. Lemke's society received contributions from such firms as the German branches of Eclipse and Gaumont[27]. While cleaning up the *Kinos*, the reformers turned their attention to the films themselves.

Production

Enjoying the easy fraternity with producers during the early years, *Kinoreformers* hoped to capitalize upon their good relations with the motion picture companies in order to increase the number and availability of reform-type productions. In 1908, Lemke suggested that his reform society act as a 'Film-Idea-Central', a clearinghouse of sorts for reform-minded scripts. Members of the society could submit ideas or scenarios and the society would negotiate with

the studios on the writers' behalf. Lemke explained, 'Because we're in good standing with the producers, such an exchange would be relatively easy to carry out. We would take on this service free of charge and only require that those who use it be members ... Perhaps this way we'll succeed in bringing the film companies up to date as well as being an influential model for foreign countries'[28]. Unfortunately, while the members of the movement itself might have held some early enthusiasm for this plan, the film companies themselves apparently did not take to it; the idea never went beyond the initial stages and no further mention is made of the 'Film-Idea-Central' in the trade press or reform publications.

The failure of the 'Film-Idea-Central' established something of a frustrating pattern for the reformers. Film companies expressed early interest in reform projects, even going so far as to sponsor events, but eventually refused more meaningful and lasting support. The end of 1908 saw the opening of Germany's first film trade show/exhibition at Berlin's Zoological Gardens. Jointly sponsored by Lemke's reform party and the leading film companies at the time, and with the rather obvious motto of 'The Ennobling of Cinema' (*Veredelung des Kinos*), it was nonetheless heavily criticized even by friendly periodicals for its lack of organization[29]. Exhibitors, manufacturers, and production companies declined the reformers' help for the next exhibit in 1912[30]. Likewise, when Lemke and Häfker attempted to muster support for their special exhibitions, the film companies were initially supportive, but lost interest fairly quickly. Realizing that domestic companies could not or would not produce sufficient numbers and variety of educational films, Häfker went so far as visiting foreign film companies, such as the Charles Urban Trading Co. in London and Eclipse in Paris, to find suitable nature films for his exhibitions[31]. Lemke even went to England and wrote film treatments in order to jump-start some sort of interest in his programme[32]. Very early on, it was quite clear that the production companies were cautious about backing the reformers and their schemes.

This did not mean, however, that the film companies wanted nothing to do with the reform movement. They were certainly willing to use the reform movement for their own ends; despite their difficulties, the reformers were still a legitimating presence – they were, after all, educators, clergy, journalists,

Fig. 3. An advertisement for *Die Irrfahrten des Odysseus (The Wanderings of Odysseus)*, 1912 identifies the film as a 'Reformfilm'.

and otherwise pillars of their respective communities. Film companies were eager to cash in on this allegiance. Advertising trumpeted this relationship, even if the reformers had nothing to do with the making of the film. A 1912 PAGU film, *Die Irrfahrten des Odysseus (The Wanderings of Odysseus)*, is labelled a 'Reformfilm' and carries this blurb: 'From a special press screening, which was attended by the most respected Berlin literary figures and art critics, came the unanimous decision: "This film signals the long-awaited reform of cinema"[33]. Aware of the potential directions cinema could take, the film companies initially went along with the reformers. But as soon as it became apparent that the vast majority of the viewing public was more interested in narrative

entertainment, the companies brushed off the reform societies' efforts to influence the product directly.

The reformers did little to help their cause with the production companies. Their regular denunciations of 'cinema drama' (*Kinodrama*) merely antagonized an industry leaning heavily toward narrative films. This prejudice against narrative films often disguised stronger rhetoric against international domination of the German film market. 'In the internationalist cinema drama [Kinodrama], the wildest passions of all nations come together for a gruesome rendezvous', charged one reformer[34]. Likewise, their complaints about capitalist interests tainting cinema's potential were thinly veiled laments about the presence of *foreign* capital. Some reformers, such as Häfker and Lange, dismissed cinema drama because of aesthetic concerns. It did not offend their sensibilities because of sloppy production qualities, although these did attract attention. Rather, the filmed drama betrayed what they saw to be cinema's primary mission: to record movement and 'real life'. The argument for filmic realism, of course, coincided with their desire to use cinema for educational purposes. As Sabine Hake notes, they did not dismiss the possibility of story elements in their educational films, but the excesses of the 'trashy film' so contradicted their stated ideals that they rallied against film drama altogether, for both political and aesthetic reasons[35].

Lemke hoped to reform the cinema through example, stressing cooperation with and from the industry. Others were not so willing to rely on this teamwork. One faction of the reform movement, led by Albert Hellwig and Karl Brunner, saw censorship and regulation as the best way to combat the deluge of *Schundfilme*. Both Hellwig and Brunner advocated a series of legal restrictions on the cinema, including censorship, entertainment taxes (*Lustbarkeitsteuer*), poster censorship, safety regulations, and child protection laws (*Kinderschutz*)[36]. Authorities tried to maintain some control over child audiences (and, consequently, theatres) by restricting their visits to specific hours of the day, regulating the length of the matinées, and requiring that children be accompanied by an adult, that police should have unlimited access to the theatre during the matinées, that the day's programme must be given prior approval, or that a 'suitable pause' separate the films[37].

Distribution and exhibition

Reformers realized early on the importance of establishing a distribution network for their educational films. For this task, Lemke and his circle enlisted the help of the *Gesellschaft zur Verbreitung von Volksbildung* (hereafter referred to as the GVV). An umbrella organization for over 8,000 local education groups, clubs, associations, and societies, it was a formidable partner in *Kinoreform*. *Bildungs-Verein*, the house publication, had a circulation of 13,000 – many times that of any film trade magazine. Yet the GVV leadership was hesitant about cinema's importance as an educational tool. Even though Johannes Tews, the director of the GVV and editor of *Bildungs-*

Verein, had attended the opening of Lemke's Friedenau reform theatre, he still considered cinema to be of minor significance[38]. The GVV resisted involvement with cinema until 1912, when it established a film distribution centre of 180 films in 16 categories, from 'History of the Fatherland' to educational films on biology[39].

The reformers found a more willing and beneficial partner in the *Lichtbilderei*, established in 1909 as a foundation of the Association for Catholic Germany (*Volksvereins für das katholische Deutschland*). The *Lichtbilderei* was the largest educational film institute before World War I, with an extensive catalogue of titles. It began as a rental source for magic lantern slides, which could be used for public lectures, but started collecting films as well after 1911. By the end of 1912, it had around 900 titles and was collecting more at about 30 films per week, and by 1913 offered 400 slide series and 1,400 film titles[40]. The *Lichtbilderei* was not limited to providing films for schools, churches and clubs; it also provided programming for many commercial theatres. Approximately 40 weekly theatres and 50 to 60 Sunday *Kinos* showed *Lichtbilderei* films regularly[41]. The *Lichtbilderei* was also involved in the distribution of more commercial dramas, actually acquiring 'monopoly' rights over such established hits as *Quo Vadis?* (Italy, 1913), *Giovanna d'Arco* (The Maid from Orleans, 1913), and *Tirol in Waffen* (Tirol in Arms, 1914)[42].

From 1912 to 1915, the *Lichtbilderei* was something of an organizational centre for the cinema reform movement. Its stock of films gave life to the community cinemas and private *Reformkinos*, and its publications – the periodical *Bild und Film* (Image and Film) and the series of books from the association's *Volksvereins* publishing company – were the principal forum for the discussion of *Kinoreform* issues after 1912.

In 1912, the GVV, in association with the *Lichtbilderei*, established the funds for two educationally oriented *Wanderkinos*. These travelling cinemas toured from town to town, playing for four to six weeks in each place, in an effort to offset the influence of commercial cinemas and unify aesthetic and educational standards across the nation. Showing between nine and eleven films an evening, accompanied by lectures concerning such topics as 'A Modern Factory', the enterprise was basically

Fig. 4. A pre-war audience (including one or two children) at the Union Theater, Berlin, 1913. [Photo courtesy of Uta Berg-Ganschow and Wolfgang Jacobsen.]

modelled after the GVV's successful *Wandertheater* and public lecture series. Between the fall of 1912 and the outbreak of war, the *Wanderkinos* offered a total of 1,279 such evenings[43].

Reformers had most success with their exhibition experiments. In addition to the reform theatres and *Wanderkinos* already mentioned, numerous communities established their own public cinemas. The first was founded in the town of Eickel at a cost to the community of 14,000 Marks. Others opened soon afterwards, in such towns as Altona, Wiesbaden, Osterfeld, Frankfurt (Oder), Gleiwitz and Stettin[44]. These cinemas became the centre of local reform activity, and provided the precedent for the state-run cinemas of modern Germany, which continue to illustrate the relation between taste and nation. The proclamations of the early *kommunale Kinos* articulate this relationship and the goals of the reform movement in general:

To oppose, for aesthetic, cultural and patriotic reasons, the trash that is offered as a general rule in the private theatres; to offer instead entertaining films of scientific and educational worth; to exert, in association with institutions with similar principles, a gradual influence on the film market, which is now almost exclusively dependent upon foreign companies; and to therefore keep here the millions that are flowing out of the country. Finally, to place the cinema in service of the youth organizations and schools by providing suitable presentations[45].

To the modern observer, the cinema reformers of Imperial Germany might seem a bit quixotic. Tilting their lances to such impassive windmills as capitalism and narrative, they only reluctantly and belatedly conceded that they were charging against the wind of public opinion. As the movies became more popular and an evening's entertainment began to look less and less like a lecture series, instead relying more heavily on 'Kinodrama', the reformers began to look more and more irrelevant. Their own 'Dulcinea' – the children of the nation – seemed oblivious to their efforts. Even those sympathetic to their cause, like this reviewer of a book on cinema and theatre reform, found the strategy somewhat naive:

> [The author] is certainly up to the task in this serious matter. But he will surely understand if skepticism prevails. An 'ennobling' of cinema by means of literature is not altogether believable and the completely different natures of the media would appear to doom this project to a bad end. The idea that theatre could be made free [of commercial influence] through the large-scale efforts of community interest groups is simply too pretty a picture for even his friendly brush to paint[46].

Others were not so kind. One theatre owner from the 1920s remembers them as 'sanctimonious folks and hypocrites, morality sleuths in male and female guise'[47]. Film histories, until recently, have been equally dismissive. Siegfried Kracauer charges simply that, with their zealous efforts to defend the literary canon of the nation, 'they yielded to the truly German desire to serve the established powers'[48]. Even if a bit condescending, Kracauer is not far off the mark. While the proclamations of the various *Kinoreformers* embraced a wide range of opinion, they never strayed far from the *status quo*. As Sabine Hake notes, 'In sharp contrast to the intellectuals, the reformers aligned themselves openly with the existing power structure'[49].

We mustn't, however, underestimate the reformers' contribution to German culture. In trying to sway what Kracauer called 'the salutary indifference of the masses', the reformers succeeded in dominating the discourse on cinema in the years before World War I. In addition to the permanent impression they left on German film culture, mass communication research owes them an especially heavy debt: their focus on media effects had a lasting influence on the vocabulary and goals of modern mass media studies[50].

Ultimately, of course, cinema reform was not completely successful. The reformers failed to meet their stated goals and, considering the extreme position of many reformers, this is perhaps all for the best. World War I changed abruptly the nation's priorities, and even though the calls for reform were heard again through the Weimar years, the urgency of the moment had passed. In 1913, lances heavy with disappointment, the movement clearly appeared to be running out of breath. Sighed Lemke, 'I had always hoped that someone would take over the chairmanship for me and assist me in further expanding the [Cinema Reform] Society, but no one was found and the result was that the Society remained stuck in its children's shoes [*in seinen Kinderschuhen stecken blieb*]'[51].

Child/crowd psychology

Lemke's metaphor is apt because it reveals the extent to which the reformers were thinking about the cinema (and themselves) through the metaphor of 'the child'. Since they were educators and teachers, this is perhaps to be expected. It is noteworthy, however, that they applied this trope to adult audiences. References to their audiences as 'children', especially in connection with mention of 'the masses', are scattered throughout the discourse[52]. One reformer, looking for the underlying causes of cinema drama's continued popularity, maintained that 'just as much blame belongs to the audience, the people, this "big child", whose horribly spoiled taste craves for cinema's dramatic trash and silly comedies; the theatre owner is pretty much forced to offer aesthetically and morally backward presentations week after week'[53]. Even Georg Lukács thought about cinema spectatorship in terms of children: 'In cinema, we forget these heights [of great drama] and become irresponsible. The *child*, which inhabits all of us, is released and becomes the master of the audience's psyche'[54].

Whether Lukács' 'inner child' was inherently good or evil depended upon one's viewpoint. Child psychology of the period fluctuated between the two claims and provides a partial explanation for the equation of children and the masses. Swedish author Ellen Key's *Century of the Child*, an enormously popular children's rights manifesto published originally in 1900, advocated a reassessment of the prevailing view that children were inherently evil. Summing up a trend in child psychology that emphasized the creative nature of the child, it called for new teaching methods to correspond to the new century, leaving behind the authoritarian methods of the old school and reassessing pedagogy 'from the child outward' (*vom Kinde aus*). If adult society, utilitarianism, and the demands of the 'real' world had determined the standards of pedagogy before, now attention turned to the child's needs and inner nature. Whereas the old pedagogy might have emphasized uniformity, now the child could expect to be treated as 'the measure of itself'[55]. As Key insisted, 'instruction should only cultivate the child's own individual nature', which Key and others assumed to be creative, good and even wise[56].

Freud, however, was less optimistic about the life of the child. His essay on 'Infantile Sexuality', published in his 1905 *Three Essays on Sexuality*, painted a darker picture of childhood as a 'hothouse of nascent psychopathology'[57]. His explanation of the importance of the child's body – describing the oral, anal and phallic stages – on mental development was ground-breaking. Its lasting contribution is manifold, but most immediately it underlined the influence of childhood development on adult mental life. While there is little indication that Freud's theories were wholeheartedly accepted by garden-variety reformers, the new child psychology of both Key and Freud does provide a clue to the urgency reformers felt when they argued for aesthetic cultivation and against the influence of sexually charged '*Kinodramas*'.

Despite Freud's seminal contributions, Darwin's evolutionary theories of child development still had a strong grip on the public imagination during this period. In particular, Darwin argued that child development recapitulated the mental evolution of the species. Accordingly, the maturing child was expected to exhibit mental characteristics of subhuman species. In *The Descent of Man*, Darwin observed, 'We daily see these faculties developing in every infant; and we may trace a perfect gradation from the mind of an utter idiot, lower than that of an animal low in the scale, to the mind of a Newton'[58].

Discussions of crowd psychology latched on to this teleological comparison between children and primitive mentalities. Gustave Le Bon, the most well known popularizer of nineteenth-century crowd psychology, characterized the masses as 'an enraged child'. Furthermore, according to Le Bon:

It will be remarked that among the special characteristics of crowds there are several – such as impulsiveness, irritability, incapacity to reason, the absence of judgement and of the critical spirit, the exaggeration of the sentiments, and others besides – which are almost always observed in beings belonging to inferior forms of evolution – in women, savages, and children, for instance[59].

Darwin's evolutionary scheme provided a quasi-scientific basis for comparing crowds to children, but even more significant for this comparison was the concept of 'suggestibility'. Le Bon devoted a chapter to 'the suggestibility and credulity of crowds', arguing that the crowd is 'perpetually hovering on the borderland of unconsciousness, readily yielding to all suggestions', a mental state most commonly found in women and children. Most serious psychologists of his time dismissed Le Bon's rather crude arguments, but the metaphorical connection between children and the masses was still quite powerful for researchers. In fact, one could argue that social psychology has its roots in child study. Alfred Binet, a follower of the famed hypnotist Charcot and one of the founders of experimental social psychology, used the observational opportunities provided by public school classrooms to test his evolving theories of suggestibility. His conclusions about children and suggestibility worked their way into his formative studies of social behaviour, which had a profound impact on the direction of modern social psychology[60].

Reformers borrowed the concept of 'suggestibility' as they described the cinema audiences and their scopophilia or *Schaulust*[61]. The Hamburg commission noted this condition in their report, complaining that:

… many cinema presentations morally endanger the children. Let's take an example: an impressionable young man sees a swindle presented with elegance and brilliant success. Wouldn't that arouse his imitative instinct? A young girl cannot help but notice how selling her honour could provide a carefree and, in her eyes, honourable life. Later, life's hardships arrive and she asks herself: 'why work at a sewing machine for 10 pfennigs an hour, why work at a factory for 10 Marks a week'?[62]

Why, indeed? These remarks prefigure persistent themes in the discourse on cinema during this period, especially the preoccupation with cinema, suggestibility and crime, not to mention female sexuality. Emilie Altenloh, who wrote one of the first sociological studies of cinema audiences, maintained that, in the absence of a strong family life or education, cinema held a mesmerizing influence on its young patrons. 'That cinema has won a certain influence over the entire thoughts and lifestyle of the impressionable is beyond doubt', she concluded. 'From the morals of criminals and fearlessness of cowboys they take a conception of life that forces them into trajectories similar to their celebrated heroes'[63].

Albert Hellwig also wrote often on the suggestive power of cinema and its dangers for the criminally inclined or morally weak. In one article, he describes a neurasthenic woman and her response to a night at the cinema. In the film, a postal clerk dreams that he is attacked by robbers; 'there appear a series of threatening faces and ghostlike hands, which reach out to others in their sleep'. This made such an impression on the young lady that she began to see hallucinations of these hands day and night. 'The apparently intelligent woman was perfectly aware from the beginning that these were merely hallucinations stemming from her own imagination. She was nonetheless quite disturbed because these gigantic hands would appear out of nowhere at different times and under varying circumstances'[64].

Hellwig implies that the cause of the woman's hallucinations is a combination of cinema's suggestive power and the woman's pathological condition, neurasthenia, a vague nervous condition in vogue during this time. It left its victims incapable of work and inflicted upon them a dazzling array of symptoms, including headaches, the fear of responsibility, graying hair and insomnia. According to Anson Rabinbach, 'neurasthenics were identifiable by their impoverished energy and by the excessive intrusion of modern urban society on their physical and mental organization'[65]. It was a form of mental fatigue that left its victims unable to resist the stimuli of the modern world; it was characterized, in short, as a weakness of the will, as moral exhaustion.

The combination of pathology and morality is significant, because the concept of 'moral weakness' metaphorically connects judgement and physical strength. The reformers' focus on both the unhealthy atmosphere of the nickelodeons and the suggestive power of cinema reveals an underlying concern for both the bodies of the audiences and their moral judgement. This concern manifested itself as a problem of 'taste' – taste lies between the realms of sensuality and reason.

As with the question of the nature of the child, reformers were divided over the nature of the masses, especially their judgement. Against those who argued that the masses were not ready for reform, that they were not interested in what interested the educated classes, Hermann Lemke argued, 'I'll give credit to the people for not having such bad taste. And even if the people are not yet mature enough [for cinema's reform], one should never be permitted to appeal to their lowest instincts – that would be dangerous to the community and must be fought against'[66]. Hellwig was less willing to entertain the idea that the masses were inherently good: 'It is the bad taste of the audience that ultimately makes the trashy film'[67]. The solution to this problem of taste and, by extension, the crisis of moral judgement, was aesthetic education.

Taste, nation and aesthetic education

Since Schiller, aesthetic education has offered a solution to the twin problems of sensuality and suggestibility. That is, Schiller suggested the category of 'the aesthetic' as a medium between alienated Nature and Reason. In an alienated world, the aesthetic provided Schiller with hope for reintegration and, thus, social harmony. The aesthetic category acted as a corridor between raw nature and a higher

Die Kultur-Arbeit
des Kinematographen-Theaters.
Gedanken aus dem Jahre 1784
von
Friedrich von Schiller
(† 9. Mai 1805).

Fig. 5. Tracing cinema reform back to Schiller: 'The Cultural Work of the Cinema Theater: Thoughts from the Year 1784' by Friedrich von Schiller.

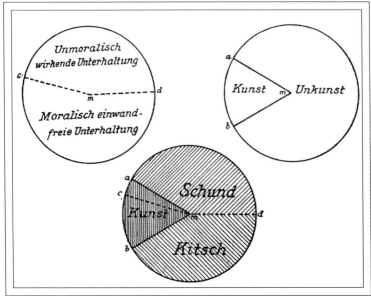

Fig. 6. The Geometry of Taste: The superimposition of morality (immorally affective entertainment' [*Unmoralisch wirkende Unterhaltung*] and 'morally irreproachable entertainment' [*Moralisch einwandfrei Unterhaltung*]) and aesthetics ('art' [*Kunst*] and 'non-art' [*Unkunst*]) reveals the nature of taste ('art' [Kunst], 'trash' [Schund] and 'kitsch').

morality. 'In a word', Schiller wrote, 'there is no other way of making sensuous man rational except by first making him aesthetic'[68].

The reformers were very interested in making 'sensuous man rational'. Schiller's importance for the reformist agenda is illustrated by an editorial in the trade periodical, *Lichtbild-Bühne*. The headline reads, 'The Cultural Work of the Cinema Theater: Thoughts from the Year 1784, by Friedrich von Schiller'[69]. The essay invokes Schiller's 'The Stage Considered as a Moral Institution' to argue that cinema could function in the same manner. The aesthetic, however, is a precondition to the moral, and cinema must first go through that transformation. An illustration from a 1918 reform pamphlet illustrates the axiomatic nature of this relationship between the aesthetic and the moral. The upper-left sphere represents 'immorally affective entertainment' and 'morally irreproachable entertainment', while the upper-right sphere signifies 'art' and 'non-art'. A transubstantiation occurs when the rather plain problems of morality and aesthetics are superimposed to reveal the nature and proportion of 'art', 'trash', and 'kitsch'. This new sphere represents the issue of 'taste'.

Schiller represents the beginning of a long tradition of aesthetic education in Germany, one that eventually became grafted on to questions of nationalism. The most famous, or infamous, example of this development was Julius Langbehn's *Rembrandt as Educator*, first published anonymously and with enormous success in 1890[70]. Like Schiller and Lagarde before him, Langbehn reacted against the excessive rationalization of the Enlightenment. The preoccupation with systemization, objectivity and book-learning had, in his opinion, brought about 'the decline of the spiritual life of the German people'. Specialization, he complained, precluded exercise of creative power: 'one thirsts for synthesis' in over-educated Germany, he wrote, and so 'one turns to art!' The German people could be rescued from this 'systematic, scholarly, cultured barbarism' by 'going back to their original source of power, their individualism'. Furthermore, if individualism is the root of all art, and he claimed it is, and if education should correspond to the nature of its students, then art education would be the most effective and natural form of instruction. Rembrandt, for Langbehn, was 'the most individual of all German artists'. 'The scholar is characteristically international, the artist national', he said, underlining the difference between science and art, word and image. The goal of art education, as Langbehn saw it, is to effect a spiritual regeneration of the German people by reacquainting them with their own inner nature as it is exemplified by the masterpieces of national art.

Alfred Lichtwark, generally recognized to be the driving force behind the art education movement, followed Langbehn's lead in his address to the 1901 art education conference in Dresden. 'Ou education still lacks a *firm national foundation*', he declared[71]. The basis for a national culture, as with Langbehn, could be found in German art. 'Up to now', Lichtwark said, 'the schools have not considered it their task to acquaint youth not only with the names, but the works of the great artists who express the German character'. And he blamed this lack of attention to 'national art' for the lack of 'formative power' in German culture. Even though Lichtwark later distanced himself from Langbehn's very nationalistic views, he still held that 'the challenge of art education' was inseparable from 'a moral renewal of our life'. This hope was certainly not limited to Lichtwark; most representatives of the art education movement held it as their ultimate goal.

But Konrad Lange was cautious of such sanguine hopes, asking at that same conference if 'with "*Kunsterziehung*" [art education] we're actually found the magic word to solve all social questions'[72]. If he seemed less concerned about the spiritual state of the people, he was very anxious about the state of German art. He acknowledged that 'we actually have masters of the first order in all the areas of the fine arts, men who are living proof that the creative German spirit is not yet dead', but claimed that this was not enough. In order for this relative good health to survive, it must have good soil in which to grow. 'And this soil can only be the people's understanding of art'[73]. Worried that the elements of the *Großstadt* could undermine their sense of culture, Lange advocated leading children to art in order to maintain a sense of artistic tradition, to bring 'the artistic education of our youth ... in closer connection to the living, creative art of the present'[74].

The education of taste was also very important to Lichtwark. To his contemporaries, he was even more well known as the director of the Hamburg *Kunsthalle*, which came into international prominence during his tenure. There he was instrumental in organizing ground-breaking exhibits of amateur and artistic photography, promoting local artists, and discovering such talents as Philipp Otto Runge. 'We do not want a museum that simply stands and waits', proclaimed Lichtwark upon assuming the directorship of the Hamburg *Kunsthalle* in 1886. 'Rather, we want an institution that actually works for the aesthetic education of our population'[75]. In that

same year he complained that 'our citizens are not yet as cultured as the English'[76]. Lichtwark envisioned his museum as an educational centre for the artistic life of the region. It would be a clearinghouse of taste, where exhibits of art from around the world would help raise the sensibilities of the general public and teach new techniques to local artists. For instance, in his introduction to the first exhibit of amateur photography in 1893, Lichtwark stated that the show's goal was to 'raise the artistic taste of the public and stir interest' in the new art[77]. The development of a national art depended upon the aesthetic education of both the public and the artists – his museum would take up that task.

Lichtwark's influence on actual educational practices came through one of his most popular books, *Exercises in the Contemplation of Art Works*. The drills consisted of Aristotelian question and answer sessions between teacher and student, demonstrating by example how the child's inherent aesthetic taste could be cultivated and guided to acceptable standards. The student would gaze upon a painting and answer the teacher's questions about its form and content until the work's meaning revealed itself to the child. For this process to be successful, Lichtwark stressed the importance of extended contemplation of single art works in a quiet, conducive environment. Consistent with the '*vom Kinde aus*' philosophy mentioned earlier, this method of aesthetic training soon gained wide favour among German educators. Lichtwark's system also confronted the important issue of national taste.

> The typical modern German is aesthetically weak. He lacks both a superficial knowledge of culture and an inner connection with visual art. He has no need of aesthetic pleasures, which presume an education of the eye and heart. His eyes see poorly and his soul not at all. For the health of our nation and our heritage, this inadequacy must be redressed[78].

Lichtwark designed his *Exercises* to provide a training programme for children and others who were 'aesthetically weak'. By teaching youngsters how to look, gaze and, ultimately, *see*, Lichtwark was following a set of presumptions common to aesthetic education: train the eye and the heart follows. For the art education reformers of Imperial Germany, then, educating public taste was a pro-

Fig. 7. Reformist Hermann Häfker. [Photo courtesy of Helmut Diederichs.]

ject in nation-building. Simply, education *through* art was a way of building a distinctly national art, while education *to* art was designed to build consensus and therefore national unity, as well as maintain traditional standards and methods of evaluation. These two directions were and are common for all art education programmes from Schiller to Dewey[79].

Kinoreformers also grasped on to this constellation of taste, nation and education. The taste of the nation was a matter of public concern because it was a symptom of both the state of national art and the political and intellectual strength of the population. For many reformers, the unity of the nation seemed fragile enough to warrant harsh measures

against foreign influences on the public's sensibility. For example, Willi Warstat, in his essay 'On the "Taste" of the Peoples', advocated censorship, entertainment taxes on the exhibitors, and tariffs on foreign films to help the fledgling German film industry, but more importantly, to protect the national sense of taste. Of Danish films and filmmakers he wrote: 'They know how to make "moral dramas" of such cunning, both unobjectionable to the censor and attractive to the lower instincts of the masses that they now present the greatest danger to the education of public taste'. But cinema is salvageable: 'That there are fairly good films now and again prevents one from despairing completely over the current depths – apparently getting deeper – of the *Kino* theatres in the matter of taste. Cinema's worth, actually still developing, depends upon its control by the forces of good taste, not just the taste of the people'[80].

Hermann Häfker's 'model presentations'

For Hermann Häfker, 'control by the forces of good taste' meant establishing alternative exhibition venues. After the failure or, at best, limited success of the attempts to create an alternative production and distribution system, the reformers realized that focusing on exhibition held the most promise for fulfillment of their programme. Miriam Hansen has argued that the peculiarities of early cinema exhibition presented the structural possibility of an alternative public sphere. The variety format, the sense of theatrical space, the combination of lectures, live music, sound effects, etc., and the uneven development of modes of production, distribution and exhibition – all contributed to 'overlapping types of public sphere, of "nonsynchronous" layers of cultural organization'[81]. Between the 'fissures of institutional development', alternative modes of reception and experience could emerge. The reformers, of course, hoped to 'synchronize' these layers, not only by coordinating the modes of production, distribution and exhibition, but also by integrating the various cultural spheres that commercial cinema was already grafting upon itself: literature, science, the tradition of the lecture series, and art.

Hermann Häfker's 'model presentations' (*Müstervorstellungen*) are the best example of the reformist exhibition programme. Some have called him Germany's first film theorist – he was certainly one of the very first to write regularly about the cinema[82]. He began the century working as a writer, journalist and translator for a number of periodicals, covering a range of topics, from Shakespeare's sonnets to his own bicycle tour of Finland. He was one of the first writers for *Der Kinematograph* and a spirited contributor to and editor of *Bild und Film*, eventually writing three books on film for the *Volksvereins* publishing company. His 'Image and Word' (*Bild und Wort*) society film exhibitions were prototypes for many 'model presentations' that reformers tried to implement on a regular basis around Germany. His 1913 book, *Cinema and Art*, is an elaborate justification of the artistic potential of cinema and an

extension of his earlier work in the reform journals. In this monograph, he describes his attempts to create aesthetically pleasing and educationally effective cinema programmes. As we have seen, Häfker was not alone in these attempts, but he was unique in providing theoretical justifications of his presentations.

Like Lange and the other reformers, Häfker was concerned with the aesthetic sensibility of the masses and the influence of bad taste. His comments about taste are directed particularly to the contemporary state of film exhibition. Of the nickelodeons of the teens, Häfker noted that 'the educated circles have been repulsed by the tastelessness of the programmes'[83]. Further, 'it's not the What of the programme, but the How of the presentation that makes the impression'[84]. Of course, he certainly did not withhold complaints about the 'sensational' films the producers presented to the audience. But unlike many of his contemporaries, such as Warstat, who felt that censorship was the proper solution, Häfker continued to express his concern for the 'tasteless' exhibition. This tastelessness referred, most generally, to the intrusion of modern life's hectic pace into the auditorium, where spectators were assaulted with a 'breathless chase of one number after another, accompanied by intertitles, the uninterrupted noise of the projector, the lights, etc'. Häfker demanded an exhibition that avoided the exciting and the extraordinary and instead tried to establish 'a quiet and natural mood'. He advised exhibitors to programme their films in accordance with classical aesthetic principles, building tension and then release by alternating comedies with dramas and 'scenes from the life of nature and simple people'. The exhibitor should also refrain from putting all the films on one reel, allowing instead a short pause between them so that 'the spectator's eyes would receive their necessary recovery time and the nerves a moment to relax'[85].

This last bit of advice points to a range of literature dealing with visual fatigue and the motion pictures. In this discourse, the equation of cinema with modernity becomes most explicit. Häfker expresses the concerns of the day quite well when he complains that 'image and form, word and sound, colour and line … rain like a hailstorm on the nerves of modern man – especially in, but not limited to, the *Großstadt*'[86]. Cinema came to epitomize this hailstorm. Some of the first articles written on cinema in Germany were medical papers on the harmful effects of 'flicker' cinema's. Other medical investigations dealt with the threat of eyestrain in the Kinos. Nearly all reformers or opponents of cinema criticized its threat to public health and vision[87].

This outcry must be seen in the context of the larger preoccupation with fatigue that characterizes discourse coming out of the late nineteenth century. As Anson Rabinbach has shown, the trope of fatigue was more than a scientific mania of the age; it expressed a profound anxiety of decline and social disintegration. In the medical, scientific, and even literary study of fatigue, there is 'a tendency to equate the psychological with the physical and to locate the body as the site where social deformations and dislocations can be most easily observed'[88]. In other words, metaphors of health and sickness were used to express national anxiety. Fatigue was more than a physical ailment – it was also perceived as a *moral* disorder, a sign of weakness and the absence of will. 'Fatigue', Rabinbach notes, 'as the horizon of the body's forces, was identified with the moral horizon of the species; the moral infirmity of the population was directly proportional to the debilitating effects of fatigue. ... Fatigue represented the membrane between morally sacrosanct labour and the violent, irrational impulses that constantly threatened to disrupt the social order'[89]. Neurasthenia, mentioned before in connection to cinema's suggestive power, was the most typical metaphor for the delicate condition of the national psyche.

Like that of Walter Benjamin, Häfker's conception of modernity is neurological, centering on the notion of 'shocks'[90]. But unlike Benjamin, Häfker seeks a haven to which he can escape the hailstorm of modernity. He just wants to rest for a while, give his nerves time to recuperate. He would like to make cinema such a haven. But cinema will never be this sanctuary, he said in 1908, 'so long as the corresponding sense of illusion is missing and the correct mood is lacking'[91]. There is so much in the modern world to disturb this mood, but treating film as an art form, especially exhibiting films 'tastefully', could slow this flood of 'the much-too-much' (*der Vielzuvielen*)[92]. He planned to do just this with his 'model presentations'. In 1910 he presented to the 'Image and Word' association in Dresden a model pro-

gramme, which was to be the prototype for other cities[93]. The selection consisted mostly of nature films, but further exhibitions planned to include travelogues, scientific films and actualités. Originally, he intended to continue the exhibitions in coordination with local schools, but the project fizzled due to lack of readily available films for continuous programming.

The 1910 presentation, entitled 'Spectacles of the Earth', highlighted Häfker's preferred form, the nature film: 'The first part showed high mountains and deserts; the second part concerned ethnological subjects (Laplanders, Chinese, Arabs, Indians, cannibals, etc.). The third part dealt with 'The Thousand Games of Water' (Victoria Falls, Niagara Falls, storms on the coast, surfs, rapids, geysers, underwater volcanoes from New Zealand)'[94]. The films were accompanied by lectures, slides, music and nature sound effects, all of which Häfker tried to orchestrate into a *Gesamtkunstwerk* of Wagnerian proportions.

The presentation began with a lecture of what to expect, what to look for, and 'in which sense to take it'. It would then alternate films with slides and lectures, carefully presenting each. Häfker provides a detailed – and obviously quite proud – description of the final section of the programme:

> Then it became dark once again. You could hear the sound of water, and as the curtain parted, you could see an actual waterfall, etc. At the end of this section there was a beautiful image – one of the rarest and most artistic ['Trip on the Avon River in New Zealand']. The spectators didn't know at first exactly where they were, and as if by magic an invisible, delicate music sounded, completely in rhythm and harmony, as if made for the image (and, of course, suited to it), accompanying it to its end. As the lights shone again on the closing curtain, the loud applause was not only for all that had been seen up to that point, but for the last image and the genuine musical enjoyment that accompanied it. The proscenium seemed a magical sphere, a mysterious land of light, life, and music (61).

Häfker's further descriptions show the pains he took to assure a proper environment and mood. He reports having three men work the slides to guaran tee precise timing; curtains were hung all around the auditorium to dampen the sound; coloured stage lights shown artistically as the audience seated themselves (59–60).

These preparations certainly have many precedents in traditions of theatrical and orchestral performance, and the format is adapted from the long tradition of lecturing in performance halls[95]. Like other reformer's, Häfker insisted that focusing on the viewing environment was the first step toward cinema's eventual aesthetic respectability. But Häfker set himself apart from his contemporaries with his claim that the entire cinematic apparatus – image, light, music, sound effects, lectures – could be used in combination for the artistic presentation of film, calling this Wagnerian use of cinema '*Kinetographie*'. Häfker's efforts to guarantee the proper conditions show his concern lay primarily with the spectator's relation to the film. The conditions of reception were vitally important to his programme and his conception of the function of art. The full effect of the 'total presentation' (*Gesamtvorführung*) – here illustrated by the audience's reported confusion/illusion that they were in New Zealand – required the spectators' complete and undistracted attention. It required, in short, their *contemplation* of the film as they would an art work. He hoped that he could educate audiences to this way of viewing the film.

Häfker took his cue from Lichtwark's *Exercises in the Contemplation of Art Works*, which provided the foundation for the training of taste and vision, a way of viewing art that Häfker transferred to film. This way of viewing was certainly not unique, having immediate precedent in the German tradition of art history, which advocated above all an unmediated, contemplative gaze, a 'silent surrender' to the art work[96]. His presentations did not simply provide an environment conducive to the passive reception of art; they set out to actually train the audience's vision. Through the lectures, Häfker guided the audience to what was important and 'in which sense to take it' – that sense being, primarily, vision. But he did not want to stop there: 'In order to draw attention to especially interesting images, perhaps one should *occasionally* employ little *signal lights*. They could be coloured incandescent lamps placed around the screen that light up shortly before surprising scenes or scenes that are difficult to see' (57–

58)[97]. These visual cues would reinforce his verbal guidance, perhaps eventually creating some sort of physiological response. Apparently, Häfker did not consider that the lights might have been a distraction.

There is also a moral dimension to this way of looking. In Häfker's discussion of approaches to art, contemplation is exemplary of a certain economy of energy, in that focused attention on the art work is a way of exercising the will against the excessive stimuli of modernity. If neurasthenia was a type of mental fatigue caused by the difficulties of dealing every day with modern life, art provided not only a haven of unity and harmony in a distracted and disorganized world, it also offered an opportunity to train the attention and exercise the taste. Art and the artistic presentation of film were workouts for the mind; museums and film theatres could be mental health clubs.

Vision and taste

Schiller, like most philosophers, was suspicious of the senses, but he was least suspicious of the sense of sight[98]. According to Schiller, knowledge of the physical world passes through the senses, and is therefore contingent on them, but vision provides the opportunity to transcend the physical world and enter the aesthetic on the way to the moral realm. The key to this journey is 'contemplation'. Schiller declared, 'As long as man, in that first physical state, is merely a passive recipient of the world of sense ... he is still completely One with that world. ... Only when, at the aesthetic stage, he puts it outside himself, or *contemplates* it, does his personality differentiate itself from it'. Upon entering the aesthetic, the subject renounces his or her passions and creates the possibility of becoming a *moral* being. Contemplation is the exercise through which this process begins. The very act of perception, the very apparatus of vision is both inextricably implicated in the sensual world and ironically outside of it. 'From the moment a man *sees* an object, he is no longer in a merely physical state', Schiller noted[99]. That is, while exercise of the other senses testifies to one's *proximity* to the natural world, vision offers the opportunity for *distance*. The aesthetic of contemplation, exemplified by what Benjamin called the 'aura' of an art work, is based on distance. The aesthetic of distraction, again illustrated by Benjamin's discussion of cinema and archi-

Fig. 8. Film in the context of the sublime: the interior of the Marmorhaus theatre, Berlin, 1913.
[Photo courtesy of Uta Berg-Ganschow and Wolfgang Jacobsen.]

tecture's tactile qualities, is based on proximity[100]. Schiller again: 'If desire seizes directly upon its object, contemplation removes its object to a distance, and makes it into a true and inalienable possession by putting it beyond the reach of passion'[101].

Thus the whole concept of subjectivity – becoming a knowing subject by objectifying and therefore 'possessing' Nature – is dependent upon the refusal of passion and sensuality. Once 'outside' this sphere, the moral becomes possible. For Schiller, the renunciation of Nature is not a goal in itself as much as a necessary step toward the fulfilment of humanity's moral potential. Like the act of vision, always in the physical world while simultaneously having the potential to transcend it, humanity balances on the fine line between the sensual and the moral. Schiller called this line 'the aesthetic'.

Taste, like vision, is both embedded in Nature

and somehow removed from it. Even more than vision, taste implies participation in the social world. An artwork affects the individual, but the exercise of aesthetic judgement implies universality. When we find ourselves agreeing that something is beautiful or sublime, we are exercising a unique and precious form of intersubjectivity based on our recognition of shared capacities for aesthetic experience. This is what Kant meant when he called taste a 'sensus communis' – a communal sense[102].

The concept of taste provides the ideal illustration of the relation between aesthetics and ideology. While society could impose moral behaviour on its subjects by appealing only to Reason, it is more efficient to employ the emotions in this task. As the medium between Nature and Reason, the aesthetic allows this operation. Schiller explains:

... the ethical State can merely make it (morally

> necessary, by subjecting the individual will to the general; the aesthetic State alone can make it real, because it consummates the will of the whole through the nature of the individual. Though it may be his needs which drive man into society, and reason which implants within him the principles of social behaviour, beauty alone can confer upon him a *social character*. Taste alone brings harmony into society, because it fosters harmony in the individual[103].

Faced with a society that they felt was becoming more alienated and fractured, reformers latched on to the promise of harmony and unity offered by the aesthetic realm. Lichtwark and Häfker focused on vision to affect a renewal in taste. Their exercises in the contemplation of art works were attempts to ward off the distractions of modernity, prophylactics against the 'much-too-much'. If spectatorship had been characterized as an addiction that lulled audiences into an impressionable somnambulism, Lichtwark, Häfker and other reformers hoped to counteract this state by inscribing cinema into an aesthetic of contemplation and reflection. The audience's vision required *training* so that mental and physical fatigue would not set in; it was a way of 'pumping up' moral weaklings. While Häfker's *Gesamtkunstwerkeffekt* would provide the illusion necessary for the aesthetic experience, it was not intended to lull the audience into distractedness. Rather, it provided access to the '*sensus communis*' through a *disinterested*, distanced aesthetic experience. Nature films were both safely asexual and reminders of potential harmony. Yet the use of nature films is ironic; the reformers' emphasis on vision and distance and disavowal of *Kinodrama* and 'sensational films' amounted to a refusal of sensuality and corporeality – in short, a refusal of Nature. Training audiences to conform to certain rules of spectatorship – an ascetic education of their vision – was part of an ideology that combined educational practices and Kantian aesthetics in order to establish some sense of social order.

This legitimation strategy – anaesthetizing/aestheticizing cinema and its audiences – was a response to modernity's perceived assault on the body and the body politic, exemplified by cinema's 'flicker'. Häfker and others felt that training the aesthetic sensibility could fend off the 'shocks' of modern life. The combined concepts of 'the child' and 'taste' served as a fulcrum for the reformers, allowing them to 'uplift' the motion pictures and incorporate cinema into their ideology. As Germany's *Kinoreformers* attempted to redeem and legitimate cinema as Art, they recognized within it the potential for recovering a lost utopia of unity and, ultimately, a means for social control.✻

Notes

1. 'Die Bremer Lehrerinnen und die Kinogefahr', *Die Lehrerin* 30 (1913): 156, qtd. in Albert Hellwig, *Kind und Kino* (Langensalza: Hermann Beyer & Sohne, 1914), 71. All translations are my own unless otherwise indicated. I would like to thank Jennifer Barker and John Belton for their helpful comments on an earlier version of this essay.

2. Stephen Kern discusses the bourgeois attitude toward sexuality in *Anatomy and Destiny: A Cultural History of the Human Body* (Indianapolis: Bobbs-Merrill Co., 1975). Cf. Peter Gay, *The Education of the Senses*, vol. 1 (New York: Oxford University Press, 1984) and Michel Foucault, *The History of Sexuality*, trans. Robert Hurley (New York: Vintage Books, 1990).

3. Konrad Lange, *Die künstlerische Erziehung der deutschen Jugend* (Darmstadt: Bergstraeβer, 1893), 12–13.

4. Pierre Bourdieu, *Distinction* (Cambridge, Mass.: Harvard University Press, 1984), 190.

5. A fuller treatment of this theme can be found in Patrice Petro, *Joyless Streets: Women and Melodramatic Representation in Weimar Germany* (Princeton, N.J.: Princeton University Press, 1989). Ann Douglas discusses the similar concern in the United States in *The Feminization of American Culture* (New York: Doubleday, 1988).

6. See Josef Chytry, *The Aesthetic State: A Quest in Modern German Thought* (Berkeley and Los Angeles: University of California Press, 1989).

7. On reform movements in general, see Norman Rich, *The Age of Nationalism and Reform, 1850–1890* (New York: W.W. Norton, 1970), 103–122; Richard Hofstadter, *The Age of Reform: From Bryan to F.D.R.* (New York: Alfred A. Knopf, 1955); Judith F. Stone, *The Search for Social Peace: Reform Legislation in France, 1890–1914* (Albany, N.Y.: State University of New York, 1985).

8. See, for instance, Gordon A. Craig, *Germany, 1866–1945* (Oxford: Oxford University Press, 1978); Hans-Ulrich Wehler, *The German Empire*

1871–1918 (Leamington Spa: Berg, 1985), 32–51; or V.R. Berghahn, *Modern Germany* (Cambridge: Cambridge University Press, 1987), as well as Jürgen Habermas, *The Structural Transformation of the Public Sphere* (Cambridge, Mass.: MIT Press, 1989).

9. On reform in Germany in general, see *Handbuch der deutschen Bildungsgeschichte*, ed. Christa Berg, (Munich: C.H. Beck, 1991) and Wolfgang Scheibe, *Die Reformpädagogische Bewegung. 1900–1932: Eine einführende Darstellung*, Ninth ed. (Weinheim and Basel: Beltz, 1984). Some have rightly argued that, despite the implications of the concept of 'reform', we should be careful not to view the educational or social theories and praxis that came out of this period as complete breaks with tradition. See Jurgen Oelkers, *Reformpädagogik. Eine kritische Dogmengeschichte* (Weinheim and Munich: Juventa, 1989).

10. A good survey of late-nineteenth-century *Kulturkritik* is David L. Gross, '*Kultur* and Its Discontents: The Origins of a 'Critique of Everyday Life' in Germany, 1880–1925', *Essays on Culture and Society in Modern Germany*, ed. Gary D. Stark and Bede Karl Lackner (College Station, Texas: Texas A & M University Press, 1982), 70–97.

11. *Verhandlung über Fragen des höheren Unterrichts, Berlin 4. bis 17. Dezember 1890* (Berlin, 1891), 770, qtd. in James C. Albisetti, *Secondary School Reform in Imperial Germany* (Princeton, N.J.: Princeton University Press, 1983), 4.

12. See Georg Kerschensteiner, 'Begriff der Arbeitsschule', in *Die deutsche Reformpädagogik*, ed. Wilhelm Flitner and Gerhard Kudritzki (Düsseldorf and Munich: Helmut Kupper, 1961), 222–238.

13. Essays expressing the themes of 'the modern', 'the healthy', and 'the national' might be, respectively: Hermann Kienzl, 'Theater und Kinematograph', *Der Strom* 1.7 (October 1911): 219–221; Robert Gaupp, 'Die Gefahren des Kino', *Süddeutsche Monatshefte* 9.9 (1911/12): 363–366; Albert Hellwig, 'Kinematograph und Zeitgeschichte', *Die Grenzboten* 72.39 (1913): 612–620. These and other representative essays can be found in *Prolog vor dem Film*, ed. Jorg Schweinitz (Leipzig: Reclam, 1992). Essays from this period are also collected in *Kino-Debatte: Texte zum Verhaltnis von Literatur und Film 1909–1929*, ed. Anton Kaes (Tübingen: Max Niemeyer, 1978) and *Kein Tag ohne Kino*, ed. Fritz Güttinger (Frankfurt am Main: Deutsches Filmmuseum, 1984). Among the numerous commentaries, see esp. Kaes' introduction, revised and translated as 'Literary Intellectuals and the Cinema: Charting a Controversy (1909–1929)', *New German Critique* 40 (Winter 1987): 7–34; Heide Schlüpmann, *Un-heimlichkeit des Blicks: Das Drama des frühen deutschen Kinos* (Frankfurt am Main: Stroemfeld/Roter Stern, 1990), esp. 189–243; and Sabine Hake, *The Cinema's Third Machine: Writing on Film in Germany, 1907–1933* (Lincoln: University of Nebraska Press, 1993), 27–42.

14. See, for instance, Fritz Stern, *The Politics of Cultural Despair: A Study in the Rise of the Germanic Ideology* (Berkeley and Los Angeles: University of California Press, 1961).

15. Paul Schultze-Naumberg, *Die Kultur des weiblichen Körpers als Grundlage der Frauenkleidung*, qtd. in Kern, *Anatomy*, 15. Schultze-Naumberg shifted easily from advocating 'natural clothing' to supporting art fashioned after natural bodies; during the Third Reich he was an architect of the campaign against 'degenerate' art. See Kern, *Anatomy*, 223–226.

16. Carl Heinrich Stratz, *Die Frauenkleidung und ihre natürliche Entwicklung* (Stuttgart: Enke, 1900).

17. Eventually exemplified by Oswald Spengler's famous *The Decline of the West*, trans. Charles Francis Atkinson (New York: A.A. Knopf, 1926–28). There are numerous commentaries, but see, for instance, Fritz Ringer, *The Decline of the German Mandarins* (Cambridge, Mass.: Harvard University Press, 1969); Klaus Vondung, 'Zur Lage der Gebildeten in der wilhelminischen Zeit', in *Das wilhelminische Bildungbürgertum: Zur Sozialgeschichte seiner Ideen*, ed. Klaus Vondung (Göttingen: Vandenhoeck & Ruprecht, 1976), 20–33; or Charles E. McClelland, 'The Wise Man's Burden: The Role of Academicians in Imperial German Culture', in *Essays on Culture and Society in Modern Germany*, 45–69.

18. See Schlüpmann, 8–25; Beth Irwin Lewis, 'Lustmord: Inside the Windows of the Metropolis', *Berlin: Culture and Metropolis*, ed. Charles W. Haxthausen and Heidrun Suhr (Minneapolis: University of Minnesota Press, 1990), 111–140; and the essays included in *Degeneration*, ed. J. Edward Chamberlain and Sander L. Gilman (New York: Columbia University Press, 1985).

19. Along with Kaes, Schlüpmann, and Hake, see Miriam Hansen, 'Early Silent Cinema: Whose Public Sphere?', *New German Critique* 29 (Spring/Summer 1983): 147–184.

20. Other periodicals included *Bild und Film* (M. Gladbach, 1912), *Der deutsche Lichtbildtheaterbesitzer* (Berlin, 1909), *Erste Internationale Film-Zeitung* (Berlin, 1908), *Film und Lichtbild* (Stuttgart, 1912), and *Die Lichtbild-Bühne* (Berlin, 1908). Helmut Diederichs provides a more complete survey of the trade press in his *Anfänge deutscher Filmkritik* (Stuttgart: Robert Fischer, 1986). On *Der Kinematograph* in particular, see Thomas Schorr, 'Die Film- und Kinore-

formbewegung und die Deutsche Filmwirtschaft. Eine Analyse des Fachblatts *Der Kinematograph* (1907–1935) unter Pädagogischen und Publizistischen Aspekten', Ph.D. diss., Universität der Bundeswehr, Munich, 1990. Hake also discusses the trade press in *Third Machine*, 3–26.

21. C.H. Dannmeyer, *Bericht der Kommission für 'Lebende Photographien'* (Hamburg: Hermann Kampen, 1907), 27–28.

22. Hellwig, *Kind und Kino*, 22.

23. See Eileen Bowser, *The Transformation of Cinema, 1907–1915* (New York: Charles Scribner's Sons, 1990), 37–52.

24. Dannmeyer, 39.

25. 'Die Eröffnung des Reform-Kinematographentheater', *Der Kinematograph* 32 (7 August 1907). *Der Kinematograph* was not paginated.

26. 'Ein kurzer Rückblick auf die erste Woche des Reform-Kinematographen-Theaters', *Der Kinematograph* 33 (14 August 1907).

27. 'Kinematographische Reformvereinigung', *Der Kinematograph* 43 (23 October 1907).

28. Hermann Lemke, 'Die Verwertung und Nutzbarmachung neuer Film-Ideen – künstlerische Films', *Der Kinematograph* 57 (29 January 1908).

29. Ludwig Brauner, 'Die Kino-Ausstellung in Berlin', *Der Kinematograph* 104 (25 December 1908).

30. Indeed, by this time the relations between the exhibitors and the reformers and trade journals were downright hostile. See 'Die Kino-Austellung und "Wir"', *Erste Internationale Film-Zeitung* 6.50 (14 December 1912): 52.

31. Hermann Häfker, 'Eine Reise an die Quellen der Kinematographie', *Der Kinematograph* 163 (9 February 1910) and 172 (13 April 1910).

32. Hermann Lemke, 'Volkstümliche Reisebeschreibungen', *Der Kinematograph* 34 (21 August 1907).

33. *Der Kinematograph* 258 (6 December 1911).

34. Paul Samulheit and Emil Born, *Der Kinematograph als Volks- und Jugendbildungsmittel* (Berlin, 1914), qtd. in Hake, 36.

35. Hake, 36–38.

36. The legal discourse on cinema in Germany is far too vast to even attempt a survey here. Albert Hellwig's reviews are the best place to start, however: *Rechtsquellen des öffentlichen Kinematographenrechts* (M. Gladbach: Volkvereins, 1913) and *Öffentliches Lichtspielrecht* (M. Gladbach: Volkvereins, 1921).

See also Gary D. Stark, 'Cinema, Society, and the State', *Essays on Culture and Society in Modern Germany*, 122–166.

37. Hellwig, *Öffentliches Lichtspielrecht*, 32–33. Not all regulations applied to the same theaters at the same time, of course.

38. My presentation of the GVV is indebted to Schorr, 81–94, and Horst Dräger, *Die Gesellschaft fur Verbreitung von Volksbildung: Eine historisch-problemgeschichtliche Darstellung von 1871–1914* (Stuttgart: Ernst Klett, 1975), 226–237.

39. Dräger, 236.

40. Willi Warstat and Franz Bergmann, *Kino und Gemeinde* (M. Gladbach: Volksvereins, 1913), 114–116.

41. Heiner Schmitt, *Kirche und Film: Kirchliche Filmarbeit in Deutschland von ihren Anfängen bis 1945* (Boppard: Harald Boldt, 1979), 41.

42. The 'monopoly' system, established in Germany between 1910 and 1911, allowed distributors to acquire sole rights to a film and pass this exclusivity to cinema managers in the form of local exhibition rights. The theatre owner's local monopoly enabled him to charge more and thus make, for the first time in Germany, a considerable profit. See Corinna Müller, 'The Emergence of the Feature Film in Germany between 1910 and 1911', in *Before Caligari: German Cinema, 1895–1920*, ed. Paolo Cherchi Usai and Lorenzo Codelli (Madison: University of Wisconsin Press, 1990), 94–113. The best survey of the role of the *Lichtbilderei* in the reform movement is Diederichs, *Anfänge*, 84–88.

43. Dräger, 234–235.

44. Volker Schulze, 'Frühe kommunale Kinos und die Kinoreformbewegung in Deutschland bis zum Ende des ersten Weltkriegs', *Publizistik* 22.1 (January–March 1977): 61–71.

45. Minutes from the meeting of the community representatives of Eickel, 14 May 1912 (Archive of the City of Wanne-Eickel), qtd. in Schulze, 64.

46. Rudolf Pechel in *Literarischen Echo* 16 (1913/14): 582, qtd. in *Hätte ich das Kino! Die Schriftsteller und der Stummfilm*, ed. Ludwig Greve (Munich: Kösel, 1976), 68. Pechel is reviewing Willy Rath's *Kino und Bühne* (M. Gladbach: Volksvereins, 1913).

47. Max Kullmann, 'Die Entwicklung des deutschen Lichtspieltheater', Ph.D. diss., University of Nuremberg, 1935, qtd. in Hake, 27. Kullmann is quoting a film theatre owner.

48. Siegfried Kracauer, *From Caligari to Hitler* (Princeton, N.J.: Princeton University Press, 1947), 19.

49. Hake, 28.

50. Helmut Kommer, *Früher Film und späte Folgen: Zur Geschichte der Film- und Fernsehenerziehung* (Berlin: Basis, 1979).

51. Hermann Lemke, *Die Kinematographie der Gegenwart, Vergangenheit und Zukunft* (Leipzig: Edmund Demme, 1911), 24.

52. Many scholars have stressed the connection between 'the masses' and 'the feminine' as an indication of the anxieties and spirit of the age. This line of reasoning is indeed extremely significant, but I would like to shed light on a relationship that has not yet been fully explored. On the masses as feminine, see esp. Susanna Barrows, *Distorting Mirrors: Visions of the Crowd in Late Nineteenth-Century France* (New Haven: Yale University Press, 1981).

53. Lorenz Pieper, 'Kino und Drama', *Bild und Film* 1.1 (1912): 5.

54. Georg Lukács, 'Thoughts on an Aesthetic for the Cinema', trans. Barrie Ellis-Jones, *Framework* 14 (Spring 1981): 3. My thanks to John Belton for reminding me of this passage.

55. This phrase and 'vom Kinde aus' are attributed to Hamburg pedagogue Johannes Gläser, one of many who popularized and realized Key's suggestions. See Scheibe, 65.

56. Ellen Key, 'Erziehung', in *Das Jahrhundert des Kindes* (Berlin, 1905) in Flitner and Kudritzki, 52.

57. Stephen Kern, 'Freud and the Emergence of Child Psychology, 1880–1910', Ph.D. diss., Columbia University, 1970, 264.

58. Charles Darwin, *The Descent of Man* (London, 1871), qtd. in Kern, 'Freud', 212.

59. Gustave Le Bon, *The Crowd: A Study of the Popular Mind* (1895. Atlanta, GA: Cherokee Pub., 1982), 16.

60. Erika Apfelbaum and Gregory R. McGuire, 'Models of Suggestive Influence and the Disqualification of the Social Crowd', in *Changing Conceptions of Crowd Mind and Behavior*. ed. C.F. Graumann and S. Moscovici (New York and Berlin: Springer, 1986), 27–50.

61. See Walter Serner, 'Kino und Schaulust', in Schweinitz, 208–214, or Kaes, 53–58.

62. Dannmeyer, 27–28.

63. Emilie Altenloh, 'Zur Soziologie des Kino: Die Kino-Unternehmung und die sozialen Sichten ihrer Besucher', Ph.D. diss., University of Heidelberg, 1913, 65.

64. Albert Hellwig, 'Über die schädliche Suggestivkraft kinematographischer Vorführung', *Aerztliche Sachverständigen-Zeitung* 20.6 (15 March 1914): 123.

65. Anson Rabinbach, *The Human Motor: Energy, Fatigue, and the Origins of Modernity* (Berkeley and Los Angeles: University of California Press, 1990), 157.

66. Hermann Lemke, 'Die kinematographische Reformpartei, ihre Aufgaben und Ziele', *Der Kinematograph* 42 (16 October 1907).

67. Albert Hellwig, *Schundfilms: Ihr Wesen. ihre Gefahren und ihre Bekämpfung* (Halle a.d.S.: Waisenhaus, 1911), 33, qtd. in Hake, 39.

68. Friedrich Schiller, *On the Aesthetic Education of Man*, trans. Elizabeth M. Wilkinson and L.A. Willoughby (Oxford: Oxford University Press, 1967), 161.

69. *Die Lichtbild-Bühne* 2.41 (4 February 1909).

70. August Julius Langbehn, 'Rembrandt als Erzieher', in *Die Kunsterziehungsbewegung*, ed. Hermann Lorenzen (Bad Heilbrunn: Julius Klinkhardt, 1966), 7–17. Stern's *The Politics of Cultural Despair* provides the standard account of Langbehn's place in history.

71. Alfred Lichtwark, 'Der Deutsche der Zukunft', in Flitner and Kudritzki, 104. Lichtwark and Langbehn were acquaintances; Lichtwark introduced Langbehn to the work of Rembrandt in 1887.

72. Konrad Lange, 'Das Wesen der künstlerischen Erziehung', in Lorenzen, 22.

73. Lange, *deutschen Jugend*, 10.

74. Lange, 'Das Wesen der künstlerischen Erziehung', 26.

75. Alfred Lichtwark, 'Die Aufgaben der Kunsthalle: Antrittsrede gehalten vor Senat und Bürgerschaft am 9 December 1886', in *Zur Organization der Hamburger Kunsthalle* (Hamburg: Meißner, 1887), 46.

76. Alfred Lichtwark, 'Unser Holzschnitt', *Die Gegenwart* 29.24 (1886): 378.

77. Alfred Lichtwark, *Die Bedeutung der Amateur-Photographie* (Halle a.d.S.: Wilhelm Knapp, 1894), 1.

78. Alfred Lichtwark, *Übungen in der Betrachtung von Kunstwerken* (Dresden: Gerhard Kühtmann, 1900), 17.

79. See, for instance, John Dewey, *Art as Experience* (1934. New York: G.P. Putnam's Sons, 1984).

80. Willi Warstat, 'Vom "Geschmack" der Volker', *Die Grenzboten* 71.6 (1912): 286–287.

81. Miriam Hansen, *Babel and Babylon: Spectatorship in American Silent Film* (Cambridge, Mass.: Harvard University Press, 1991), 93.

82. Helmut H. Diederichs, 'Naturfilm als Gesamtkunstwerk: Hermann Häfker und sein "Kinetographie"-Konzept', *Augenblick* 8 (1990): 37–60. If Häfker is known at all to English-speaking readers, it is through Kracauer's characterization of him in *From Caligari to Hitler* as the man who 'praised war as the salvation from the evils of peace'. Häfker saw World War I mainly as an opportunity for the state to take control of cinema and put his plans into action. While there is no doubt that Hafker was conservative, nationalistic, and blind to the horrors of war, it would be unfair to depict him as a war-monger with the pre-fascist tendencies implied by Kracauer. Häfker earned a 'heart attack' in a concentration camp for his resistance to the Nazi government. All biographical information comes from Diederichs' article and his entry on Häfker in *Cinegraph*, ed. Hans-Michael Bock (Munich: edition text + kritik, 1984). My presentation of Häfker is indebted to these essays and my conversations with Diederichs.

83. Hermann Häfker, 'Zur Dramaturgie der Bilderspiele', *Der Kinematograph* 32 (7 August 1907).

84. Hermann Häfker, 'Meisterspiele', *Der Kinematograph* 56 (22 January 1908).

85. Häfker, 'Dramaturgie'.

86. Hermann Häfker, *Kino und Kunst* (M. Gladbach: Volksvereins, 1913), 5.

87. See, for instance, Robert Gaupp and Konrad Lange, *Der Kinematograph als Volksunterhaltungsmittel* (Munich: Callwey, 1912); R. Stigler, 'Über das Flimmernüder Kinematographen', *Archiv fur die gesamte Physiologie des Menschen und der Tiere* (Bonn) 123 (1908): 224–232; Naldo Felke, 'Die Gesundheitsschadlichkeit des Kinos', *Die Umschau* 17 (1913): 254–255.

88. Rabinbach, 21.

89. Rabinbach, 43.

90. On Benjamin's neurological conception of modernity, see Susan Buck-Morss, 'Aesthetics and Anaesthetics: Walter Benjamin's Artwork Essay Reconsidered', *October* 62 (Fall 1992): 3–41.

91. Häfker, 'Meisterspiele'.

92. Hermann Häfker, *Kino und Kunst*, 9. Hereafter cited parenthetically.

93. Ernst Schultze, *Der Kinematograph als Bildungsmittel* (Halle: Buchhandlung d. Waisenhauses, 1911), 118.

94. Max Brethfeld, 'Neue Versuche, die Kinematographie für die Volksbildung und Jugenderziehung zu verwerten', qtd. in Diederichs, 'Naturfilm', 41.

95. On the Urania lecture hall influence, esp., see Gerhard Ebel and Otto Luhrs, 'Urania – eine Idee, eine Bewegung, eine Institution wird 100 Jahre alt', in *100 Jahre Urania: Wissenschaft heute für morgen* (Berlin: Urania Berlin, 1988), 15–74. There are also structural similarities between Hafker's presentations and the presentation of early cinema's passion plays. See Charles Musser, *The Emergence of Cinema: The American Screen to 1907* (New York: Charles Scribner's Sons, 1990), 208–218.

96. I am thinking esp. of Johann Friedrich Hebart's psychological aesthetics and his influence on Conrad Fiedler's notion of 'visibility' and Robert Vischer's theory of empathy. See *Empathy, Form, and Space: Problems in German Aesthetics, 1873–1893*, ed. Harry Francis Mallgrave and Eleftherios Ikonomou (Santa Monica, Ca.: The Getty Center for the History of Art and the Humanities, 1994).

97. Heide Schlüpmann notes that, ironically, narrative structure eventually assumed the task of guiding the spectator through the film. *Unheimlichkeit*, 266.

98. Schiller was an exception among philosophers in this respect. See Martin Jay, *Downcast Eyes: The Denigration of Vision in Twentieth-Century French Thought* (Berkeley and Los Angeles: University of California Press, 1993).

99. Schiller, *On the Aesthetic Education of Man*, 183.

100. Walter Benjamin, 'The Work of Art in the Age of Mechanical Reproduction', in *Illuminations*. trans. Harry Zohn (New York: Schocken Books, 1969), 217–251.

101. Schiller, 183.

102. Immanuel Kant, *Critique of Judgement*, trans. James Creed Meredith (Oxford: Oxford University Press, 1952), 150–154 (§40).

103. Schiller, 215. For for my discussion of aesthetics and ideology I am indebted to Terry Eagleton, *The Ideology of the Aesthetic* (Cambridge, Mass.: Basil Blackwell, 1990).

Film History, Volume 6, pp. 470–486, 1994. Copyright © John Libbey & Company
ISSN: 0892-2160. Printed in Great Britain

Forgotten audiences in the passion pits: Drive-in theatres and changing spectator practices in post-war America

Mary Morley Cohen

n 1947, Reverend J. Virgil Lilly drafted an ordinance limiting the operation of drive-in theatres in Montgomery County, Maryland, claiming that they had 'a demoralizing influence leading to promiscuous relationships'. Co-author Mrs. Thomas M. Bartram, of the League of Women Voters, warned that the 'invasion of such amusements into the country would increase juvenile delinquency'. The ordinance imposed a $1,000.00 license fee and set an 11.00 p.m. curfew on the theatre being built by the aptly named exhibitor, Sidney Lust[1]. Lilly's concerns were echoed in many popular magazines and trade journals, and the reputation of drive-ins as 'passion pits' remains to this day.

Drive-in theatres have always occupied a marginal position in relation to other more 'legitimate' places of film exhibition, and they have been viewed with suspicion by the film industry and critics alike. Throughout the post-war years until the late 1950s, mainstream distributors avoided renting first-

run films to drive-ins, arguing that these theatres would 'cheapen' films shown in them and lower earnings in subsequent runs. Even cinema historians have overlooked outdoor theatres as a serious object of study, viewing them more as an anomalous part of 1950s popular culture – a humorous novelty and not much more. Those who have written about drive-ins tend to underestimate their importance. Douglas Gomery, one of the few scholars to include them in exhibition history, for example, argues that 'The lone attraction of the drive-in seemed to be that it was cheap entertainment for baby boom families wanting the occasional night out'[2]. Another writer attributes its popularity to conservative attitudes to-

Mary Morley Cohen is a Ph.D candidate in the English Department at The University of Chicago. Please address correspondence c/o The University of Chicago, Department of English, 1050 East 59th Street, Chicago, IL 60637, USA.

ward sex, saying, 'Things are so much more wide-open sexually today that who needs a drive-in'[3]? Such an analysis simply re-circulates the stereotype of drive-ins as 'passion pits'.

However, drive-in theatres cannot be discarded as mere novelties nor can their enormous popularity be explained adequately by their appeal to families or amorous couples. As this essay will argue, drive-ins represent an overlooked but pivotal institutional stage in cinema's development. They therefore provide rich material for rethinking the trajectory of film history as it is currently conceived. For example, drive-in theatres developed a hybrid mode of exhibition that does not fit neatly into current historical periods. Specifically, the post-World War II explosion of drive-in construction occurs somewhere between the period of so-called 'classical' cinema and that of current or post-classical film practice. Taking advantage of this relatively unregulated transitional moment, drive-in theatre owners drew upon the traditions of early cinema and amusement parks as well as the privatized, media-generated entertainment of the emerging television industry. The many activities available at the drive-in reflect an understanding that film audiences have a variety of needs and interests that cannot always be distilled into a single product. During the post-war years, then, drive-in theatres helped to challenge and expand the industry's conception of the movie-going public by moving away from the fiction of a homogeneous, easily defined, urban audience. Drive-ins were among the first theatres in the South to desegregate, and in some areas they were the only non-segregated public spaces. In addition, drive-in theatre owners actively solicited audience members forgotten or deliberately overlooked by mainstream theatres, such as children, housewives, people with disabilities, labouring men and teenagers. Drive-in theatres, then, are indispensable to a thorough understanding of the ways in which exhibition, audiences and the film industry itself changed during the decade following World War II.

Drive-in spectatorship: attractions and distractions

The period just after World War II was a watershed in American film history. The five major Hollywood companies that had dominated the film industry in the 1930s and 1940s were gradually losing their monopoly of distribution and exhibition[4], and film audiences were moving away from urban centres to the rapidly expanding suburbs, trading picture palaces for television and, significantly, drive-in theatres. Because the drive-in thrived during this period of transition, it provides important insight into the ways in which spectator practices changed.

Drive-in theatres challenged classical conceptions of spectatorship that dominated film practice during the so called 'golden age' of Hollywood of the 1930s and 1940s. Many critics have observed that classical cinema imposes middle-class standards of consumption, preventing audiences from interacting with each other and reacting collectively to the film. It imposes a 'discipline of silence' whereby audience members are asked to sit politely in the darkened theatre and are discouraged from talking or commenting aloud on the film. Far from demanding this type of genteel spectator, drive-in theatres encouraged their audience to do all the things proscribed in conventional theatres. At the drive-in, spectators could smoke, eat, talk, and make out, and many ads and programmes encouraged them to do so. In 1951, *Hollywood Quarterly* maintained that the typical outdoor theatre had a 'special sense of informality' and that this relaxed atmosphere attracted an altogether different audience from that of downtown picture palaces[5].

Drive-in theatres altered the prevailing system of spectatorship primarily by re-introducing spectator practices common during the pre-classical period, when films were shown in industrial expositions, vaudeville theatres, nickelodeons, dime museums and fairgrounds. Like these older sites of film exhibition, drive-in theatres were 'entertainment centres' where patrons could choose among a variety of activities, only one of which was the film. The Walter Reade drive-in circuit, for example, offered a playground, pony rides, a dance floor, shuffleboard and horseshoe pitching tournaments, cartoon carnivals, midnight spook shows, baby parades and 'beautiful child' contests, dare-devil car rides, circus acts, high-tower dives, anniversary and birthday celebrations (with special ceremonies and cake available for all patrons), fireworks, a picnic and play area open free of charge for community use during the day, potato-sack races and television[6]. The Reade theatres and other deluxe drive-ins made use of a style of programming known in early cinema as

Fig. 1. A typical Walter Reade Drive-In: The Woodbridge Theater, Woodbridge, NJ, ca. 1960. Something for the whole family: a Disney cartoon, *Eyes in Outer Space* (1960) for the kids and *Psycho* (1960) for teens and grown-ups.

the variety format[7]. This loosely-structured format supplied disconnected attractions and allowed theatre owners to mix as many styles, moods and traditions as possible. As Tom Gunning has observed, 'Such viewing experiences relate more to the attractions of the fairground than to the traditions of the legitimate theater'[8]. In other words, the variety format encouraged a mobilized, discontinuous mode of reception that Siegfried Kracauer and Walter Benjamin have called 'distraction'[9], which is contrary to the rapt attention demanded by the structure of classically conceived films.

This exhibition context was often so distracting that many observers worried that audiences didn't come to outdoor theatres to see the films at all. Suspecting this, Herbert Ochs, owner of an Ohio drive-in periodically omitted the name of films being shown and advertised the theatre only. On these occasions, apparently, few people bothered calling

to find out what movie was showing. In fact, when Ochs asked his customers why they came to the theatre, he discovered that 'in almost every instance, they said they did not know what picture was being shown when they drove into the parking space'[10]. The film, then, was very often secondary to the theatre's many other attractions.

Another attraction of the drive-in was the opportunity to meet and play with other spectators. The Reade Theaters' potato sack and three-legged races, for example, encouraged both bodily and social contact among the audience. In addition, with its anniversary and birthday celebrations for patrons, the Reade Theater attempted to recreate what Alexander Kluge has called 'the village principle' which is 'characterized by the absolute predominance of intimacy'. In a village, 'everyone cares for each other; everyone keeps an eye on each other'[11]. The Reade Theaters created this sense of

Fig. 2. The car becomes a private box at the theatre. The San Val Drive-In, Burbank, CA, ca. 1945.
[Photo by Malcolm Keele.]

intimate community by inviting all patrons to share one's birthday cake. Many other theatres tried to foster reputations as community gathering places by renting out space to local religious groups. Three drive-ins in Jacksonville, Florida, for example, rented their theatres to area churches, which conducted services on top of the projection booth while parishioners listened on their in-car speakers[12]. While this may not have been a typical practice, most outdoor theatres had a playground and full-service snack bar where audience members could meet before and during the show. This highly sociable atmosphere was quite different from sitting quietly in a darkened, indoor theatre.

But if drive-in theatres had the atmosphere of villages, they were at best post-modern versions in which the community was often fragmented into small, isolated groups. The whole concept of the auto-theatre is, clearly, based on the premise of watching a film from the enclosed and private space of one's car. As Richard Hollingshead, the inventor of these theatres, describes it, 'The Drive-In theater idea virtually transforms an ordinary motor car into a private theater box'. During the post-war period, when television or 'home theatre' inspired interest and curiosity, this concept was especially appealing. Like television, drive-ins allowed spectators to be 'at home' – to relax and ignore the conventions and constraints of public behaviour. Writing in 1933, Richard Hollingshead boasted that the privacy of one's car would liberate the audience. 'Inveterate smokers, for example, who were pro-hibited from smoking in downtown theatres, were free to smoke in their own cars. 'People may chat', he continued, 'or even partake of refreshments. ... without disturbing those who prefer silence ... Here the whole family is welcome, regardless of how noisy the children are apt to be'. A more recent article on drive-in viewing habits shows that the privacy of the drive-in allows audience members to interact with each other to a much greater degree than in conventional theatres. 'At a walk-in theatre you can't analyse the movie ... You have to wait till you get home. Here, you can analyse it while you're watching'. Not only did drive-in theatres take advantage of television's form of spectatorship, many also exhibited early television. At the Reade theatres, for example, a television was set up at the foot of the screen for curious patrons who did not yet have one. Of course, this was not the thoroughly privatized experience of home viewing, but it did provide a transition to what was to become the media-generated entertainment of the future. At the Reade Drive-In, the audience was introduced to television spectatorship in the more familiar and public context of the movie theatre[15].

However, comparing drive-in spectatorship to that of television does not fully describe the unique experience of attending an outdoor theatre. The car was not merely a private space, but was a medium through which people saw their environment in a new way. The car helped create a new spectator whose awareness of street life alternated with the intensely private space of the car's interior. Driving down a highway with the radio on, for example, one is simultaneously cognisant of the world outside and the cocoon-like space of the car. As Roland Barthes describes this phenomenon, driving frames and de-realizes the scenes that speed by the window:

> If I am in a car and I look at the scenery through the window, I can at will focus on the scenery or on the window-pane. At one moment I grasp the presence of the glass and the distance of the landscape; at another, on the contrary, the transparency of the glass and the depth of the landscape; but the result of this alternation is constant: the glass is at once present and empty to me and the landscape unreal and full[16].

In this description, the landscape becomes de-realized and appears as a projection on a screen. Jean Baudrillard takes this same concept and links it more overtly to film and television spectatorship: 'the vehicle ... becomes a bubble, the dashboard a console, and the landscape all around unfolds as a television screen'[17]. In the car, then, not only the distinction between public and private spaces but also between simulation and reality gets blurred.

One's experience as a driver-spectator was manipulated and heightened at the drive-in theatre. First, as one drives to the theatre, the landscape through which he or she passes is de-realized and appears to be a projection. This sensation becomes literal once one has parked in front of the drive-in screen and begins to watch the movie, to 'travel' through its diegetic space. Drive-in theatres thus literalized the cinema's illusion of mobility by addressing its spectators as voyagers. Even the names of many drive-in theatres reinforced this illusion of travel and adventure: El Rancho, Prairie, Go West. The Oasis in Bensenville, Illinois carried the travel theme one step further. It was designed around a desert motif: 'a turbaned "Arab" directs traffic under a neo-Taj Mahal archway and past waving palms and burbling waterfalls'[18]. Here one could travel to India (or Saudi Arabia, it doesn't matter which) in the familiar space of one's automobile. These and other drive-in theatres harnessed the mobility of the car and allowed spectators to 'travel' to distant places in cinemas near their homes.

Although I have suggested that drive-in theatres were the first theatres to conceive of their spectators

as travellers, in fact, they were adapting a long tradition of film practice. Hale's Tours, for example, was a common attraction at many amusement parks and expositions from 1905 through 1907. It was a chain of movie theatres designed to look like a railway car, and created the illusion of moving through space on a train. These theatres featured railroad and trolley 'trips' through Ted Rock Canyon, Pike's Peak, Niagara Falls, Chicago, Palm Beach and the Black Hills, among other tours[19]. These travelogues, shot primarily from the cow-catcher of a moving train, were projected on to a screen at the front of the theatre/car and were accompanied by the grinding sound of railway wheels regulated to match the speed, stops and starts of the film. An artificial rush of air was provided, and the entire car jolted from side to side during the ride[20]. Although the cars in drive-in theatres were not so literally tied to the content of the film, they, like Hale's Tours, took advantage of the spectator's desire for the increased mobility that each mode of transportation offered. At the turn of the century, the train offered the possibility of a new mobility and opportunities to see distant places, opportunities which were also satisfied, at one remove, by the cinema. Hale's Tours epitomized and literalized the thrill of travel while remaining within the scope of one's home town and limited leisure time. Similarly, the automobile, which was quickly becoming the dominant vehicle of post World War II America, offered the means for greater personal mobility. And both exhibition practices appropriated the desire for personal mobility and travel.

However similar they may appear, though, there is an important difference between Hale's Tours and drive-in theatres. In the former, the site of exhibition, the train car, served to reinforce the reality-effect of the film and to bind spectators psychologically and physiologically to the film. In the latter, the car served to distance one from the events unfolding on the screen. This distanciation occurs on several levels. First of all, films shown at drive-ins were not literally tied to the exhibition site in the same way as Hale's Tours[21]. In addition, the car placed drive-in spectators at a physical remove from the screen, and the windshield created, in effect, a second screen on which a distorted version of the image played. This experience of distance was reinforced by the drive-in's sound system. Rather than emanating from the screen, the sound was displaced into the car, and if one opened the car windows, the sound echoed from the other cars at different rates and created an eerie and very unrealistic effect. Finally, because of the relaxed attitude of most drive-in audiences, one's view of the screen was often obscured by people walking in front of the car or turning on their headlights to wash out the film image.

Drive-in theatres, then, revised and adapted an early spectator practice that ended around 1907; however, their particular version of spectator-as-traveller also made use of the 'atmospheric' aesthetics of the picture palaces. Like the Oasis Drive-In, the theatres of the 1920s also evoked themes of exotic travel. The lobbies were often decorated with tropical palm trees, water fountains, and elaborate neo-Grecian archways. Even the moon, stars and clouds above the drive-in theatre may have evoked memories of the elaborately painted ceilings of the picture palaces. Douglas Gomery has gone so far as to say that 'from a design standpoint, the "interior" of the drive-in represented an extension of the stars-and-clouds atmospheric theatres of John Eberson'[22]. Drive-ins therefore adapted and mixed as many spectator practices and traditions as possible.

The variety format allowed the Reade Theaters and other drive-ins to draw upon older, newer and transitional forms of entertainment and provided a context for the configuration of different and competing modes of spectatorship. Drive-in theatres, then, functioned as heterotopias – in Foucault's sense – as 'spaces apart' or 'counter-sites' within which established social rules and institutions are mixed, inverted or contested[23]. For example, these theatres juxtaposed several spaces (the private space of one's car, public space of the theatre, and diegetic space of the film) in a single place. Drive-ins also jumbled time by mixing elements of the pastoral village, turn of the Century amusement parks, early cinema, picture palaces of the 1920s, and the very current television entertainment. These temporal and spatial transitions were not always smooth. In fact, they allowed radically different attractions to compete with and critique each other. Thus, the pony ride highlighted the mechanization of the merry-go-round; the desire for face-to-face contact on the dance floor provided a counterpoint to the privatized consumption of films; the need to go to a

drive-in to find people with whom to celebrate one's birthday betrayed the impossibility of creating a true community at the theatre; and, finally, going to church in the same place where one watched a B-movie the night before redefined the experience of both church- and movie-going.

Context: creating a 'cinema without walls'

It's difficult to know what to do with the many odd and competing discourses present in the post-war drive-in, which is why so many critics tend to discard the theatres as anomalous and absurd; but, in fact, if one studies these theatres in the context of a culture in transition, they make more sense. Although the first drive-in theatre was invented in 1933, the industry did not take root until the years just after World War II, when America underwent massive changes in spatial, social and temporal coordinates. The rise of the automobile and the concurrent explosion of highways cutting through the landscape broke down older spatial and temporal barriers; television both theatricalized domestic space and brought public entertainment into the home; and picture windows, glass doors, and other alterations in domestic architecture pointed to a blurring of the boundaries between public and private space. Drive-in theatres participated in these cultural transformations by bringing cars into the theatre space, replicating the private reception of television, and manipulating the tension between the private, interior space of the car and the public, outdoor space on the other side of the windshield.

All of these changes point to a revaluation of public and private parameters in the late 1940s and 1950s. Perhaps the best way to understand the post-war years is to consider that many Americans, soldier and civilian alike, had to re-orient themselves from being part of a communal war effort to settling back down to being private citizens. In other words, the period can be characterized by the overt preoccupation with privacy. Lynn Spigel has observed that middle-class families during the postwar period had 'a new stake in the ideology of privacy and property rights', which was expressed most profoundly in the massive migration to the suburbs. Spigel characterizes this departure as an expression of postwar isolationism and xenophobia, in which the home functioned as 'a kind of fall-out shelter from the

Fig. 3. A post-war phenomenon: The Paducah Drive-In, Paducah, KY, 1949.
[Courtesy of the American Museum of the Moving Image.]

anxieties and uncertainties of public life'[24]. The 1949 Housing Act encouraged contractors to build single-family homes, and the GI Bill and low interest VA loans made it easier for families to buy a home in the suburbs. During this time, the Federal Housing Administration established red-lining practices which were ostensibly designed to stabilize property values, but which also prevented African-Americans from joining the suburban migration. Thus, as Spigel points out, 'in the postwar years, the white middle-class family, living in a suburban tract home, was a government-sanctioned ideal'[25]. As I will soon show, the ideology of suburban living was central to discussions of drive-in audiences at the time.

With the rise of the suburbs, domesticity became a primary preoccupation. The popular media encouraged women to stay at home on a full-time basis, and the home became an important site for leisure time activities for the whole family[26]. As Sydnie Greenbie recommended in his book *Leisure for Living*, the home should be 'a nook for personal living and intimate self-amusement, a kind of miniature clubhouse for a little family group'[27]. Families became preoccupied with new appliances and labour-saving devices, and Americans spent more time at home barbecuing, gardening, and doing

home repairs[28]. Television played an important role in these cultural transformations by shifting spectator amusements from public theatres into the private sphere of the home.

The postwar retreat to the suburbs, however, did not prevent public contact; it did, however, help create a radically new form of publicity. During the period of migration to the suburbs, for example, community groups such as the PTA grew. Spigel describes the suburbanites as securing 'a position of meaning in the *public* sphere through their new-found social identities as *private* land owners'[29]. Even their position as private land owners was slightly ambiguous due to the pre-fabricated, mass-produced nature of their houses, making it difficult to tell one family's home from another. So, the private spheres were joined to one another by their similarity. And because these homes were not isolated, the suburbanites' privacy was enjoyed in the company of their neighbours. Television further offered people the opportunity to become linked from the private space of their homes – to an electronic community or network of spectators across the country. According to Daniel Boorstin, 'the normal way to enjoy a community experience was at home in your living room at your TV set'[30]. In other words, television gave audiences a private way to participate in a community.

The growth of the suburbs, the viability of the detached, single family home, and the development of the drive-in industry were all dependent on the rise of car culture and with it the possibility of greater mobility. In 1945, 69,500 people bought new cars; in 1950, the number jumped to 6.7 million; and by 1957, over 7.9 million Americans bought new cars[31]. On the one hand, these cars were perceived to be part of one's property – as an extension of the home and its private space. As the drive-in industry described it, the car was one's 'domain on wheels'[32]. On the other hand, as the population became more mobile, Americans gained greater access to recreation outside the home. Family outings to public recreation areas, beaches, parks, etc. increased, and vacations to national parks nearly doubled[33]. Also, outdoor recreation industries, such as hunting, fishing, and boating surged. This meant that in the 1950s, the ideology of suburban home ownership and privacy often clashed with Americans' impulse to get out of the house and engage in outdoor entertainment.

One important issue raised by the public/private tension in the expanding car culture was social control. In other words, while cars allowed greater personal mobility, they also brought previously isolated communities together and allowed others to flee from each other. In his book entitled *America and the Automobile*, Peter Ling discusses the tremendous class anxiety precipitated by the car. It broke down spatial barriers between the city and urban farm communities, which were considered 'ignorant, economically uncompetitive, [and] socially backward'. Ling describes middle-class motorists who were 'disgruntled at the inconvenience of sharing road space with the low-income motorist' while at the same time fearing that their own expensive car might fuel class hatred[34]. Social reformers, on the other hand, viewed the automobile as a means by which they could 'extend middle-class standards of hygiene and morality to lower-class, frequently immi-

Fig. 4. Located on the borderline between suburban (bottom centre) and rural (top centre) communities, drive-ins drew audiences from both groups. [Author's collection.]

grant, Americans' by dispersing them to 'detached single-family residences located further out from the city's core'[35]. While this impulse to better the conditions of the city appears to be altruistic, it did not always have a positive result. Cars could dispatch undesirable elements of the community to the outskirts of the city. And as later became the case, cars allowed the middle class to escape from the rabble of the city to the suburbs. So, the car functioned both to bring people into contact and to protect them from each other.

This rather long digression was necessary, I believe, in order to show that drive-ins were not an isolated or freakish phenomenon, but were part of larger cultural changes, including the blurring of the distinction between public and private experience.

Drive-in theatres participated in, reflected, and at times subverted this societal reorganization. Outdoor theatres, for example, tended to be built on the fringe of suburban developments and drew a portion of their audience from the suburbs. At the same time, the open-door policies and sociable atmosphere of most drive-ins stood in sharp contrast to the redlining and other xenophobic practices of suburban communities. But then again, like the PTA, this sociability was based on one's identity as a private home- or car-owner. And like the car itself, drive-ins could bring people together and keep them apart.

The 'forgotten audience'

The unique combination of attractions at drive-in theatres allowed theatre owners to expand their markets beyond that of the bourgeois picture palace and appeal to audiences that would not normally attend the cinema. Instead of providing one product for an audience conceived of as having uniform desires, drive-in theatres aggressively solicited a diverse audience with widely different interests. Also, by virtue of their location on the edges of towns, drive-ins drew an audience which cut across class and social lines, a mixture of people from rural, urban and suburban locations. This rather heterogeneous audience posed a significant challenge to standards of cultural consumption based on the model of the picture palace in the city's centre.

The great majority of journalistic articles I came across talk about drive-in theatres as special sites of mixing, where people encountered new populations:

> To the amazement of even the drive-in theatre owners, in came a type of patronage rarely seen at indoor theatres; the physically handicapped, invalids, convalescents, the aged, deaf people, expectant mothers, parents with infants and small children – whole families, dressed as they pleased in the privacy and comfort of their own domain on wheels. They are continuing to come in increasing numbers from rural, suburban, and city areas – a new clientele representing a long neglected but highly important segment of some 30,000,000 people of the 'Forgotten Audience ...'[36]

This and other articles describe drive-in audiences as a sort of side show where one could see strange aberrations in the human species. In general, drive-ins became sites in which the excitement and anxiety surrounding new social formations were played out.

'Negroes flock to the open air theatres', announced one *Variety* writer[37]. Because the private space of one's car already segregated audience members from one another, many drive-ins overlooked Jim Crow laws. Articles on the Southern drive-ins suggest that they were completely desegregated, meaning that the restaurants and amusement parks in the drive-in may have been the only places in certain areas where a black and white public could mix. At a time when segregation was still strictly enforced in many cinemas, particularly in the South[38], the drive-in theatre policy would have seemed quite radical. Whether or not African-American audiences 'flocked' there as a result is debatable; this rhetoric may well be a symptom of surprise at black and white audiences coming together for the first time; it may also have been part of the strategy to discredit drive-ins. Finally, although drive-ins were not considered to be as reputable as the downtown movie palaces, they were often superior to the theatres generally available to African-Americans at the time[39], so they may well have been attractive to these audience members.

Drive-in theatres also actively solicited obese people and people with disabilities, although, again, it is not clear to what extent this potential audience actually attended. Early advertisements for the Camden, New Jersey Drive-In, for example, showed a drawing of a rotund woman squeezing through a conventional theater aisle, disturbing patrons along the way. The caption reads: 'Even Kate Smith would have no trouble getting a seat in the world's first automobile movie theatre[,] where you see and hear talkies without leaving your car'[40]. Drive-in theatres were accessible to anyone who could get into a car. This was not true of conventional theatres, as one would have to park and use a wheel chair to get to the theatre door. The stairs, dark theatre aisles, and seats were rarely accessible. Drive-ins also offered an in-car speaker system with individual volume-control so that patrons with impaired hearing could turn up the sound without disturbing their neighbours. The ways in which drive-in theatres accommodated people with disabilities was of particular interest to Americans after 1945, many of whom were disabled – or knew someone who was – as a result of the war.

Another 'new' audience the drive-in theatre attracted was housewives and their families. The two entertainment forms in direct competition with the drive-in, television and movie theatres, were in many ways unsuited to this constituency. Although television was convenient, it did not show current movies and was located in the same space in which the housewife worked all day. It therefore did not provide an escape. And although indoor movie theatres would have provided a social arena outside her experience of domestic isolation, most did not provide entertainment for both adults and children. Drive-in theatres, then, offered the perfect solution. Kids could go to the playground or sleep in the back seat while their parents enjoyed the film, and parents could bring even very young children without worrying about disturbing their neighbours.

Drive-in theatres also appealed to working-class families, primarily because they were more affordable and informal. Many articles placed special emphasis on the fact that men would not have to shower or change their clothes after a day of manual labour in order to go to the drive-in, and they could 'avoid a second struggle with the razor'[41]. Because of the private space of one's car, one could act as he or she would at home and overlook the rules of etiquette for most other public spaces. In this respect, drive-in spectatorship was very similar to that of television. Indeed, the private interior of one's car was not unlike the living room at home, where spectators could take off their shoes, put up their feet, and nod off to sleep in front of the screen.

Finally, the most infamous of the new audience was teenage couples. Nearly every popular article mentions them, but not one gives an adequate explanation as to why young lovers might be drawn to these theatres. Most articles assume that privacy of the car was the main incentive; however, if they had a car, there were countless other places couples could go which were much more private. Home may not have been an option, but a quiet country road certainly was an option – cheaper and much more private. If drive-in theatres were 'passion pits', they were also very well lit, and many had bouncers who patrolled the parking lots with flashlights to

prevent any inappropriate behaviour[42]. On the other hand, exhibitionism had a certain appeal, and some couples enjoyed being seen and the danger of being caught. Drive-in theatres thus encouraged a form of sociable narcissism and gave a new twist to what Laura Mulvey calls the contradictory pleasures of cinema: scopophilia and narcissism. Whereas cinemas usually 'appropriate all motion and sound to themselves, allowing only the furtive, private rendezvous of lovers or of autoeroticism'[43], drive-ins allowed spectators to enact their arousal in the open[44].

The anxiety that spectators and theatre owners may have experienced upon seeing 'forgotten audiences' in public for the first time was reflected in their hyperbolic accounts of the audience in general: 'a familiar sight in many Drive-Ins is a car driven by an adult and crammed with happy children … Fat persons and cripples, who find it inconvenient to attend indoor movies, flock to Drive-Ins'[45]. Such descriptions reveal an attempt to come to terms with the diverse population seen at the drive-in, coupled with the tendency to code this population as strange or other.

Drive-in theatres appealed to this diverse audience for very different reasons, some of which were contradictory. On one hand, the drive-in theatre offered the informal, private, segregated space of home. On the other hand, it offered an escape from home and the opportunity to interact with people in a social environment – while at the same time offering a certain protection from the effects of this interaction. So the experience of attending a drive-in combined watching television and attending an amusement park, and this mixing of public and private reception often had odd results. Since patrons by no means had to remain in their cars, unshaven men were seen standing in a concession-stand line, and children were often seen running around the theatre in their pajamas. It is this element of forbidden mixing which, I believe, led to the perception of drive-ins as 'passion pits', places of illicit contact.

As a site for testing relationships created by social changes and by the shifting distinctions between public and private, drive-in theatres became sites of intense battles to determine by whom and how their public would be controlled. Because the fiction of a homogeneous American audience was

Fig. 5. Privacy in public: a newspaper ad emphasizes privacy, comfort, and multiple attractions. Ad from *The McHenry Plaindealer* (23 September 1948).

the drive-in, many conventional theatre owners made concerted efforts to discredit them. In Minneapolis, for example, Minnesota Entertainment Enterprises (MEE) provided financial and other support to residents' efforts to keep out drive-in theatres 'on the grounds that they create traffic hazards, cause juvenile delinquency and lower property valuations'[47]. It was later discovered that several members of the MEE themselves owned drive-in theatres, which significantly weakened their moral position against them and made it clear that they were merely trying to limit competitors. This was the only article I came across which admitted the financial motivation behind the efforts to discredit drive-ins. Most reports simply reiterated allegations of indecent behaviour.

eroding, there was much anxiety among cultural, moral and business leaders and the film industry itself over how to monitor private and potentially subversive reception of 'public' entertainment. Throughout their history, drive-in theatres occupied a liminal position in relation to the film industry as a whole. Despite their immense popularity, they were never able to overcome the perception that they were unsavoury, uncivilized theatres unworthy of claiming first-run status.

The battle for recognition

The combination of the drive-in's unique mode of spectatorship and its appeal to a highly diverse audience proved to be a very successful strategy at a time when attendance was dropping at conventional theatres. According to one survey, 4,000 indoor theatres closed between 1948 and 1958. Approximately 3,200 drive-ins opened and thrived during the same period[46]. Alarmed by the success of

Seemingly concerned by these negative reports, mainstream distributors carefully scrutinized drive-ins to determine if they met with Hollywood standards. They conducted elaborate studies of outdoor theatres before they even considered releasing films to them. These studies were conducted 'not only to check on the efficiency of the management of different theatres, but to show theatre officials how their own place looks to an *unbiased* paying customer'[48]. Of course, this 'unbiased' hypothetical spectator imposed certain normative restrictions. These studies, then, allowed distributors to rate drive-ins according to the standards of indoor picture palaces. Not surprisingly, one such study argued that 'the new drive-in theatres have created some questions in the minds of distributors and theatre operators who have been confronted with conflicting statements concerning the audiences of this new form of exhibition'. The study concluded that drive-in

Fig. 6. Regulating relations between the sexes with a Dickensian respectability: the Pickwick Theater, Burbank, CA, 1948. [Photo by Malcolm Keele.]

theatres did not cater to the 'average' or conventional spectator. Rather, their audiences constituted an 'entirely new patronage'[49]. One would think that distributors would jump at the chance to rent their product to this new, rapidly expanding industry; however, many decided to forego short-term market interests in favour of traditional relationships with indoor theatres. This choice can be explained in part by the fact that despite the Paramount case, many studios owned theatres until about 1956. This meant that some distributors had a financial interest in selling only to their theatres. However, early on, drive-ins had a hard time getting first-run fare from anyone, so a further explanation is necessary. I believe that distributors were worried about the effect of showing their films – which were designed with a conventional audience in mind – in the unpredictable, distracting, and somewhat irreverent atmosphere of the drive-in.

Drive-in theatre owners worked very hard to combat their increasingly negative reputation and tried to convince distributors of their mainstream appeal. Many argued that 'nothing happens [in drive-ins] that doesn't go on in a balcony'[50]. Others tried to clean up their image more directly. An owner of a theatre chain in Memphis, for example, hired 'police patrons' or undercover officers to monitor couples' behaviour in cars. They followed guidelines to help them define indecent behaviour and warned patrons when they went too far. David

Flexer, the owner, described the rules as follows: 'If a man puts his arm around a girl that's all right. But if she puts her arms around him, too, and they go into a clinch – well, that's out'[51]. Flexer thus attempted to lend this theatre an atmosphere of respectability by imposing sexual standards and monitoring, in particular, the sexual behaviour of women.

Drive-in theatres also tried to combat their reputation as 'passion pits' by arguing that the white, middle-class, nuclear family was the primary unit of spectatorship. Early information and education manuals designed for drive-in owners and patrons consistently showed very traditional family configurations in the cars. One manual, reproduced in the *Motion Picture Herald*, for example, showed several drawings of Mom, two Children, and Grandma crammed in the back seat with Dad enjoying a soda by himself in the front. Many drive-in ads focused on the family-oriented amenities such as laundry and shopping services and ads often featured a photograph of a whole family gathered around a bottle-warming table. Others overtly solicited housewives by offering laundry services. One ad in *The New York Times*, for example, reads, 'While mother is lost in a romantic Hollywood dream the laundry is tossed into an automatic machine. By the time the show is over the wash has been damp-dried and ready to take home'[52]. Such amenities were designed to make the local drive-in seem like an extension of the audience's domestic sphere, and the drive-in staff was groomed to seem part of the ideal family: friendly, courteous, and ready to help with the chores.

Also, drive-ins launched a campaign to promote the drive-in as a wholesome family activity. They suggested, for example, that drive-ins were healthy, outdoor recreation – despite the fact that audiences sat in their cars. Many articles also claimed that drive-ins were safer than conventional theatres, particularly for parents. There was no need to entrust the safety of one's children to baby-sitters. Also, during a polio epidemic in California, many children were quarantined from movie theatres. Drive-ins took the opportunity to promote themselves as safe and hygienic: '[parents] who fear to expose their children or themselves to local epidemics of flu, measles or whooping cough feel safe in the privacy of their own cars'[53]. Many drive-ins went so far as to make a spectacle of these family-spectators. The obligatory playground was always prominently placed directly under the screen. The idea was that parents could watch the film and monitor the children at the same time. Its location also meant that the rest of the audience was constantly reminded that children were present. By constructing the wholesome family as the predominant spectator and by actively luring such an audience, drive-in theatre owners sought to lend their theatres respectability. The emphasis on children, especially the beautiful baby contests, created a spectacle of innocence, youth, and old-fashioned family values. Such an exaggerated emphasis on wholesomeness, however, had little effect on distributors or city officials.

On 4 April, 1949, the Chicago City Council passed an ordinance banning drive-in theatres, arguing that 'the unregulated operation of such theatres would be detrimental to the best interests of the City'[54]. Nine months later, drive-in theatre entrepreneurs brought their case before Circuit Court Judge Harry Fisher. Representing the City, Attorney Mort Nathanson contended that such theatres invited immoral behaviour. The exchange that took place over the effect of drive-in theatres was reprinted in the *Motion Picture Herald*:

Mr. Nathanson: It is a question of whether or not this is a lawful business.

Judge Fisher: What is unlawful about it?

Mr. Nathanson: Now there are features of a outdoor theatre that are different from an ordinary theatre. They are out in the country with the moon shining, in automobiles. Why, some of the things that happen there, Judge – it's terrible[55].

Nathanson does not describe immoral audience behaviour but, rather, argues that the theatre space itself is unlawful, that there is something perverse about a theatre which is at once outdoors, in the country, under the moon, in the private space of a car, and open to the public.

These legal battles echo similar battle cries made by moral reformers who believed the earliest cinemas were places of dangerous heterosocial mixing and illicit behaviour. In *Cheap Amusements*, Kathy Peiss describes the amusement park and the cinema in turn-of-the-century New York City as places of contact between the sexes. Cinemas in particular were feared to be 'public spaces for undue familiarity between the sexes', where women were in danger of being drugged and sold into 'white slavery'[56]. Drive-in theatres were similarly labelled 'passion pits', showing indecent movies and encouraging sexual promiscuity.

Mainstream distributors for the most part accepted this view of the drive-in. In fact, they proved to be so reluctant to rent their films to drive-ins that a number of drive-in owners brought conspiracy suits against them – and won. In one such case, *Milgram, et at. v. Loew's, Inc., et al.*, theatre owners claimed that distributors were engaging in conspiracy by refusing to rent first-run films[57]. In arguing his case, David Milgram, owner of the Boulevard Drive-In, claimed he had been operating his theatre 'along lines consistent with the highest grade of moving picture entertainment'[58]. In their defence, the distributors argued that:

... the showing of a feature on first run at a drive-in would reduce the income derived from subsequent runs. They asserted that first run showings are, in a sense, showcases for subsequent runs, in that the first run showing at a downtown theatre gives a picture prestige which is important in 'establishing' it in the neighbourhood area[59].

This prestige was so important, in fact, tha

distributors refused to rent first-run films even when theatre owners offered to pay extra for them. Behind the argument that drive-in theatres were sub-standard and would thus 'cheapen' the films shown in them was, I believe, a suspicion of the drive-in audience which did not conform to the 'ideal' spectator of most Hollywood films.

In the midst of these rhetorical and legal battles, several independent production companies and distributors emerged to fill in the market gap created by the crisis: American International Pictures (AIP), Crown Pictures, and others. AIP, in particular, was an independent, low-budget production company designed specifically to take advantage of the drive-in market. Created in 1954, AIP produced inexpensive double bills for what they viewed as the drive-in audience: teenagers. At a time when other companies were suffering from antitrust actions and decreased ticket sales due to television and other leisure activities, AIP thrived. It produced low-cost, hastily-made science-fiction, horror and melodrama films, and 'between 1954 and 1960, not one AIP film lost money'[60]. AIP saturated drive-in circuits with films particularly produced for them at a time when conventional distributors were reluctant, and thus helped perpetuate drive-ins' image as a disreputable medium suitable only for B-movies[61].

Because they often found it so difficult to rent first-run pictures, drive-in theatre owners also had to come up with creative ways of promoting their less than current and less than quality fare. For example, they often booked films which were specially suited to their form of exhibition. Outdoor films, such as westerns and beach or surfer movies were seen as particularly appropriate, for obvious reasons. Because the theatre was itself in the open air, it was thought that audiences would favour the same qualities in the diegetic space. They also tried to appeal to specific constituencies. For example, the Skyline was the first drive-in designed specifically for an all-black audience. Located in Compton, New Jersey, where segregation was not officially practiced, the Skyline featured 'a mixture of white and Negro bills and other entertainment angles aimed particularly at the coloured patron'[62]. But these methods of 'exploitation' or advertising were somewhat old-fashioned when compared with the generic appeal of conventional theatres. So these selling strategies, along with the unconventional

movies they tried to sell, helped relegate drive-ins to the margins of film practice.

The malling of drive-in theatres

During the post-war years, the drive-in industry was able to survive its marginal position, and many theatres even profited from it. They were able to do so, in part, because the entire culture, including Hollywood, was in transition. No one knew precisely where film practice was headed, spectators bracketed many preconceived notions of what the cinema should be like, and the new practices that did emerge were not yet codified and therefore had latitude to develop. However, towards the end of the 1950s and early 1960s, it became increasingly clear that the film industry as a whole was moving away from deluxe theatres — both picture palaces and drive-ins — and towards the smaller and cheaper theatre in the mall.

Ironically, many drive-ins were quite directly supplanted by the new theatres. In 1972, one drive-in owner explained, 'Taxes are high, property values are out of reach and road patterns have attracted shopping-centre developers'[63]. Because drive-ins were built at the intersection of rural, urban and suburban communities, their property was the ideal location for shopping malls. Here malls could be accessible to the largest range of consumers. In addition, because drive-ins were designed as entertainment 'shopping centres', there was a pre-established clientele who might return to the same site and resume their shopping patterns when the drive-in was replaced by a mall. It is not surprising, then, that there were concerted efforts on the part of shopping mall owners to buy up the drive-in property, and drive-ins were replaced by shopping malls and parking lots: 'in Paramus, the Route 4 Drive-In may be purchased by the owners of the Garden State Plaza to create a larger parking lot for the proposed expansion of the shopping area'[64]. Thus the drive-in was relegated to its most literal function, that of the parking lot, and the transitional spectatorship of the drive-in was appropriated by an even more privatized form of consumption: the cleaner, pre-fabricated, and indoor malls.

It would be a mistake, however, to assume that drive-ins have completely disappeared. These theatres still appeal to a diverse audience that feels constrained by mainstream exhibition practices. This

Fig. 7. The dinosaur lives on: children in a makeshift bed wait for the film to start at the Grayslake Outdoor Theater, Grayslake, IL., 1993. [Author's collection.]

Drive-in theatres, then, are gradually being replaced by the very industry they attempted to exploit. In the early 1950s, when television and other privatized amusements were not yet affordable on a mass-level, the privacy at the drive-in was a novelty. Drive-ins allowed audiences to experience the new pastimes in a familiar, cheaper, and more public context. They exploited a liminal moment in the history of entertainment and were designed in such a way as to incorporate both obsolete and emergent amusements. As time went on, privatized entertainment became more and more accessible and legitimate – until television, video and computer games became the norm and drive-ins were shoved even further toward the margins of exhibition practice.

This marginal position, however, should not discourage film scholars from studying drive-in theatres. On the contrary they must be examined further precisely because they offered an alternative to standard viewing practices. They provided a positive critique of and alternative to mainstream spectatorship and proved that not everyone was satisfied with classical film-going practices. Studying drive-in theatres and other liminal practices can serve to re-focus attention on to the interstices of film history. This will not only help us revise and expand the narratives we have constructed for cinema by adding fascinating material and crucial transitions; it will also allow us to reformulate the concept of spectatorship by adding practices and audiences long forgotten. ✳

past summer, five drive-in theatres showed films around Chicago, which has a poor climate for outdoor theatres. And according to a Department of Commerce survey, drive-in theatres constituted 26.9 per cent of the total number of US movie theatres as late as 1977[65]. Although their numbers have dwindled since then, there were approximately 1,000 theatres running during the 1987 census[66]. By 1994, this number had fallen to 837[67].

In addition to the theatres still operating, the home video and cable television industries have created a new market for what are commonly known as 'drive-in movies'. Joe Bob Briggs, author of the 'Joe Bob Goes to the Drive-In' column in *The Dallas Times Herald*, is now releasing videos of his favourite drive-in films. Even Blockbuster Video stores have a special sub-section of horror films under the category 'Drive-In Horror', which features the cheapest and goriest of the genre whether or not they were ever shown in drive-ins. Cable TV's Comedy Central has a drive-in movie show that shows excerpts from the bloodiest horror films. Also, the funniest of AIP movies are regularly shown on Mystery Science Theater 3000, a show in which characters interrupt the films with commentaries and stupid jokes. The films themselves are so ridiculous that they seem to demand this type of irreverent reception. In many ways, home video and television seem to me to be the proper place for drive-in movies, since outdoor theatres were among the first to exploit the trend towards private entertainment.

Acknowledgements: For their invaluable comments and suggestions, I wish to thank Tom Gunning, John Belton and, above all, Miriam Hansen. I also wish to thank the owners of the Family Outdoor Theater in Grayslake and the McHenry Outdoor Theater, Tom and Hank Rhyan, who were kind enough to loan me their family scrapbook. An earlier version of this article was presented at the Approaches to American Mass Culture(s) Conference at the Chicago Humanities Institute on 19 February 1994.

Notes

1. 'Drive-Ins Labeled Only' Licensed Petting Places', $1,000 Fee, Curfew Set', *Variety* 17 December 1947: 5.

2. Douglas Gomery, *Shared Pleasures: A History of Movie Presentation in the United States* (Madison: University of Wisconsin Press, 1992) 93.

3. 'The Disappearing Drive-In', *Newsweek* 9 August 1982: 65.

4. The Paramount Case, an anti-trust suit brought against five major studios by independent exhibitors and producers, was settled in 1946 and prevented the studios from maintaining a monopoly on exhibition sites through price fixing, block booking, and blind bidding. By 1948, the 'Big Five' signed consent decrees, agreeing to separate their production and distribution activities from their theatre circuits. See Michael Conant, 'The Paramount Decrees Reconsidered', *The American Film Industry* ed. Tino Balio (Madison: University of Wisconsin Press, 1985) 540–541.

5. Rodney Luther, 'Drive-In Theatres: Rags to Riches in Five Years', *Hollywood Quarterly* 5, No, 4 (Summer 1951) 406.

6. 'Drive-Ins are Showbusiness' – But That Ain't All!, *Motion Picture Herald*, Better Theaters Section 4 February 1950: 28–29.

7. For a more in-depth discussion of the variety format, see Miriam Hansen, *Babel and Babylon: Spectatorship in American Silent Film*, (Cambridge, Mass. & London: Harvard University Press, 1991) 29–30.

8. Tom Gunning, 'The Cinema of Attraction: Early Film, Its Spectator and the Avant-Garde', *Wide Angel* 8.3 & 4 (1986): 65.

9. Siegfied Kracauer, 'Cult of Distraction: On Berlin's Picture Palaces' (1926), trans. Thomas Y. Levin, *New German Critique* 40 (Winter 1987): 91–6; Walter Benjanmin, 'The Work of Art in the Age of Mechanical Reproduction' 1935–36 and 'On Some Motifs in Baudelaire" (1939), *Illuminations* trans. Harry Zohn (New York: Schocken, 1969).

10. Kerry Segrave, *Drive-In Theaters: A History from Their Inception in 1933* (Jefferson, North Carolina and London: McFarland & Co., 1992) 38–39.

11. Alexander Kluge, 'The Assault of the Present on the Rest of Time', *New German Critique* 49 ([1985] 1990): 15.

12. 'Church Services at Three Drive-Ins Builds Goodwill in Jacksonville', *Boxoffice* 18 July 1953: 23.

13. Segrave, 7.

14. Quoted in Segrave, 7.

15. Drive-in theatres thus sidetracked the genealogy of in-home entertainment from radio to television by re-introducing communal reception.

16. Roland Barthes, *Mythologies*, trans. Annete Laves (New York: Hill & Wang, 1972) 123. See also Margaret Morse, 'An Ontology of Everyday Distraction', *Logics of Television: Essays in Cultural Criticism*, ed. Patricia Mellencamp (Bloomington and Idianapolis: Indiana University Press, 1990).

17. Jean Baudrillard, *The Ecstasy of Communication*, trans. Bernard & Caroline Schutze, ed. Sylvére Lotringer (New York: Semiotext(e), 1988), 13.

18. 'The Drivein Liein', *Newsweek* 8 July 1963: 78.

19. Raymond Fielding, 'Hale's Tours: Ultrarealism in the Pre-1910 Motion Picture', *Film Before Griffith*, ed. John L. Fell (Berkeley, Los Angeles & London: University of California Press, 1983) 127. See also Charles Musser, 'Exhibition Practices in the Early Nickelodeons', *The Emergence of Cinema: The American Screen to 1907* (New York: Charles Scribner's Sons, 1990) 428–433.; and Lauren Rabinovitz, 'Temptations of Pleasure: Nickelodeons, Amusement Parks, and the sites of Female Sexuality', *Camera Obscura* 23 (1990): 79–82.

20. Fielding, 122.

21. Peter Bogdanovich's 1968 film *Targets* is a notable exception.

22. Gomery, 92.

23. See Michel Foucault, 'Of Other Spaces', *Diacritics* 16.1 (1986): 22–27.

24. Lynn Spigel, 'Installing the Television Set: Popular Discourses on Television and Domestic Space, 1948–1955', *Camera Obscura* 16 (January 1988): 13,14.

25. Lynn Spigel, *Make Room for TV: Television and the Family Ideal in Postwar America* (Chicago and London: The University of Chicago Press, 1992) 33.

26. See Betty Friedan, *The Feminine Mystique* (New York: W.W. Norton, 1963).

27. Qtd. in Spigel, *Make Room for TV*, 34.

28. John Belton, *Widescreen Cinema* (Cambridge, Mass and London: Harvard University Press, 1992), 71–74.

29. Spigel, *Make Room for TV*, 101.

30. Boorstin, Daniel, *The Americans: The Democratic Experience* (New York: Vintage Books, 1973) 393.

31. Belton, 72.

32. Charles R. Underhill, Jr., 'The Trend in Drive-In Theaters', *Journal of the Society of Motion Picture and Television Engineers* 54 (February 1950): 162.

33. Belton, 74.

34. Peter J. Ling, *America and the Automobile: Technology, Reform and Social Change* (Manchester and New York: Manchester University Press, 1990), 6.

35. Ling, 6–7.

36. Underhill, 162.

37. 'Ozoners' Big Negro Draw', *Variety* 3 August 1949: 4.

38. Mainstream cinemas were not desegregated until about 1965 (See Gomery 155–170).

39. 'The open air theaters … are attractive deluxe affairs as compared to the second-rate flickeries generally available to them. This holds true particularly in Texas' ('Ozoners' Big Negro Draw', 4).

40. Segrave, 6.

41. Thomas M. Pryor, 'Movie Novelty Develops into Big Business', *New York Times* 4 September 1949.

42. A friend told me she preferred to go on dates at the drive-in because it placed an automatic limit on sex and therefore provided a sense of protection and safety.

43. W.J.T. Mitchell, 'The Violence of Public Art: *Do the Right Thing*', *Art and the Public Sphere*, ed. W.J.T. Mitchell (Chicago: University of Chicago Press, 1992), 39.

44. It has been suggested to me that conventional theaters also offer the promise of the public display of sexual acts. Thus, the 'make out' scene at the back of the theatre has the faint trace of an orgy rather than that of a private rendezvous.

45. 'Stars', 117.

46. Cobbett Steinberg, *Reel Facts: the Movie Book of Records* (New York: Vintage Books, 1978) 361.

47. 'Fight Drive-Ins as Traffic and Juve Headaches, *Variety* 1 September 1948: 5.

48. Leo A. Handel, *Hollywood Looks at its Audience: A Report of Film Audience Research* (Urbana: The University of Illinois Press, 1950) 209 (emphasis added).

49. Handel, 210.

50. 'All This', 84.

51. Segrave, 41.

52. Pryor.

53. Cullman, 3.

54. *Journal of the Proceedings of the City Council of the City of Chicago*, 4 January 1949: 3670.

55. 'Chicago Court Rules City Cannot Bar Drive-Ins', *Motion Picture Herald*, 28 January 1950: 22.

56. Kathy Peiss, *Cheap Amusements: Working Women and Leisure in Turn-of the Century New York* (Philadelphia: Temple University Press, 1986) 151.

57. Defendants in the case were: Paramount, R.K.O., Warner Bros., Twentieth Century-Fox, and Loew's, referred to as the 'Big Five'. Columbia, Universal, and United Artists were referred to as 'minor defendants'. *Milgram, et al. v. Loew's, Inc., et al.*, 192 F.2d 579 (argued 19 June 1951).

58. *Milgram, et al.*, 581.

59. *Milgram, et al.*, 582.

60. Robert Stanley, *The Celluloid Empire: A History of the American Movie Industry* (New York: Hastings House, 1978): 243.

61. Even when an A-grade film was shown, it was often on its second or third run. Thus, in drive-in theatres, even Hollywood pictures took on an outdated or out-of-step quality.

62. Bill Brogdon, 'No Brakes on Drive-In Lures: Indoor Exhibs Plenty Worried', *Variety* 13 July 1949: 18.

63. Martin Gansberg, 'Drive-in Movies Go Dark as Costs Rise', *New York Times* 6 October 1974.

64. Gansberg.

65. Dennis Giles, 'The Outdoor Economy: A Study of the Contemporary Drive-In', *Journal of the University Film and Video Association* 35.2 (1983): 68.

66. Segrave, 202.

67. Brett Pauly, 'Drive up to the dinosaur', (L.A.) *Daily News*, 21 July 1994.

Film History, Volume 6, pp. 487–501, 1994. Copyright © John Libbey & Company
ISSN: 0892-2160. Printed in Great Britain

The K-mart audience at the mall movies

William Paul

During the late 1970s, a crisis sensibility began to overtake Hollywood. In 1977, there was a mild panic in response to a sudden 7½ per cent decline in movie theatre attendance in 1976 after a two-year surge in 1974–75. After a decade of almost continuous growth and record revenues, the years 1990–91 saw ticket sales decline sharply, in fact to their lowest level since 1976[1]. A similarly bleak sense of crisis lowered over Hollywood, one that has continued even after box office began to pick up again in the following year[2]. Never before in the history of Hollywood has an individual film been able to make as much money as it can today. But the demand for sure-fire blockbusters and commensurately escalating budgets has also meant that never before had any individual film been able to lose so much money. As a consequence, it's very easy to go from a buoyant boom to a gloomy bust in a very short time.

Crises come very easily to Hollywood since movie production is probably the world's largest crap shoot, or, as a *Variety* writer surveying 1993 box office put it, 'What keeps the movie business so interesting and media pundits so busy is that the search for a sure thing has a success rate right up there with playing slot machines in Vegas'[3]. Every new film is like a roll of the dice or a spin of the slot machine with every player trying to calculate odds that might well be incalculable. The extraordinary success of Arnold Schwarzenegger movies was enough to make Columbia willing to gamble $80 million on *The Last Action Hero*, but it turned out to be a bad bet, with a $28 million loss[4]. Still, 20th Century-Fox saw sufficiently good odds in previous

Schwarzenegger successes to place a $100 million-plus bet on *True Lies*, even though Schwarzenegger is completely miscast in that film. The stakes are enormous, far beyond what anyone might have imagined during the crisis of the late 1970s. Furthermore, the intervening seventeen years saw radical changes in distribution, marketing and exhibition that make the crisis of the early 1990s different. In fact, the current situation arises from changes brought about by a response to the crisis of the 1970s, which was really a crisis of confidence in Hollywood's sense of its audience[5].

In the late 1970s, an apparent fickleness of audience taste coupled with an increasing selectivity in moviegoing raised new questions for Hollywood's executives: who were these viewers and why did they go to the movies? Not only did Hollywood wonder why they went to a movie, but why they went to *any* movie? In the mid-1970s Ned Tanen, executive vice president of Universal, could declare, 'The truth is, although nobody likes to bring it up, we can't find twenty-five films a year worth making'[6]. What this executive actually meant was they could no longer find twenty-five films a year that would appeal to an audience they felt increasingly remote from them and unpredictable. The crisis of 1991 also has to do with uncertainty about what motivates

William Paul is the author of *Laughing Screaming: Modern Hollywood Horror and Comedy* (1994). He is Associate Professor of Film at the University of Michigan. Address correspondence c/o Film/Video Studies, University of Michigan, 2512 Frieze Bldg., Ann Arbor, MI 48109, USA.

an audience, but it is of a different order in large part because it reflects changes in the way Hollywood addressed its audience over the last couple of decades.

Exploitation psychology

Changes in exhibition practices that were a response to the previous sense of crisis have led to a consequent transformation of the *kinds* of movies that get produced. In effect, exhibition has become the tail that wags the dog as it inescapably makes demands for product that can most appropriately fit new modes of exhibition. There is a kind of reciprocal influence that exists between film producing companies and their audience that is determined by the way the companies address their audience: new exhibition practices which occur in response to changing demographics (shifts in geographic and age distribution of the audience) and market pressures, in turn, help transform audience expectations of the moviegoing experience. The period I am concerned with here presented one of the clearest examples of this process in American film history, largely because it saw the most radical break with past exhibition practices: favourable audience reaction to a number of films whose subject matter would once have marked them as exploitation product led to an exploitation releasing strategy that eventually became applied to all films. The films in turn became marked as exploitation product by virtue of the releasing strategy[7]. The responses of the audience may help determine marketing strategies, but the marketing strategies effectively reconstitute the audience. The manner in which the films are presented to the audience effectively tells us something about who Hollywood thinks its audience is.

While there had been a general decline in movie theatre attendance from the mid-1960s through the early-1970s, with 1973 representing the worst year since the leveling off of the post-World War II decline in the late 1950s, individual films were reaping theatrical revenues on an unheard of scale, generally surpassing the grosses of even the biggest blockbusters from the 1950s. And the success of these individual films led to lopsided box-office returns. There was a striking example of films released in 1975 that had earned more than $2 million, which was then considered the minimum necessary to break even: out of seventy-nine films

that reached the magic $2 million figure, a mere fifteen accounted for fifty-seven per cent of combined domestic rentals, monies returned to the producing companies from the US-Canada market.

Moving away from the golden age of theatrical exhibition when the margin of economic difference between success and failure was of a much smaller scale, this new development proved to have such lasting effect that an astute movie business observer writing in *Variety* in 1986 could state flat-out:

> In the film business, an unchanging parameter is that the top 10 per cent of films account for 40–50 per cent of the business of *all* films in concurrent release. If there are 200 films released in a year, 20 of them will generate nearly one-half the b.o. of all 200[8].

This was a statement, however, that could only apply to post-television Hollywood, when the regular moviegoing audience had disappeared. Every film had to succeed in the marketplace entirely on its own, but in a crowded marketplace how could it attract the attention that was a necessary prelude to success? It was in this period that it became a commonplace in Hollywood to think that every film had to be an event to succeed in this marketplace. So, even though individual films in the seventies could make enormous amounts of money, production dropped sharply as each producing company tried to concentrate its production on the event films, the films that would land in the top 10 per cent to generate half the company's income.

Within a decade, the cries of product shortage common throughout the seventies were succeeded by new concerns about product glut[9]! This shift came about through the development of the aftermarket, the videotape as a major form of distribution and the continuing growth of pay-cable television. The majority of films might still have trouble making their cost back from theatrical distribution, but video in its various forms buoyed confidence by promises of profit margins in the post-theatrical market. Since the number of people buying tickets remained remarkably steady throughout this period, video did not so much cut into active moviegoing as expand the market for feature films[10]. And since theatrical exposure is often a key factor in the success of a film on video, theatrical exhibition was actually given a new *raison d'être* in this period: a necessary spring-board for the lucrative tape market.

Saturating the market

For all the changes that videotape would help introduce, the mid-1970s product shortage and its concomitant sense that every film had to be an event did itself have a lasting impact on film exhibition in one striking way. In June of 1975, Universal simultaneously opened *Jaws* in about 500 theatres at once, promoting the film with a massive television ad campaign. The very way in which the film was exhibited helped make it an event, something of a necessary strategy for Universal because it was the only film the company released for the next three months. Mass releasing was a mode of exhibition distributing companies had been experimenting with ever since it proved successful with the low-budget *Trial of Billy Jack* in 1971, but *Jaws* was the first time since *Duel in the Sun* that the strategy had been applied to a big-budget, glossy production, and it seemed to work.

Significantly, the *Duel in the Sun* release was unusual in 1946, one which producer David O. Selznick described as a revolutionary 'multiple-booking plan' involving 'enormously and unprecedentedly heavy newspaper and radio advertising by territories'. Selznick, realizing he had not come up with another '*Gone With the Wind*', used the mass release as a way of capitalizing on advance audience interest and countering potential bad word of mouth. Nevertheless, he eventually came to regret it, writing in a memo that 'the advertising and ballyhoo on *Duel* was damaging, and was a complete contradiction of our former "Tiffany" standards ... even if am wrong in exaggerating the extent of the loss to my position, there is the matter of my family to think of ...'[11]. But if the release strategy contradicted the kind of movie Selznick thought he had produced, *Jaws* truly was material that in the past would have been considered exploitation; what made it different was the big budget, the major stars, and a change in the cultural environment that made no one connected with the film worried about sullying their families. The film might have had the trappings of A films in the past, but its exploitation release was appropriate to its content and genre[12].

Nowadays when *The Lion King* can première in 2,552 theatres simultaneously, 500 theatres

would count as a limited opening, but *Jaws* at least helped established the future method for distributing films, one that would become set in stone by the middle of the next decade: extensive advertising on prime-time national television to generate name-recognition followed by opening of the film in as many markets as possible to take advantage of all the national advertising[13]. Once advertised this way, the film should be easily available to its audience, as easily as any other mass produced item. To say this method became set in stone is to be quite literal in that it effectively became institutionalized by the ascendancy of a new institution: the multiplex. There are, of course, a number of reasons for the multiplex, but the one of most interest to me here is the way it provided the perfect set-up for the new releasing strategy since it could make readily available all mass advertised films to their mass audience in the most convenient form. Viewers wouldn't have to search for the film they saw advertised on television. All they'd have to do is show up at the local multiplex.

This exhibition strategy turned out to be, for the most part, a radical reversal of past releasing patterns, and with this reversal, the movie distributors effectively changed the way they had addressed their audience in the past. Up through the 1970s, distribution was based on principles of exclusivity. Virtually every major release was tiered through a series of runs, with each tier effectively inscribing a somewhat different audience. The movie might be the same, albeit a bit older, but seeing it in your small neighboured movie theatre in second-run made of it a different experience from seeing it in one of the big downtown movie palaces. If executives in the mid-1970s began to worry about how to position each movie as an event, they could turn to an earlier model when the first-run theatres of the post-war era attempted to transform exhibition into an event.

The culmination of this booking strategy came in the 1950s and 1960s when the most lavishly produced films of the year would open solely in the biggest cities in the country, on a reserved-seat basis and with only two shows a day, imitating the classy pattern set by live theatre. Exclusivity had its own marketing value by effectively lending an aura to each film: the small number of first run theatres – they accounted for only a quarter of the total theatres in

Fig. 1. Mass-marketing at the multiplex: the Lloyd Cinemas in Portland, OR (1986), a ten-screen multiplex. [Photo courtesy of the American Museum of the Moving Image.]

the United States – gave anything that was seen in those theatres a distinctive stature. And when they were shown in even fewer theatres with advanced ticket purchases required, they were immediately made even more special.

The value of giving special value by exhibition practices was thrown into question by the disastrous 1969–70 seasons that eventually saw the ledger books of all the major film companies turn red. *The Sound of Music*, released in 1965 on a reserved-seat, limited run basis, ended up with over $70 million in rentals, an extraordinary figure for the period, far outdistancing every other film of the decade and effectively setting a goal for every studio to try to reach. Unheard of losses turned out to be the eventual destination, however, as every studio found its monies tied up in a small number of megabudget musicals that failed to duplicate the *Sound of Music*'s success. The immediate response of the major studios was to limit costs and product. Exclusivity had seemingly lost its value in marketing films.

At the same time that the studios were moving towards disaster with the megabudget musicals,

theatre chains were trying to shore up their economic base through the discovery of the suburban market. Even with the growth of the suburbs after World War II and the intensified suburban flight of the 1960s, big downtown movie theatres continued to exist as important venues for first-run. But they lost some of their dominance with the building of new suburban theatres. Located near new shopping malls or in isolated spots along interurban highways, these theatres followed the model set by downtown theatres since it was appropriate to the tiered releasing policies of the major studios: they were generally freestanding structures with large auditoriums of 500–1500 seats, and most often with single screens.

Multiplexing

The first twin theatre was built in 1964, but single screens dominated in this period of building; the aim was to duplicate in scaled-down fashion the experience of the downtown theatre. Exclusivity was still the aim, but now it was an exclusivity that the downtown had to share, often against its will, with the suburb[14] Within two decades, however, the exclusive down

Fig. 2. Predecessor to the multiplex: Cinema I and II, New York City, NY, 1962. [Photo courtesy of the American Museum of the Moving Image.]

town theatre would virtually disappear from most mid-sized cities and become an endangered species in large cities. The suburban theatre became so dominant that currently a trip to the suburbs is necessary in some urban areas in order to see first-run product[15].

If the development of a network of first-run suburban theatres made the mass booking of films like *Jaws* feasible, this kind of booking strategy effectively helped change the course of theatre building. The second wave of theatre growth, beginning in the late 1970s, moved in a different direction. In 1978, only 10 per cent of indoor theatres were multiplexed, with twin theatres accounting for 80 per cent of those[16]. Freestanding theatres built in the 1960s were cut down the middle to create, however awkwardly, twinned theatres, and downtown movie palaces, if they continued to survive, did so by turning their balconies into separate theatres or abandoning movies altogether to become performing arts centres. This tentative move towards multiple screens escalated during the 1980s when one of the greatest explosions of new theatre building in the history of motion pictures took place[17]. Multiplexes,

some so large they became malls unto themselves, began to ring cities throughout the US in rapidly increasing numbers[18]. In 1979, there were 16,901 'screens' in the United States; by 1990, the number had grown to 23,689, as *Variety* triumphantly noted, 'the highest count in the nation's history', even though 'screen' in the past always referred to a single theatre[19]. Multiplexes had become such a dominant form of exhibition that the Motion Picture Association of America now just lists screens rather than theatres. It's as if the actual number of theatres in the country had become the irrelevant statistic. The screen is the defining factor.

The very structure of these theatres created a new kind of moviegoing experience for film patrons. No longer offering just one film, these theatres, more in the mode of a television set than older film theatres, offered up at least six to ten different films and, in more extravagant outbursts, as many as twenty. Film began to be merchandized like wares in a variety store, with everything to please a range of interests and tastes, in theory at least, available under one roof. Much as Kresge's, once an also-ran to Woolworth's, transformed itself into one of the country's pre-eminent retailers as 'K-Mart' by abandoning downtown locations for more expansive suburban plants, the multiplex cinemas became the dominant force in film exhibition by following a similar retailing strategy.

But there was also one clear advantage the multiplexes had over K-Mart: since most of these theatres are first-run, they inescapably defined themselves as quality theatres. In the past, the quality of a theatre might be defined by its elaborate architecture which designated it as the appropriate venue for the biggest and best films of the year. The building lent its aura to the product. Now the process is reversed and the quality product lends its aura to the undistinguished settings. Second-run became the province of home video, some of it sold by K-Mart in fact, while subsequent runs were handled by the various stages of television distribution: pay-per-view, pay cable networks, network television and syndication. But the very different venue at which first-run also arrived in this period has effectively changed our notions of what constitutes a first-run movie.

Marketing fallout

The marketing strategy of mass distribution has clearly made the multiplex a particularly viable exhibition form for the distribution companies. With the average film now costing $29.9 million to produce with an additional $14 million for prints and advertising, the multiplex offers a couple of key advantages. The heavy investment in television advertising, often, now, at the expense of local newspaper ads, requires that the film be non-exclusive, as readily available for immediate consumption as any other nationally advertised product. Further, the very high costs of producing and releasing films demand a quick return on investments to avoid ever-mounting interest payments on loans used for production and distribution.

The economic pressure is supported by industry wisdom that a strong first week is essential for the success of a film. Oddly, this is more a matter of faith than fact. It's actually impossible to prove that a film could not build slowly, as it often did in the past, but the current system actively discourages that. If the release of each film becomes something of a national event by virtue of the media blitz, every first week that does slow business must necessarily seem

like a failed event: the film fizzles before it's given the chance to fizz[20]. In a sense, the audience is no longer allowed to discover films on its own, and the only real 'sleepers' are films that do better business than advance marketing research had anticipated.

Any film which does not manage to survive the first week blitz, is liable to disappear from theatrical life very quickly. This is actually a reverse of what was expected as multiplexes began to dominate exhibition. Initially, there was some sense that the great number of screens would enable 'underperforming' films to hang on and build up an audience. This might in fact work during a period of product shortage, but now there are always other films waiting to take their place. And even films with $40–$50 million dollar budgets like *I'll Do Anything* and *Wyatt Earp*, to take two recent examples, can find themselves out of distribution within a month of release.

National advertising may help impulse buying to the extent that a title may come to mind when the patron reaches the box office. The theatre chains seem aware of this to the extent that many of them now print brochures that contain guides to current releases to help guide the patron through the plethora of choices that the average multiplex offers. But there is impulse buying of another sort that is crucial to theatres, and that centres around the concession stand. The multiplex theatre is a boon to the concession stand because it promotes more foot traffic by it than a single-screen theatre does[21]. And the concession stand is a major source of profit for theatres, with 'the proportion of profit in refreshment revenue ... considerably greater' than that of the box office[22]. In 1989, for example, tickets cost patrons $5.03 billion, while concessions hit them for $1.35 billion. Furthermore, because the distributor may take away a good deal of the ticket receipts for the film rental, 'At some theatres, [the concessions] account for 90 per cent of the profits'[23]. In most multiplexes, the candy counter is central to the building's architecture: it is generally the first thing you see upon entering, and something you generally move by in leaving.

Every theatre is a piece of real estate, and the escalation of land values in the 1980s helped put the final nail in the coffin of downtown movie palaces. As downtowns across the country became primarily business centres valued for their potential

Fig. 3. In the mall, one of the anchor stores, J.C. Penney (left), receives prominent signage, while United Artists Theaters (right), unlike movie palaces of the past, must content itself with second billing and a smaller sign (Briarwood Mall, Ann Arbor, MI). [Photo by the author.]

as office space, the large spaces given over to theatres became increasingly cost ineffective. The per square foot value of office space was simply a better investment. If theatres offered the lowest return per square foot in the centre of a city, they could nonetheless have a real value for indoor malls since they could bring people into them and help promote foot traffic[24]. As a result malls generally give theatres preferential treatment in their leases, and they place the theatres in such a way that their exact location remains somewhat mysterious[25]. Where the anchor stores are always clearly visible from the exterior, the only external sign of a multiplex is generally a marquee placed near the entrance to the mall. The theatre itself is often off in an obscure corner, usually unmarked on the outside, and often requiring an extensive trip through the mall to find.

The K-mart look

The other way out of the real estate bind of downtown theatres is the theatre *as* mall. Although population and other shopping centres might eventually grow up around them, these theatre malls are built at remote locations that have easy access to highways. They are often found on the sites of the former drive-ins that went up in the post-war period to accommodate both the move to the suburbs and the baby boom. Two of the largest theatre chains now operating, General Cinema and National Amusements, in fact began as chains of drive-in theatres, and many of their multiplexes stand on the grounds of former drive-ins. Further, these theatre malls play up 'the movies' rather than any individual movie. Externally, they tend to be generally nondescript, with large marquees simply listing film titles next to auditorium numbers. If there is anything special about the product, no moviegoer would know that until getting inside the lobby where one poster might dominate another, but not often. It's in the theatre mall's interest to sell all films equally, although it must also realize that some films can act as come-on draws for others. This is the reason they hand out the guides at the box-office.

Finally, the theatre malls offer the big theatre chains the cost-effectiveness of uniformity. They are made up of a common and infinitely repeatable architectural design, somewhat modular in approach so that the number of screens actually contained within the multiplex won't change the overall look of the theatre. These chains create theatre malls with as familiar a look as K-Mart or McDonald's or other retail outlets with a national base[26]. The uniformity in effect helps give the theatre a kind of brand-name recognition designed to assure an audience by its very familiarity.

Fig. 4. The typical mall theatre box office is located at the end of a side corridor in the mall; anchor stores occupy a more central space. Unlike the box office, the entrance to the theatre (here just to the left of the glass door exit) is relatively invisible. Patrons must walk from the box office past four fast-food outlets in order to reach it (Briarwood Mall, Ann Arbor, MI). [Photo by the author.]

So, what does this form of exhibition have to do with the kind of audience that goes to these theatres? For one thing, the theatres certainly posit an audience familiar and comfortable with mass retailing strategies. And in fact the publicizing of movies has changed as radically as the exhibition strategy over the past couple of decades. Where publicists working in Hollywood studios once generally rose up through the ranks of the studio hierarchy, more and more frequently Hollywood has begun to draw on outsiders, on people with extensive backgrounds in advertising and with little experience in the movie industry[27]. One of the key aspects of this shift in the nature of both movies and the movie-going experience is the way the film industry addresses its audience through commercials. There is now a concern to treat each individual movie as a brand and try to build up a kind of brand-name recognition for it before it opens. In effect, the various auditoriums in a multiplex function like a chain store's showroom displays of competing products: the strategy of exhibitors is to try to get potential patrons to recognize and purchase their brand.

There is, of course, one problem with this super-market analogy, as there is with all the industrial and retailing analogies that have been applied to the 'dream factory' in the past. The movies represent a peculiar 'industry' since each product which that industry turns out is unique and has a very limited 'shelf life'. This life has been extended by the growth of the aftermarkets, but compared to other kinds of products, movies achieve a 'brand name recognition' that is decidedly short-term. In a 'secret' staff memo that was almost immediately leaked to *Variety*, Disney Studios head Jeffrey Katzenberg put it this way:

> Thanks to the dictates of the blockbuster mentality, the shelf life of many movies has come to be somewhat shorter than [that of] a supermarket tomato[28].

Katzenberg is clearly correct, but his language is also quite revealing. If you do think of your 'product' in terms of shelf life, then the logical next step is to think of it in terms of modern marketing techniques[29]. Katzenberg can see something wrong with this system, but he can't really step outside of its way of thinking.

In the classical studio period, the companies

themselves as well as the stars they held under contract might have functioned like brand-names to assure audiences of a certain quality in their pictures, but there was little sense at that time that an individual film might have become a brand name that could fuel a wide variety of ancillary markets. Today's ancillary markets and cross-promotion tie-ins help lead to the treatment of the individual film as a brand name: if a studio can get McDonald's to spend $40 million to help promote *Dick Tracy* by setting up a 'Dick Tracy Crimestoppers Game' as a promotion for itself, then it has to treat *Dick Tracy* the film, as opposed to the game, the lunch box, the contest, or the tee shirt, as the flagship object that establishes the brand[30]. One 'old time' Hollywood executive quoted by *Variety* objects to the new approach for the simple reason that the product is different: 'When you have people talking about brand identification and product launches, you forget what you're selling ... These guys think they're selling toothpaste. It's just a movie! You sell it like a movie'[31]. The executive has a point, but his response also begs the question: how, exactly, do you sell something like a movie? Is the product itself ever the sole determining factor?

Mass advertising was initially a response to an exhibition strategy, not to the product itself. That strategy has now become so entrenched that it must effectively drive marketing. In the past, the slow release of a film through a system of tiers depended primarily on local advertising and, the most intangible of all Hollywood marketing strategies, word-of-mouth. Now, in effect, the word-of-mouth must exist before any moviegoer has actually seen the film, a peculiar situation to be sure. If a movie opens wide, as most major studio movies do now and the very exhibition system demands that they do, there must already be widespread interest in it[32]. Hence, the rise of mass-media advertising. But if the advertising was a response to exhibition, it inevitably had both to impact on the way we understand the product and ultimately affect the nature of the product as well[33]. Something that is exclusive and hard to see will necessarily seem different to us than something readily available for mass consumption. The object must eventually be able to fit the selling strategy.

In the early days of multiplexing, there was some thought that the multiple theatres would make for the availability of more diverse product[34]. A stronger, more popular film in a larger auditorium would help a specialty film in the smaller hall either because of overflow from the more popular film or because of the kind of impulse buying the multiplex, like any other mass retailer, tries to encourage. As it has turned out, the reverse seems to be more the case: speciality items tend not to make it to mall theatres[35]. K-Mart might offer everything under one roof, but there are definite limits to what it might sell. There are, of course, no mink coats or sterling silver, but even in other areas there are definite limitations dictated by the kind of marketing strategy behind mass-driven chain stores. In the book section, for example, you are most likely to find Danielle Steele, Stephen King, John Grisham, and their epigones. There are items that simply do not sell well within the mall theatre system. Most strikingly, foreign language film distribution has greatly declined since the advent of the multiplex. There are a number of reasons for this, but the lack of speciality theatres remains a major one. A foreign language film really needs an art house to promote it; its location makes it something special. In the context of a multiplex, it becomes merely another product, and one for which the mass audience holds little interest. In the early 1960s, Federico Fellini's *La dolce vita* could move through first-run art house showings to a wider distribution that would eventually enable it to take in ca. $70 million in current dollars. It's impossible to imagine anything like that happening in the current market.

But if the decline in foreign language film distribution defines what can't survive in a multiplex market, what films are especially well positioned to thrive in it? Most older films were released in tiered fashion. Most, but not all. In 1953 Warner Bros. premiered *The Beast From 20,000 Fathoms* in 1,422 theatres and, a year later, *Them* in 2,000. In both cases, the word 'theatres' means something a good deal larger than what we would now think of[36]. These bookings were high enough to rate brief items in *Variety*, but they were not entirely unheard of. Rather, they represented a very particular type of exhibition policy of the period, one strictly reserved for exploitation movies. Exploitation films, as their name indicates, were made for quick turn-over. They were low budget works that would draw on highly marketable features, like sex, violence, technical gimmicks, or timeliness, to ensure a quick turnover

Fig. 5. Unlike the mall theatre, the theatre mall does not share space with other stores. In order to get to one of the 14 theatres in this theatre mall, audiences must walk past a four-sided concessions stand which dominates the lobby (Showcase Cinema, Ann Arbor, MI). [Photo by the author.]

Fig. 6. Gameability: past years' successes – or even flops – might be this year's videogame. Audiences waiting to see *True Lies* can play the *Terminator 2* game in the lobby (Showcase Cinema, Ann Arbor, MI). [Photo by the author.]

and tidy profit. They were targeted at a large num-ber of initial patrons titillated by the exploitable elements. Exceptional films might emerge from the exploitation market every now and then, but for the most part they could not expect to increase box office through word of mouth. In these movies, the come-on was what sold them.

In the 1950s, exploitation was firmly entren-ched in the realm of B-genres like horror and science fiction, which account for the two titles cited above, *policiers*, and lurid crime melodramas. By the 1980s, an exploitation marketing strategy had been set in place to exhibit films, but the films themselves were different at least in terms of budget. Exhibition became dominated by megabudget exploitation films. Film types once considered almost exclusively B-movie fare became the most touted genres of the year: horror, science fiction, cop movies, films based on comic strips and cartoons, films based on old TV/radio shows. The most explicit recognition of this trend came with *Raiders of the Lost Ark* in 1981. The film openly acknowledged its roots in B-film production, but did so with an A-film budget, lavish-ing millions of dollars on set design and special effects.

The reasons for this shift are complex since it is grounded in a striking change in audience taste. Taste itself is a consequence of too many factors, social and personal, to warrant explanations of simple economic determinism. Nevertheless, as mar-keting and exhibition have affected audience experi-ence of a movie, they have clearly played an important role in the transformation of what an audi-ence *wants* from a movie. The marketing system required by mass exhibition calls for a product which has highly exploitable elements, one that can effectively establish its flavour and its excitement within the constrictions of an extremely brief televi-sion commercial. It's not very easy to make an intimate drama look exciting in the context of a 30-sec spot, so questions of how to market the 'product' necessarily come into play before the 'pro-duct' is put into production. If it won't play well as a TV spot, there's a good chance it won't get pro-duced. Furthermore, the wide opening demands an audience at the very beginning that will have a precise set of expectations which the movie will pay off one by one. The whole system of marketing and exhibition simply favours exploitation fare.

Exploitation and the aftermarket

To say that Hollywood production decisions are driven by the marketplace is hardly news. What is new in the 1990s are the ways in which the market-place has reconfigured itself through a massive ex-pansion. One reason offered by the product shortage of the mid-1970s was the 'somewhat inelastic overall market potential'[37]. Within a decade, however, the market became a good deal more elastic than anyone in the 1970s might have anticipated. As I noted earlier, the product shortage that became an unexpected product glut in such a short period of time owes everything to the rise of home-video. Since income from sales and rentals of videotape now surpass those of first-run theatrical exhibition, home-video by a change of venue has effectively made second run economically primary, an impossible feat for theatrical second run. Home-video certainly changes the way an audience experiences a movie, but it remains difficult to determine if home-video affects the kind of movies that get made[38].

It is clear, however, that other aspects of the aftermarket are helping to determine what gets pro-duced[39]. Can a movie be turned into a theme park attraction that a producing studio owns? What are its chances for being reconfigured as a video game? The latter is a question made important by its market: as *Variety* noted, 'videogames, mostly pro-duced by companies outside the Hollywood loop, now earn more than movies domestically ... Domes-tically, videogames generated between $5–7 bil-lion dollars in 1993, while total US box office for features was closer to $5 billion'[40]. With the after-market surpassing the 'primary' market, demand grows for the former to impact on the latter. Dan Gordon, screenwriter on *Surf Ninja*, partially fin-anced by the videogame company Sega, stated bluntly, 'I try and write action sequences that will serve the movie and provide the spring-board for the videogame'[41]. If a movie has sufficient 'ga-meability', a premise that can produce a challeng-ing videogame, then even a flop might achieve success as an arcade game[42]. With movie com-panies ever increasing their corporate involvement in a multimedia universe, it is perhaps inevitable that the ability to translate a film project into another medium will be a key factor to greenlighting its production[43]. The videogame machines that line the lobby walls of the multiplex theatres best signal the synergy between movies and videogames, the fact that both seem to offer comparable experiences to some of their patrons[44].

In this new expanded media universe, what is the future of the theatrical feature film? Hollywood has effectively changed the way it addresses its audience over the last two decades, and that change has become institutionalized by the building boom in multiplex theatres. If audiences tire of the exploitation fare encouraged by the exploitation market, can Hollywood once again change its manner of address? Certainly, a number of executives like Katzenberg have attacked the 'event' mentality that they feel led to the earlier crisis of 1970 and has now returned with a vengeance. But to acknowledge this is also to ignore how different the marketing of films is now. Other executives simply worry what the next event will be, and that might well be a more realistic approach to the current situation. The decline of science fiction, horror and actioners, in that order, has left them uncertain what the audience actually wants. The success of *Pretty Woman* and *Ghost* back in 1990 and more recently *Sleepless in Seattle* in 1993 suggested that there might be value in films aimed more directly at women, who tend to be left out of the exploitation market, but, according to *Variety*, 'Studios are also hesitant to bank on female audiences to turn a profit. 'Most moviegoers are men,' says 20th Century-Fox production exec Melissa Bachrach'[45]. If a Hollywood executive says this, there are no doubt demographic studies to prove it, but the observation contradicts the consensus of old Hollywood that most audiences were women. If men dominate now, it might well be a consequence of the exploitation market which has always been aimed primarily at them.

Can this change? Years ago, the future of the movies seems to lie in the then newborn video-cassette market. But that industry has turned out to be as market driven as theatrical movies. Still, the oft-predicted demise of Hollywood and the theatrical film has yet to occur. Perhaps there is simply a need to change marketing strategies every couple of decades. The top tier of exclusive, theatrical-style exhibition that was added to release schedules via reserved seat showings in the 1950s was one such change, but it was easy to establish within existing structures of exhibition. How much the multiplex phenomenon dictates exhibition strategies remains to be

seen. The only certainty is that the need for change will lead to change. Change might be as minimal as the move to reserved seats in the 1950s, extending the tiering system to its farthest reaches, or it might be as radical as the dramatic revamping of production, distribution, and exhibition that has taken place over the last fifteen years. Whatever happens, it's likely that Hollywood will be speaking to us in a different way over the next decade, and what we expect when we go out to a movie then will be different from what we expect today.✣

Addendum

As this issue was going to press, *Variety* ran a lead story headlined 'Here Come the Megaplexes: Exhibs Usher in 24-Screen Destinations'. The story reports a new wave in theatre building that confirms the trends in exhibition outlined in the preceding article: super multiplexes – or 'megaplexes' in *Variety*speak. Every possible thing is contained under one roof, with free-standing theatres independent of malls that can operate as destinations in themselves by being 'coupled with entertainment centres encompassing everything from miniature golf and virtual reality games to "food courts" and toddler compounds'[46]. This new trend runs counter to industry fears of overbuilding, but the *Variety* writer speculates that the new theatres – a logical extension of the 'theater malls' described in the current article – might render the original mall theatre obsolete and ultimately replace rather than add to them.

Notes

1. According to the Motion Picture Association of America, attendance declined by 5.9 per cent in 1990, then by another 4.0 per cent in 1991. The rebound in 1992 and 1993 still did not bring attendance levels back to the 1989 record.

2. A recent *Variety* article on the weak first quarter of 1994 suggests that anxiety levels continue. Following a subtitle, 'Glorious Summer Start Can't Erase Spring of Discontent', the article begins, 'It's difficult to recall a time when relations between exhibitors and distributors have been more brittle'. Leonard Klady, 'Exhibs' Hard Feelings Linger', *Variety*, 6–12 June 1994.

3. John Brodie, 'Franchise Frenzy in H'wood', *Variety*, 3–9 January 1994, 1, 66.

4.   John Evan Frook, 'Sony Calculates Comeback: "Hero's" Flameout Was Not Rocket Science', *Variety*, 2–8 May 1994, 1, 103.

5.   For a more detailed discussion of this earlier 'crisis', see William Paul, 'Hollywood Harakiri: Notes on the Decline of an Industry and Art' *Film Comment* 13, No. 2 (March–April 1977), 40–43, 56–62.

6.   Robert Lindsey, 'Hollywood Scenario: Boom and Bust', *The New York Times*, 26 September 1975, 28.

7.   I have written more extensively about the rise of the gross-out and the high-budget exploitation film in *Laughing Screaming: Modern Hollywood Horror and Comedy* (New York: Columbia University Press, 1994).

8.   A.D. Murphy, 'Ancillaries No Alibi for B.O. Blahs', *Variety*, 16 July 1986, 26. Murphy also claimed this was not a distinctive feature of the film business: 'All broad-based art forms are driven and sustained by a handful of successes. There are lots of books, records, films and TV shows offered each day to the public; only a few make it big'. Still, it should be noted that the difference in revenue between a successful film and a weak film grew immeasurably larger in the post-studio period.

9.   Lawrence Cohn's analysis of the increase in production makes clear that homevideo was the driving force: 'While a very low budget project can successfully bypass theatrical and earn back its cost in strictly ancillary markets (such as the made expressly for homevideo exercise programs), most features require theatrical exposure to justify their existence and get the ball rolling. As a result, many of the new indie distribs are merely walking their pictures through the theatrical release, at minimum cost, en route to the more lucrative ancillaries'. Cohn, 'Overproduction Hurts Distribs', *Variety*, 25 February 1987, 1, 86.

10. As A.D. Murphy noted in analyzing a box office recession of the mid-1980s, 'For a quarter of a century, the number of tickets sold annually by US theaters has ranged up and down around 1.03 billion ... By 1962, the impact of television (and an enlarged leisure-time spectrum) on film attendance had exhausted itself ... Instead of looking at new video gadgets as a threat, it should be kept in mind that the combination of old and new exhibition markets results in more people, watching more films, more often, than at any other time since the invention of film and camera nearly 100 years ago'. Murphy (1986), 3, 26.

11. Selznick, *Memo from David O. Selznick* (New York: The Viking Press, 1972), 356–9.

12. The obvious precedent for the release of *Jaws* was another high budget horror film from two years earlier, *The Exorcist* (1973). See my discussion of the release of *The Exorcist in Laughing Screaming* (287–290) for how audience response led Warner Bros. towards more of a mass booking release than they originally intended.

13. Advertising costs offer the clearest evidence of this shift in marketing. According to a Motion Picture Association of America chart, average advertising costs between 1980 and 1993 nearly quadrupled, from $3.5 million to $12.1 million. In 1991, a studio executive complained to *Variety*, 'Movie marketing has become totally media driven, neglecting the exploitation of publicity, promotion and word-of-mouth'. Anne Thompson, 'Studios Shifting to Mad Ave's Savvy Sell', *Variety*, 1 April 1991, 87.

14. Difficulties experienced by the exclusive first-run theaters of Chicago in the Near North Side and the Loop by the mid-1970s are exemplary of this shift: 'Whereas outlyers here once had to fight to get major bookings on a first run basis, that situation has been reversed, with near north exhibitors and an occasional Loop house now seeking track product and suppliers looking for additional track houses'. Lloyd Sachs, 'Near North Side Vis-A-Vis Loop and Suburbs; Chicago Altering, *Variety*, 31 March 1976, 19. See also Lloyd Sachs, 'Loop Comes To Day-Date Policy; Downtown Grief', which makes clear that marketing strategies were affecting the booking policies of downtown theaters: 'Distribs have backed away from exclusive runs in the Loop, he [Plitt theater booker Jerry Winsberg] said, because 'There just aren't enough pictures that lend themselves to spending money in the Loop and then in outlying houses, in terms of advertising'. *Variety*, 2 June 1976, 7.

15. 'What we have found today is that many, many of the prime theaters in the country are in shopping malls', says marketing consultant Martin Levy, 'and that's a major revolution in distribution in the last five or ten years. There are many cities in which a first-run, quality film will only open in four or five theaters, and they will all be out in [suburban] communities, and generally they will be in shopping centers'. This quotation is from a 1983 article; since this point, most of the downtown movie palaces have disappeared as venues for first-run exhibition. William Severini Kowinski, 'The Malling of the Movies', *American Film*, September 1983, 55.

16. Gary R. Edgerton, *American Film Exhibition and an Analysis of the Motion Picture Industry's Market Structure 1963–1980* (New York: Garland Publishing, 1983), chart on p. 139.

17. A *Variety* article published in 1984 noted that 'Totals (of screens) had gradually risen from 1964 to 1984', with 1984 seeing the 'highest number of

screens since 1948'. Furthermore, 'Scores of additional screens' that had recently been added to the nation's total were 'almost entirely in new multiplexes ...' Will Tusher, 'US Exhibs Showing New Growth', *Variety*, 28 November 1984.

18. Because it did not have the same kind of suburban flight as most other American cities, New York City remains the largest urban film market in the country, but the fate of the oldest Broadway theaters reflects changes taking place elsewhere. In the 1970s, these old palaces turned themselves into twin theatres by adding a screen to the balcony. By the 1990s, a theatre of only two screens was no longer a viable use of real estate: the Criterion, which had not only twinned its auditorium but added four small theatres to its basement, became the only one of the original Broadway film palaces that was not torn down. In fact, the Loew's chain tore down its three remaining large-scale movie theatres in Manhattan to replace them with newly built multiplexes.

19. Will Tusher, 'Nation's Screen Tally Reached a New High in '90', *Variety*, 28 January 1991, 3.

20. 'The hundreds of new theaters that can present anywhere from 6 to 18 movies at a time provide opportunity for the increasingly important independent filmmakers and small distribution companies. But the peril in such numbers is that failure can be quicker and have more impact ... "Since there is so much film for exhibitors to choose from, you have to open strong or exhibitors will pull your movie", said the president of distribution and marketing at 20th Century-Fox, Tom Sherak. "A year ago a movie used to have a minimum shelf life of two weeks. Now it's only one week, and then the movie is double-billed. In and out"'. Aljean Harmetz, 'New Movies Battle for Theaters', *The New York Times*, 14 October 1987, C23.

21. A measure of the concession stand's importance is the quick reaction of theater chains to reject claims about theatre popcorn made by the Center for Science in the Public Interest. See Paul F. Young, 'Popcorn Peril Puts Theater Owners on the Hot-oil Seat', *Variety*, 2–8 May 1994, 13, 20.

22. Thomas Guback, 'The Evolution of the Motion Picture Theater Business in the 1980s', *Journal of Communication*, Spring 1987, 63–64. Guback reprints a chart from the US Department of Commerce that shows concession revenue as a percentage of admission revenue rose from 14.62 per cent in 1967 to 23.26 per cent in 1982.

23. Charles Fleming, 'Snackbar Slowdown Bitter Pill for Exhibs', *Variety*, 21 January 1991, 3. An article on shopping center theatres in a real estate journal from the same year notes, 'in a theater it often is not the movie, but the ancillary concessions that generate the most revenues available to the theater operator'. Earl L. Segal, Edward M. Rogers, 'Negotiating the Shopping Center Movie Theater Lease', *Real Estate Review*, Summer 1991, 84.

24. Guback points out that the building boom of the 1980s 'is closely tied to the growth of shopping malls and does not necessarily represent a significant capital investment on the part of exhibitors themselves'. Some of this building boom, then, was spurred on by the desires of the shopping mall developers, who put up much of the cost of theatre building. Guback, 71.

25. Guback notes, 'In cases where the exhibitor advances some construction money to the developer, the rent for the premises is reduced accordingly'. Guback, 69. Segal and Rogers detail the special arrangements shopping centers make in their rental agreements with theatres, 82–87.

26. In writing this, I do not intend to update Douglas Gomery's assertion that the movie theatres chains forming in the mid-1910s followed the pattern set by chain stores such as Sears-Roebuck, Woolworth's, and A&P because I think this analogy needs some qualification. While the theatre chains might have followed some of the marketing and accounting strategies of the chain stores, they also aimed to position themselves as high class, which made them something quite different. Gomery himself seems to recognize this in his discussion of Balaban & Katz as the chain that set the mode for nationwide chains: 'Balaban & Katz proved that the movie entertainment business was not one of simple *mass* market appeal'. Furthermore, while the retail chains Gomery cites managed to establish themselves by offering low prices, 'Prices [in Balaban & Katz theatres] were higher than the usual five and ten cents and sometimes reached a dollar for the best seats on the best night of the week for the top attractions'. While similar designs for these movie palaces might be used in different cities, the theatre chains for the most part did not aim for the kind of uniformity that is typical in multiplex building since that itself would have denied their aspirations to quality. Where the movie palaces might have imitated the Paris Opera, there was no confusing the interiors of Woolworth's stores, all uniform, with the very distinctive downtown Chicago Marshall Field, itself an imitation of a Paris department store. Gomery, *Shared Pleasures: A History of Movie Presentation in the United States* (Madison: The University of Wisconsin Press, 1992), 35, 36, 55.

27. 'For the first time, top-level advertising decisions are being made, not by old movie hands, but by marketing professionals, recruited from agencies or other industries ... While marketing chiefs traditionally rose

through studio publicity and ad departments, four major studios now have looked outside in filling their top posts and a fifth is expected to be announced shortly'. Thompson, (1 April 1991) 1.

28. 'The Teachings of Chairman Jeff', *Variety*, 4 February 1991, 24.

29. One of the oddest examples of this is the use of the word 'franchise' as in 'franchise picture' to denote a film that holds out the possibility for endless sequels if the original has sufficient drawing power. See Brodie (3–9 January 1994), 1, 66.

30. Thompson (1 April 1991), 87.

31. *Ibid.*

32. Some films that will admittedly have a more limited appeal, like *Barton Fink* and *The Commitments*, may be 'platformed', which means opening at a limited number of theatres and moving out from there, something in the manner of the tiering system, but the timing of these platforms is often fairly short, and the aim is still to move the film into a kind of mass market system. Of course, if these films fail in limited release, they never make it to the mass market.

33. See Cameron Stauth, 'The Cineplex Complex', *American Film*, December 1990, 16.

34. Even as late as 1986 Jean Picker Firstenberg could write, hopefully, 'The multiplexes greatly increased the number of small venues that could support – without filing a Chapter Eleven – experimental films, artistic films, foreign and independent films'. Firstenberg, 'A Renaissance in Film Exhibition', *American Film*, November 1986, 73.

35. Guback has written, 'Clearly, the proliferation of screens has not necessarily meant a great choice of films for consumers but merely more locations at which to view a smaller number of films. Moreover, release strategies in recent years have turned virtually all theaters into first-run houses in many communities. The second run, therefore, begins with home video and pay TV'. Guback, 76.

36. 'Plan Fast Playoff For WB "Beast"', *Variety*, 17 June 1953, 3, and '2,000 Playdates for WB's "Them" Within a Month'! *Variety*, 2 June 1954, 5.

37. A.D. Murphy, 'Pinch Picture Playoff Patterns', *Variety*, 17 March, 1976,

38. Certainly sale of home-video rights has been a factor

in facilitating niche marketing, production of films aimed at limited audiences. This might also mean, simply, that independent cinema has greater visibility than ever before in the past.

39. It is a fair measure of how much the market has changed that A.D. Murphy, one of the most astute observers of Hollywood economics, could write in 1978: 'A major diversified film production-distribution company – active in music, recreation parks, telefilming, whatever – cannot be expected to lose money on theatrical filmmaking ... and make it up on the diversifications. Nor can the secondary markets for features – TV, pay-TV, etc. – be required to create the overall pix profit ...' Murphy, 'Hits Alone Nourish Biz; More Non-Hits Too Risky', *Variety*, 14 June 1978, 3.

40. John Brodie, Marx, 'Two Can Play This Game', *Variety*, 27 December 1993, 1, 74.

41. *Ibid*, 74.

42. 'Gameability Can Elude Even a Blockbuster Pic', *Variety*, 27 December 1993, 74.

43. Over a decade ago, William Severini Kowinski wrote of the mall movie theatres: 'The marriage between Americans and the mall is changing not only how movies are promoted and exhibited but perhaps even which movies get made. More films these days are being shown in theaters that are located in shopping centers; not only are the movies themselves available in malls, but so are the books, records, games, toys, mugs, kites, clothes, and dolls that make-up the tie-in merchandise for a growing number of films ...' In the intervening period, the potential for tie-ins as a factor in determining production has remained high, so it is likely that the video-game will be an equally potent force in production decisions. Kowinski, 55.

44. These machines also point to the radical difference between the multiplex of today and the movie palace of the past in the deliberate downscale atmosphere. Much as the videogames seem fitting in the multiplex, it would be impossible to imagine the grand lobbies of the old palaces full of pinball machines.

45. Anne Thompson, 'Studios Stick to their Guns over Sex Appeal of Pics', *Variety*, 7 January 1991, 109.

46. Paul Noglows, *Variety*, 22–28th August, 1994: 1.

Film History, Volume 6, pp. 502–521, 1994. Copyright © John Libbey & Company
ISSN: 0892-2160. Printed in Great Britain

Stepin Fetchit: The man, the image, and the African American press

Charlene Regester

he African American press of the early 20th century was highly critical of its own community, and seemed to assume a race-conscious attitude toward members of the black community. This was especially true of its reportage of newsworthy black citizens. Coverage of African American filmstars thus took the form of a 'message', praising and/or scolding the actor. Coverage of Stepin Fetchit played that dual role to the hilt, reporting generously on his successes, but exposing his failures in detail, perhaps to warn other African American actors of behaviour they should avoid. The press assigned to any black actor during this era of segregation a share in the responsibility of presenting the race at its best. This paper will develop the theme of the interrelationship between that African American press and the life and career of Lincoln Perry, also known as Stepin Fetchit, one of the first major black screen stars.

Stepin Fetchit is the epitome of a comedian who provided unflattering imitations of the African American. James Baldwin who classified Stepin Fetchit with Willie Best and Mantan Moreland stated, 'all of [these actors], rightly or wrongly, I loathed. It seemed to me that they lied about the world I knew, and debased it, and certainly I did not know anybody like them – as far as I could tell; for it is also possible that their comic, bug-eyed terror contained the truth concerning a terror by which I hoped never to be engulfed'[1]. Undoubtedly, aimed at appealing to white audiences, Fetchit's demeaning portrayals often confirmed whites' pre-existing views. Fetchit used these self deprecations to provoke laughter among whites and thereby soothe their fears and insecurities regarding the African American. Fetchit skilfully played on these fears and insecurities by perfecting his characterizations; yet these characterizations would ultimately consume him, as the Stepin Fetchit in real life became more like the Stepin Fetchit on the screen. Unfortunately, what evolved was an imitator who became his own imitation; the Fetchit who attempted to deceive his audiences, ultimately became the Fetchit who deceived himself. The buffoon character he portrayed on the motion picture screen was internalized by Fetchit as he became more like this buffoon in real life. Fetchit was so gifted at perfecting such characterizations that he could not separate his character roles from his own personality and, therefore, engaged in intrapersonal conflict.

Charlene Regester is co-editor of the *Oscar Micheaux Society Newsletter* published by Duke University, and author of an unpublished manuscript on African American Newspaper Coverage of Films, Filmmakers, Actors and Actresses, 1900 to 1950. She is a visiting Assistant Professor at the University of North Carolina, Chapel Hill, in the Curriculum in African and Afro-American Studies. Correspondence c/o African and Afro-American Studies, CB #3395, 401 Alumni Bldg., UNC, Chapel Hill, NC 27599-3395, USA.

Fetchit, whose real name was Lincoln Theodore Monroe Andrew Perry (named after four presidents)[2], 'earned more money than the combined salaries of fifty equally able actors and actresses, and [he] earned it by pandering to the most demeaning white myths about blacks'[3], according to Gary Null, who continues, 'It was felt that [Fetchit] was more interested in living well at the expense of [his] race than in making any attempt to combat [his] typecasting'[4].

Fetchit's metamorphosis throughout his career as a motion picture actor has rarely been examined, because his demeaning portrayals are considered so offensive that he was often viewed as being undeserving of such study. However, Donald Bogle contends that Fetchit's 'place in black film history remains significant'[5]. Bogle argues that Fetchit is of importance when examining black cinema history because Fetchit, in his time, was among the most popular black actors in the industry. According to Bogle:

Fig. 1. Fetchit as caricature: an imitation of himself. [Courtesy of the John Ford Collection, the Lilly Library, Indiana University.]

In the year of 1934 – at the age of thirty-two – Stepin Fetchit was already a legend and one of movieland's few authentic oddities. Only a few years earlier, no one could have predicted that this actor who gave the appearance of being a lanky, slow-witted, simple-minded, obtuse, synthetic, confused humbug would take an entire nation and an era by storm. But Stepin Fetchit went far beyond anyone's predictions or expectations, and in his own inspired way did so brilliantly. In the early 1930s he was the best known and most successful black actor working in Hollywood ... He popularized the dim-witted, tongue-tied stammer and the phenomenal slow-lazyman shuffle. So successful was he with his slow gait that for years audiences thought Stepin Fetchit actually could not run[6].

In the 1920s and 1930s, the African American press often provided the only coverage of the suc-cesses and failures of all African Americans in the motion picture industry. Particularly during the early years, African Americans frequently found themselves invisible, excluded, alienated, isolated and ignored by the white press. More importantly, the African American press was instrumental in articulating the views and concerns of the African American community regarding their portrayals on the motion picture screen. The black press was outspoken in denouncing demeaning portrayals in motion pictures; outspoken in condemning African Americans who participated in perpetuating these objectionable images; and outspoken in expressing opposition to the treatment that African Americans received in the motion picture industry. In view of Fetchit's star status as well as his disturbing portrayals, it was inevitable that the African American press would cover him extensively.

However, Fetchit, one of the outstandingly successful figures among black actors of the 1920s and 1930s, remains one of the most under-reported figures in current black film history. His painful portrayals were so scarring that African Americans have practically removed his image from the history of motion pictures. According to Bogle, 'Today because his films are seldom shown and often neglected – to the point where his scenes are even cut when shown on television – the credit due to him is generally denied'[7].

Fetchit as entertainment reporter

This present examination is not an attempt to re-open wounds, but to critically examine the development of Fetchit's image as screen star and man, an image that was reflected in and influenced by the African American press. His career and his life were commended and condemned in the press while he became a man consumed by his successes and failures. Because Fetchit was so extensively covered by the black press of his day, the black press becomes an obvious and viable resource for research and examination. It is interesting to note that in the mid-1920s, Stepin Fetchit was himself a columnist for the *Chicago Defender* newspaper. Fetchit, whose debut into the entertainment industry started as a stage entertainer, later served as an entertainment reporter for the *Chicago Defender* where he wrote a column entitled, 'Lincoln Perry Writes', also titled 'Lincoln Perry's Letter'. This column, printed from the mid-to-late 1920s, provided news on various stage and vaudeville performers including Fetchit's own performances.

In December 1926, Fetchit reported in his column '... I have joined hands with Ed Lee, formerly owner and manager of Ed Lee's Bathing Beauties, and after a successful engagement in Muskogee, Okla., we are now completing a very successful week's run here at the Dreamland theatre. Our act alone is packing them in every night'[8]. Fetchit apparently was an entertainer who had a considerable amount of appeal, as was evident by the size of the crowds he managed to attract. In a later column, Fetchit reported that his original partner, Buck Abel, was confined due to medical complications and that Ed Lee would replace Abel as part of the 'Step and Fetch It' Act[9]. Fetchit had become quite busy not only as a performer but also as a reporter. In July of

1927, Fetchit wrote that he 'had a mailing list of 1,000 [which he had to circulate], ... business [dealings] with the office, which ended with a route until August and [he had to fulfil] an option on the 100 weeks [contract on] the West Coast [enabling him] to offer acts in the near future; in other words, I am going to forsake vaudeville and take to presentations'[10]. (It can be speculated that presentations may have referred to motion picture work, while vaudeville referred to stage performances).

In the early years of Fetchit's career his views continued to be welcomed by the African American press. During this period he was also being recruited by the major studios as an actor, and his achievements in the motion picture industry were noted. Fetchit reported in his own column:

> I am writing this from the Metro-Goldwyn-Mayer studio and at present I am sitting on a platform where Lon Chaney, Henry Walthall and Marceline Day are shooting a scene in a garden of one of Mr. Chaney's latest pictures ... My reason for being here is due to a contract I have to play a very prominent part in a picture entitled *In Old Kentucky*, and am working on the opposite stage. I have been guaranteed four weeks work at a salary that has only been exceeded by Chas. [Charles] Gilpin and [James] Lowe and Noble Johnson. Carolyn Snowden is working in this picture with me[11].

Here and elsewhere, Fetchit seemed to be often articulating his approval of the treatment that African Americans received in Hollywood. For example, Fetchit described the atmosphere at the Metro-Goldwyn-Mayer studio lot. 'Everyone including president, stars, extras ... eat[s] together in one big dining room, no partitions, no sign of prestige and to think these people make thousands a week salary, have the best of everything and feel at home to eat beside you regardless of colour'[12]. But then, Fetchit inserted a personal aside: 'What an example this could be to the white supremacy of the South'[13]. Fetchit applauded the treatment that blacks received in Hollywood, but did not hesitate to simultaneously comment on the inability of the South to accommodate blacks in the same manner. A question arises about Fetchit's motives. Was he disingenuously patronizing the Hollywood white establishment to further his own advancement, was he honestly striving

Fig. 2. Fetchit with Frank Morgan in *Dimples*, (1936). [Photo courtesy of Twentieth Century-Fox.]

to 'needle' the Southern white establishment, or both?

In a later column, Fetchit assumed an authoritative position as an experienced actor in motion pictures as he provided advice to aspiring black actors. It is interesting to note that Fetchit condemned certain black actors for actions and behaviour that ironically he would later adopt and that would ultimately result in his virtual demise as a screen star. First, Fetchit urged black theatre managers to secure the Tiffany Stahl productions 'because they have taken the first step toward our people's progress in becoming real motion picture stars with the same privileges and chance of advancement as the whites'[14]. He added, 'I don't mean that they have succeeded, but they have taken the first step in preference to the many promising announcements Cecil B. DeMille [has] been making and failed to put into action'[15]. Second, while encouraging these theatre managers, he warned black actors that the personal behaviour previously exhibited by promi-

nent African American actors explained why major motion picture producers were reluctant to cast black actors in major roles.

> For instance, the action of Charles Gilpin when cast for the important role of Uncle Tom's Cabin only increased in the producer's mind that the Race artist would be hard to get along with and that he would allow his pride to encourage him to misuse the advantage he possessed for personal gain.

> Then although James Lowe did much to assure them of our ability as actors, yet on the other hand, he increased the belief that we would take advantage of our powers as if our personal gain meant all regardless of the fact that we would make the road harder for our fellow artist. I don't mean to condemn the action of these two Race professional history makers, but to remind that our action, although not intentionally, plays sometimes two-thirds of the parts in

our 'nonadvancement' and the victory for us lies first in the phrase 'Conquer oneself and the rest is easy'[16].

Fetchit asserted, '[It is necessary] to correct the great mistake that is made by so many Race papers in calling a movie actor a movie star'[17]. Yet Fetchit himself was concerned with his image as an important African American actor. Fetchit's outspokenness on issues that affected black actors struggling to survive in an industry dominated by whites would continue. At this stage in his career, Fetchit seemed to accept without question the demeaning characterizations imposed on most black actors attempting to penetrate the major motion picture industry since he himself filled such roles. Yet even though he was limited to such dehumanizing portrayals on the screen, off the screen he could and would continue his denunciation of segregated practices that existed for African Americans.

The beginnings of a career in Hollywood

In 1927, in his first motion picture, Fetchit landed a role in *In Old Kentucky* in which he was cast with African American actress, Carolyn Snowden. Of his appearance in this film, Fetchit reported, 'Although Miss [Carolyn] Snowden and I have a very prominent part, and I think I will get all screen credit for the picture, neither of us were starred. Still we are mentioned in the cast and have positions never before attained by Race performers in a white production'[18]. Fetchit, after previewing the film reported his impressions of his appearance on screen:

> ... what a thrill it was to myself to sit in a million-dollar theatre and watch and laugh at myself taking a feature part in a feature picture! Miss Carolyn Snowden and myself closed the picture with a love scene, which is something that has never happened before in a big ofay [white] production. Then, after the showing of the picture, yours truly was congratulated with the warm and unprejudiced hand-shake of the big officials of a firm ... and feeling that one has really earned such a rare reception, 'Ain't that a grand and glorious feeling'[19]?

In Old Kentucky was also favourably reviewed by the *Chicago Defender* reporting that 'Carolyn Snowden and Lincoln Perry, who played her shiftless

sweetheart, almost steal the show'[20]. This newspaper further praised the performances of both Fetchit and Snowden, stating, 'Carolyn Snowden as Lily May, and Stepin Fetchit as High-Pockets, not only act their parts well, they live up to them. And by doing so they have opened wide the gates of a new field for Race talent on the screen. They have created a like sensation in Hollywood to that "Shuffle Along" created on Broadway, and producers and directors all over, are clamouring for their contracts'[21].

Fetchit's success with this picture led to such a flood of other motion picture offers that by the end of the 1920s Fetchit no longer had time to compose his column. The demand for Fetchit as an actor would interrupt his journalistic career. But at this period, also, his persona as a screen actor would begin to undergo change. Fetchit, who in the early stages of his career was genuinely concerned with the African American image in motion pictures, now became more concerned with making the big money. Fetchit began to be criticized by the black press for distancing himself from black actors, as is evident in an article in the *Chicago Defender* in 1928 entitled 'Actor Too Proud to Work in Films With Own Race'[22]. This article stated:

> ... all was not so well between Fox and his new protege. According to the studio's version the trouble began when Fetchit decided he did not belong in a picture made wholly by members of his Race.
>
> He does not like to be surrounded by black actors. He prefers to be an actor in a white cast, it is said. One story represents Fetchit as cast to represent a lazy roustabout lying along a fence, whose duty in one scene was to rise regretfully and yawn. He did his part so well that he always fell asleep and failed even to do the rising and stretching parts of his assignment, this accusation said, even after the other actors had built up to this bit of business[23].

He responded to this criticism by submitting a letter that was printed in the *Pittsburgh Courier* that stated, '... I am quoted as saying that I don't like to be surrounded by coloured actors, but prefer to be an actor in a white company. This makes it appear that I am trying to high-hat my own race, which is untrue'[24] Fetchit added, 'What I really said was that I much preferred to work as comedy relief in a company of white people rather than an all-coloured picture, because in the former company I have no competition as to dialect and character, and, therefore, have a much better chance for recognition'[25]. But in fact, this criticism would signal the beginning of a deterioration in Stepin Fetchit's public relations.

Hearts in Dixie

Following his role in *The Ghost Talks* (1929), however, Fetchit changed his stance and did take a part in *Hearts in Dixie* (1929), one of the first experiments by a major motion picture studio to produce a film with an all-black cast. But 'big money' could have been interpreted as his reason for accepting the role, for which he reportedly earned $1500 a week, making him one of the highest paid black actors ever. By the end of the 1920s Fetchit's portrayal in the black press began to fluctuate between condemnation and commendation. For example, the *Pittsburgh Courier* praised him and described his performance in *Hearts in Dixie* by noting that 'the only laugh of the evening'[26] was provided by Fetchit. His performance in this film was further commended by the *Opportunity*, which reported 'I see no reason for even hesitating in saying that he is the best actor that the talking movies have produced. His voice, his manner, his timing, everything that he does, is as near to perfection as one could hope to get in an essentially phony medium such as this'[27]. [Other films in which he appeared in 1929 include: *Thru Different Eyes* (1929), *The Kid's Clever* (1929), *Showboat* (1929), *Fox Movietone Follies of 1929*, *Big Time* (1929), and *Salute* (1929).]

But even as his film portrayals were once again receiving praise, Fetchit's controversial off screen behaviour again became exposed and targeted by the African American press. Fetchit was being held to the same standards he had earlier invoked. The black press was concerned about the effect his off screen behaviour would have for other blacks in Hollywood and elsewhere. Fetchit was considered a role model of sorts for black success in motion pictures and was criticized for self-indulgent behaviour. For example, concerning his private life, the African American press reported, 'Stepin Fetchit is again in the limelight and again with unfavourable notoriety. This time the name "Bubbles" of the famous team of Buck and Bubbles is linked with his as the result of a knock-down, drag-out, house-and-alley battle that had half of California's Harlem excited'[28]. The article continued, 'The brawl started through a joke that Step suggested that Bubbles help him play on [Step's] fiancee, Miss Dorothy Stevenson, [a] 17-year-old ... girl. They were to stage a fake quarrel over her affections, but it seems that Bubbles was too good an actor and Step, detecting a note of sincerity in Bubbles' statement, grew angry and the battle began in real earnest'[29]. Fetchit thus exhibited much of the same behaviour he had previously condemned and warned other African Americans to avoid in their pursuit of a motion picture career.

Fetchit again became an object of condemnation when the newspaper reported he was being sued for $100,000 for breach of promise because he had allegedly promised to marry a 17 year-old woman, Yvonne Butler[30]. In 1929 Fetchit married Dorothy Stevenson of New Orleans, Louisiana, and their marriage was reported on extensively in the black press.

Becoming a star

Fetchit's success as a motion picture actor escalated at an amazing rate. According to Bogle, between 1929 and 1935 Fetchit appeared in some twenty-six films and also performed on stage[31]. When he performed at the Lando Theatre in Pittsburgh he was described as having 'a brand of comedy all his own' and was hailed 'as the successor to the late Bert Williams' (a black vaudeville entertainer who performed in blackface)[32].

Fetchit's talents even extended to songwriting; he composed two songs – 'Member Mandy' and the 'Step Fetchit Strut'[33]. The *Pittsburgh Courier*, returning to the commendation mode, noted that, 'The famous singing comedian is said to have accepted a contract from the Radio-Keith-Orpheum people to appear in a series of vaudeville engagements in various parts of the country. Fetchit will tour the country, it is said, in one of the three special made Cadillacs which he uses'[34].

Throughout Fetchit's steady rise as an entertainer, his coverage in the black press continued to fluctuate as they reported and also editorialized on both his private and public failures and his successes. The press condemned his ostentatious dis-

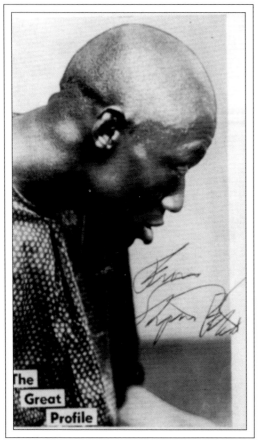

Fig. 3. The lord mayor of Harlemwood: Fetchit presents himself as 'The Great Profile'. A postcard sent to John Ford. [Courtesy of the John Ford Collection, the Lilly Library, Indiana University.]

play of wealth. These media reports, it seems, contributed to his image as a buffoon off the screen, because they gave the impression that this African American actor lacked the sophistication to be at ease with his newly acquired wealth. Fetchit's flamboyant lifestyle was often exposed by the African American press; the *Chicago Defender* reported that he 'had the biggest house on Central Ave., four autos, each [had chauffeurs who wore] different uniforms ... The uniforms were a cross between those of Bolivian admiral and the Emperor Jones. On the back of his cars were signs bearing Stepin's name; at night they blazed with electric lights'[35]. A later article that appeared in the *Chicago Defender* stated, 'In his heyday, Fetchit ... had 21 servants, 12 automobiles and a wardrobe that contained suits costing up to $1,000'[36]. Other sources reveal

that Fetchit had a caddy who even accompanied him when he played on a miniature golf course and that he acquired a Jewish valet[37]. While appearing at the Cotton Club, Fetchit allegedly requested that 'the club build him a special dressing room containing a bath and kitchen. It was reported that Fetchit was asking for an electric refrigerator for his use in the club'[38]. Fetchit is said to have had an all-day party on a specially built roof-top that had been made to resemble a beach. The *Chicago Defender* reported that in attendance at this party were 'George Garner, noted tenor soloist and choral director; ... US. (Slow Kid) Thompson, widower of the late Florence Mills; ... El Fetchit hissef, squire and lord mayor of Harlemwood ... Other well-known personages are seen in the background surrounded by Chinese servants'[39].

Even Fetchit's stage-name met with press disapproval. Sylvester Russell, a film reviewer for the *Pittsburgh Courier*, charged that 'Lincoln Perry ... should use his own name rather than the slang 'Stepin Fetchit', which could be better applied to dogs and horses, much less human beings. Where do they get that nickname stuff and what will we have next'[40]? Obviously, some members of the black press resented artists who were willing to compromise their personal integrity to promote themselves in the entertainment world by assuming such demeaning names. In an interview conducted in 1929, Fetchit revealed that he had adopted his name from a horse he bet on at a Texas race track. Fetchit, commenting on the race horse, stated:

> Well, Step and Fetch It stepped home ahead in Lawn Martin, thereby saving my wardrobe and pin and netting me some cash.

> I was a dancer and singer and after that I teamed with a fellow. We took the name of the horse. He was called 'Step' and I was called 'Fetch It'[41].

In spite of the personal criticism Fetchit received from the black press, his talent as an actor was often applauded. When Fetchit appeared in *Fox Movietone Follies of 1929*, the *Chicago Defender* reported, 'Stepin is what is called a natural born comedian. He is funny without effort. The type shown in his lazy roustabout shuffle, his piously sly humour and his innocent whining voice is the pattern from which all minstrel characters have been drawn'[42]. The article concluded, 'Stepin is emphatically not an imitation, but a personification'[43]. When he appeared in *Big Time* (1929), Kenneth Hawks, who directed Fetchit in this motion picture, stated 'If all the laughs that Stepin Fetchit, the inimitable comedian of the talking screen, caused in *The Ghost Talks* (1929), *Hearts in Dixie* (1929), *Fox Movietone Follies of 1929*, and other all-talking Fox productions, could be gathered into one big laugh, the roar of Niagara Falls, by comparison, would sound like pouring a thimbleful of water into a bale of Alabama cotton'[44]. Similarly, the *Defender*, regarding his portrayal in *Salute* (1929), noted that Fetchit 'steals the picture because he has proven to be the outstanding comedian of the day'[45].

Unsuitable behaviour

As Fetchit's successes in his film life increased, in his private life he was clearly becoming more like the buffoon he portrayed on the screen. In January of 1930, the *Pittsburgh Courier* reported that Fetchit had been arrested for drunk driving. The article stated that during the court proceedings Fetchit fell asleep and had to be awakened to be informed that he was acquitted of the charge[46]. Another report added that in order to perfect the character that he often portrayed on the screen, Fetchit '[did] not sleep more than two hours nightly for ten days [prior] to his actual work in [a] production'[47]. That, according to Fetchit, explained his courtroom behaviour.

Many of these reports that appeared in the black press were relayed to Hollywood studio executives and added to Fetchit's deteriorating image. When it was announced that Fetchit had signed with Columbia pictures to appear in the film, *Lover Come Back* (1931), his unsuitable behaviour was mentioned. The *Pittsburgh Courier* reported that 'Fetchit, according to stories emanating from the coast, is hard to handle. He has ideas of his own, despite his droll mimicry, has defied producers who attempt to ridicule his race. Clean and wholehearted fun fits in his scheme of things, but anything else is taboo'[48]. It seems that Fetchit's 'hard to handle' behaviour could perhaps be interpreted as a form of resistance to the negative screen roles that he was so often forced to play, in addition to the fact that he was already considered a complicated person. His complicity was exacerbated when he engaged in

behaviour that studio officials considered to be defiant. A report followed shortly thereafter that Fetchit had been fired from Columbia. The *Pittsburgh Courier* printed an announcement regarding Fetchit's dismissal, which read:

> Stepin Fetchit is out over at Columbia. He had been cast in an important role in *Lover Come Back*, which Eric C. Kenton is directing, but after two days his temperament got the best of him. Harry Cohn, rather than put up with him, let him out and scrapped the film that had been shot up to the time Fetchit went 'haywire'. Clarence Muse, well-known coloured actor, steps into the role. ... Of course, this announcement does not give Fetchit's side of the story, which your correspondent is at present seeking to obtain, but there have been circulated frequently stories of his irresponsibility and some of his feats have landed him in the police station. It is generally regarded as a step forward to have Clarence Muse selected to take the Fetchit role[49].

After Fetchit's dismissal from Columbia, the black press wrote that the black 'actor's chance in Hollywood will probably be killed by the slightest indiscretion of one or two fellows who become intoxicated by success in a comparatively small way. The action taken by the Columbia people in Fetchit's case is described by Walter Winchell as "one cure for inflated skulls", but in plain old Harlem ling, "big heads"'[50]. Further condemnation of Fetchit was provided by the *Chicago Defender*:

> The boy could not conform. It seemed that a stupid director insisted upon having his actors on the set at 9 a.m., at which hour the rare spark of Stepin's genius did not burst into flame. If it pleased him to wander off the set and make personal appearances at a local theatre he did so without consulting anybody.

> Nor could he be made to realize that he was being paid to act. Stepin acted only when inspired.

> Sometimes he had to wait for inspiration for days. ... How long this studio will put up with Step remains to be seen. The sensation of

Hearts in Dixie was, I'm afraid, just a flash in the pan and it was all his own fault[51].

Fetchit's career, careening between successes and failures made him a commodity waiting to be acclaimed or denounced. When he was offered an opportunity to appear with Hal Roach Comedies in 1930, the *Pittsburgh Courier* reported that Fetchit had signed a contract for five years with Hal Roach, receiving an increase in salary[52].

In spite of Fetchit's difficulties and the growing alienation he was beginning to experience in Hollywood, African American audiences, spurred on by the African American press, continued to acknowledge his talent. When Fetchit appeared on stage at the Regal Theater in Chicago, the *Pittsburgh Courier* reported, 'Fetchit made his biggest hit with his singing and dancing. He can't sing, nor do much playing, but his attempt is so ludicrous and so much according to the genre that it takes with the audience. However, the boy can dance'[53]. This report continued, 'He put on the Stepin Fetchit Shuffle which the audience forced him to repeat ...'[54]. The report concluded, 'Fetchit seems to have made much more of a hit as a legitimate performer than Miss Nina Mae McKinney, the pretty star of *Hallelujah* (1929)'[55].

However, audience approval is not to be relied on. One newspaper account notes that when Fetchit appeared on stage in Baltimore he had been promised a salary of $2,500, but when he failed to attract a sizeable audience, one-fourth of his salary was withheld ...[56].

Returning to a supportive tone, the *Afro-American* (Baltimore) wrote, 'It seems that Stepin Fetchit and the movie producers, who haven't spoken in a long time, have made up as Stepin is now back in the talkies. His latest picture is *The Big Fight* (1930)'[57].

But, reporting upon the birth of his son, the press qualified the good news with the bad. One article, after announcing the birth of his son, switched from the birth to his stormy career: 'Mr. Perry, after years of mediocre work on the stage, in 1929 was assigned the comedy role in the Fox film *Hearts in Dixie*, and suddenly skyrocketed to success. After appearing in a number of films without the success of his first venture in the films, Mr. Perry

[had to leave] Hollywood and headed East for personal appearances in theatres'[58].

Bankruptcy

After a few successful years between 1927 and 1929, Fetchit's career began to fluctuate erratically, ranging from bankruptcy in 1930 (while still a popular star) to a three-year absence from the screen (the end of 1931–34). The *Chicago Defender* reported:

> Stepin Fetchit is broke. ... he has filed a petition of bankruptcy in the New York courts. The Scribe can remember only a year ago when the lazy-voiced comedian used to have to pull straws to make up his mind which car he wanted to take out and numerous other displays of unlimited wealth. Alas, such is fame and fortune. It leaves as fast as it comes. Step lists his liabilities as $17,444 and his assets as $6,505. And more than half of his assets are tied up in salaries which as yet have not been paid[59].

In November of 1930, the *Chicago Defender*, continuing to expose the scandalous Fetchit, reported, 'Lincoln Perry, better known as Stepin Fetchit, bad luck's favourite son, is in hot water again'[60]. Fetchit had been named as the defendant in a $2,500 lawsuit for breaking a contract with the State Theater located in New York. The *Afro-American* (Baltimore) followed, reporting on the troubles that plagued Fetchit, castigating him as a buffoon who had fallen victim of his own buffoonery. This source noted that Fetchit was facing two lawsuits, one for breach of promise, the other for overdue rent[61]. The news account continued 'Playing in a good part opposite Lawrence Tibbett in *The Southerner* (1931), [Fetchit] has been showing spells of stubbornness and temperament. After wasting nearly an hour of the studio's valuable time for him to read certain lines as Director Pollard wanted them, he is said to have been given this ultimatum: "Either go on with your part in ten minutes, or we'll have you put off the lot"'[62].

In 1930, Fetchit attempted to redeem himself with the African American community by providing advice to actors and actresses to avoid his mistakes, vowing to reform himself. 'The talkies actually knocked the pride and swellhead out of many and brought many to realize that money and influence are not as powerful as sincerity, diligence and courage', he pontificated[63].

Despite landing roles in the motion pictures *The Prodigal* (1931), *Neck and Neck* (1931), and *Wild Horse* (1931) his personal life remained troubled. The African American press reported that Fetchit's wife would file for divorce alleging that Fetchit had kidnapped their son Jemajo (named for Jesus, Mary and Joseph), that Fetchit had physically assaulted her and charges that also included 'desertion and non-support'[64]. The *Afro-American* (Baltimore) philosophized, 'The screen comedian is Hollywood's paradox among movie stars. A fanatic on the scriptures he has an uncanny faculty for getting into one scrape after another'[65]. The *Chicago Defender* headlined Mrs. Perry's charge that Fetchit was a 'brutal husband'[66] and later again attacked Fetchit when a battle surfaced at an annual benefit for the Boy Scouts of America, between Fetchit and another prominent black actor, Clarence Muse[67]. The *Chicago Defender* posited that although Fetchit was at one time in demand in motion pictures, his popularity had declined, and he had fallen upon disfavour with studio executives because:

> After Fox had signed him to a contract with a sizeable salary, he went 'ritzy'... did not show up at the studio when ordered to do so ... kept directors waiting and all that sort of thing. He also branched out in a silver Rolls Royce, they say, and began living on a ridiculously elaborate scale[68].

By the end of 1931, Fetchit pursued filmmaking for himself. His efforts were again reported on in the black press. One report asserted that Fetchit was touring the country to find talent to appear in his film designed to be a sequel to *Hearts in Dixie*. Fetchit explained his launching of this venture by saying, 'I have been able to find men willing to cast me in certain types of films, but whenever some mention is made of placing me in a picture that contains real class they turn the other way and it is for that reason that I intend to write my own story and produce my own film'[69]. Evidence to support this assertion was provided by the *Chicago Defender*, which noted that in one of his last films before leaving motion pictures, Fetchit was 'cast in the role of a man catching bugs that troubled camels. This, of course,

was not a fine role but it gave producers the chance to curtail some of the Fetchit popularity which many figured they were trying to do'[70]. Fetchit's filmmaking skill and talent remained undisputed; however, one film producer and the *Chicago Defender* claimed that although Fetchit portrayed a lazy character on the screen, he was indeed quite intelligent[71].

In hot water
But the black press continued to remind its readers of Fetchit's failures and his mischievousness. The *Afro-American* (Baltimore) once reported that Fetchit:

> ... did many things that made Hollywood mad. One was the day they were making a film and stopped [for] lunch. In the interim, Step went to the barbershop and had his head shaved bald. When the company resumed work an hour later Step looked like a different person. The director faced the alternative of holding up production for a week while his hair grew back or trying to put hair on his head from the makeup kit. They called out the finest makeup experts who worked for hours trying to put the hair back. High-powered stars, drawing huge salaries, sat around and twiddled their thumbs. Step's haircut cost the company thousands of dollars[72].

In 1934, after a three year lull in his career, which could be attributed to studio officials who had become disenchanted with Fetchit's on screen and off screen behaviour, the *Afro-American* (Baltimore) reported that Stepin Fetchit would return to motion pictures, entitling their article, 'Can Lazy Bones Come Back'? According to this report Fetchit's return had been credited to:

> Charles Legters, wealthy insurance broker, in whose employ Stepin's mother has been for years, [and who] gave him a lift, only recently – an old automobile and funds with which to get to New York. In New York, so the story goes, Stepin ran into Winfield Sheehan on Broadway ... [who] is said to have replenished his anaemic exchequer and hired him for a role in *Carolina*, with other roles to follow – *provided Stepin can manage along without any more of his peculiar didos*[73].

This time Fetchit's contract contained a clause

Fig. 4. Fetchit is sold with a horse by Will Rogers in *David Harum* (1934).

'that forms a screen around his conduct and actions – which is supposed to guarantee his showing up when needed'[74]. Harry Levette, columnist for the *Afro-American* (Baltimore), took the opportunity to 'rub salt into the wound', reporting 'Incidentally he promises not to break the studio lot's speed laws of 12 miles an hour; report to the set on time; listen to his director; cut out street brawls; and the diverse and sundry things that got him in bad and held back his fellow players before'[75].

During the year of 1934 screen appearances for Fetchit included: *Carolina* (alternately titled *The House of Connolly*) (1934), *Follies of 1934*, *David Harum* (1934), *The World Moves On* (1934), *Stand Up and Cheer* (1934), *Judge Priest* (1934), *Marie Galante* (1934), *Bachelor of Arts* (1934), and *Helldorado* (1934). When he appeared in *Carolina* the question was raised as to whether he exceeded Bert Williams, blackface comedian, in comic talent. The *Chicago Defender* returned to commending Fetchit, reporting that Lionel Barrymore, who appeared in this film with Fetchit claimed

that, 'Stepin, without even trying, could steal a scene from any living man or woman'[76]. The film *Carolina* apparently provoked controversy within the African American community about Fetchit's role. In this Civil War drama, Fetchit portrays the character Scipio, and according to a film review in the *New York Times*, 'Stepin Fetchit, who could probably get a handicap from a tortoise or a snail in a race, gives a comic exhibition as a stable worker and butler'[77]. *Variety* added that in this film he was 'still funny in action, but continues to be as incoherent in speech'[78]. Undoubtedly, the black press was disturbed by his subservient, comic and demeaning portrayal of African Americans. A letter in defence of Fetchit's portrayal, submitted by Moxley Waldo Willis, Sr., stated:

By no stretch of the imagination can the character portrayed by Stepin Fetchit and the coloured woman appearing with him be made to fit, for instance, Ben Davis or Mrs. Mary Bethune. Yet, there are coloured people in the South, on

Fig. 5. 'The screen's laziest comedian', in a poster for one of his short race-film musicals, *I Ain't Gonna Open That Door*, c. 1948. [Courtesy of The Carson Collection.]

every hand, who are prototypes of the characters portrayed. Therefore, such portrayals are artistic.

And if the bulk of us did not have such an annoying inferiority complex, or weren't so supersensitive, we could perceive what is artistically true, and not believe that in every instance some white man is bent on dealing with us disparagingly'[79].

The screen's laziest man

As for his portrayal in *David Harum*, it was reported that he enjoyed his role because 'he was associated with horses, though he did not fancy the idea of being sold with the horse by Will Rogers, who enacts the title role'[80]. In response to Fetchit's obvious attempt to justify taking this role, the *Afro-American* (Baltimore) was condescending in its review describing Fetchit as 'Black, slow, big-eyed and Ubangi lipped, [as]

he provided much hilarity in the character of a stableboy …'[81].

During this same year of 1934, the *Afro-American* (Baltimore) reported that a bench warrant for Fetchit's arrest was made 'when the comedian refused to appear when cited to show cause for the failure to pay a bill of $1,404 … for rent and the wrecking of an apartment which was owned by George Williams. Fetchit and another actor are reported to have engaged in fistic combat in the apartment and all [movable] objects were used'[82].

In 1935, although Fetchit scored successes in several films, including: *The County Chairman* (1935), *One More Spring* (1935), *Charlie Chan in Egypt* (1935), *Steamboat Round the Bend* (1935), and *The Virginia Judge* (1935), he continued to encounter problems off the screen, as the buffoonery he perfected on the screen also became a stereotype for his off-screen life. The *Afro-American* (Baltimore) reported that:

> Stepin Fetchit may be as slow as molasses in January when it comes to stepping around a motion picture set, but it is hardly possible that anyone could beat him in a race for getting into trouble. The screen's 'laziest man,' here for a seven-day engagement at the Apollo Theater last week, managed to get himself into two scraps in three days, and as a result was forced to put in personal appearances at both Harlem and Washington Heights courts, Thursday. In Harlem court the comedian was charged with slugging Philip Kauchers, white, a process server … when Kauchers tried to serve him with a summons over an alleged debt. … As soon as the bail had been arranged for, Stepin went to Washington Heights court to answer a second charge of assault brought against him by James Madison Parker, the comedian's 'stooge'. … In Boston he got into difficulty with the police. The following week he was locked up in Philadelphia when police raided a number of night clubs'[83].

According to the *Chicago Defender*, Fetchit was arrested in Baltimore, Maryland, for attacking two valets, though he pleaded not guilty to these charges. He was later acquitted of charges filed against him in the incident at the Apollo Theater[84].

Fetchit, annoyed by a press he considered

hostile, struck back. In an interview with the *Afro-American* (Baltimore), Fetchit asserted, 'My real following is ninety per cent white and the coloured public had very little to do with my universal success on the stage or in pictures'[85]. He added, 'There are certain corners that I strive, live, and am comfortable in that the coloured press cannot reach. If the press does not cater to me, who definitely is news, who will the press cater to'[86]?

Fetchit made it clear that he knew he would always be a newsworthy item in the African American press, implying that they needed him.

In 1936, Fetchit was reportedly the only African American actor who had an annual contract with Twentieth Century-Fox Studios. During this year, Fetchit appeared in: *36 Hours to Kill* (1936), *Dimples* (1936), and *On the Avenue* (1936), an appearance following an automobile accident in which he suffered a fractured skull. The film was reviewed by the *Chicago Defender* which stated: 'Stepin is at his best, as he reels you with laughter, and through his droll manner of provoking laziness and intelligence, easily steals several important scenes from his co-stars, Dick Powell, Alice Faye and [Madeleine] Carroll'[87].

Fetchit's contract allowed him to work as a free-lance artist, to perform on stage in a number of theatres. When he appeared at the Howard Theater, the *Afro-American* (Baltimore) did a combination praise–scold review: 'Stepin Fetchit, screen comedian, likes the stage because he can hear the applause, but he doesn't want too much of the latter, for he 'would have to walk all the way back on the stage for an encore'[88].

The *Afro-American* (Baltimore) commented on Fetchit's life in its usual condemnatory style, reporting in 1937 that Fetchit had married for a second time to Minnie Johnson, a Broadway dancer, that the two eloped, but that it was rumoured that Fetchit had been engaged to Elsie Roxborough, niece of John Roxborough, manager for Joe Louis[89]. Another report followed, after his marriage, that Fetchit and his new wife were in dispute over the name of their newly born son, Donald Martin[90]. Fetchit's second marriage was short-lived and ended in scandal with Fetchit accusing his wife of infidelity insisting that their child was not his. This report on his personal troubles was followed by one on his career, which alleged that Fetchit was being hit with a $25,000

lawsuit for failing to appear at the Orpheum Theater. This lawsuit was later withdrawn[91]. During this year he managed to appear in the following motion pictures: *Love Is News* (1937) and *Fifty Roads to Town* (1937).

In 1938 it was reported that Fetchit would return to Hollywood after an absence of a year. During his absence Fetchit had performed on the stage in theatres throughout the country, and again had provoked attention, as the African American press reported that Fetchit had allegedly been involved in an attack when he was delivered a steak with which he was dissatisfied while on tour at the Oriental Theater in Chicago[92]. In 1939 he appeared in the movie *Zenobia* (*Elephants Never Forget*), but as before, his private life garnered a great deal of uncomplimentary attention. It was revealed that in 1940 Fetchit's 'wrangle with the Federal Government ended quietly last week when Fetchit paid $469 to the Government. This amount represented duty and penalties on three suits which the comedian is alleged to have brought in illegally after a trip to Canada'[93]. In the same year the *Afro-American* (Baltimore) reported that Fetchit, engaged in a brawl with his ex-valet who was suing him for failure to pay back wages after the court ruled against the former valet[94]. A third lawsuit was reported for alleged legal fees Fetchit owed, involving an auto damage suit[95] and in a fourth in 1941, Fetchit was again sued, for failing to appear for a performance that had been scheduled[96]. As a result, according to the *Chicago Defender*, Fetchit 'filed a bankruptcy action for $4 million dollars which [in 1951] still stands as an all-time record'[97].

At war with the black press

In view of Fetchit's success as an African American screen actor in the early days of American filmmaking, the African American press' coverage of Fetchit was certainly warranted. Fetchit, however, condemned the black press' coverage, particularly of his private life, claiming in the *Chicago Defender* that the papers had greatly exaggerated his troubles. For example, he cited the Cotton Club: 'Sure I had a fight with Herman Starks, manager of the place, but the story that I tossed bricks at half of the Cotton Club crew is entirely false'[98]. In a letter in the *Chicago Defender*, Fetchit wrote:

Kindly try and show your dislike for me in some other way other than abusing my name by allowing it printed as in your last issue as being in the employment of people whom I employ as I can see no other reason than dislike of me that would allow your paper to print things about me so detrimental when you have been advised better and should know better or I suggest you dig up the real bad things I do and give me bad publicity that is true and not be so unjust and try to belittle me with unjust and impossible statements[99].

Even as early as the late 1920s, Fetchit was disenchanted with his portrayal in the African American press. According to Harry Levette, 'Step used to feel mistreated when this column condemned his misbehaviour back in 1928 and made "hot copy" of his frequent escapades. In fact, he consulted Atty. Curtis Taylor concerning the matter. "Should I sue that guy Levette for slander, or should I beat him up"? he asked'[100]. Fetchit was advised to improve his behaviour and thus avoid ridicule in the black press[101].

As his failures increased in number, the black press continually subjected him to censure, and his relationship with them continued to deteriorate. In 1943, Fetchit was arrested on a charge of 'contributing to the delinquency of a minor' when he was found in a hotel room with a sixteen year-old girl[102]. Following his arrest, reports circulated that Fetchit had a double who posed for him while he was incarcerated for 30 days and that he was actually residing in California[103]. Such reports prompted an investigation by the Assistant State Attorney, which resulted in Fetchit's agent declaring, 'Fetchit hasn't a double nor a brother and he's the boy who's in the Bridewell right now. He's written me three letters from his cell'[104]. A report in the *Afro-American* (Baltimore) that may have reflected the black community's sentiments stated, 'Folks of the stage and movies always rated Step as the "laziest" of actors. He cashed in on his characterization to the dismay of those seeking to have coloured portrayed in healthier roles. They don't have to worry now; the axe has fallen on Step'[105].

From 1945, as Fetchit's screen career slowed to a halt until his death in 1985, Fetchit began defending his screen portrayals. According to the *Afro-American* (Baltimore), Fetchit asserted:

The role of Stepin Fetchit, the slow-moving, lazy man who shuffles through life in a half-sleep, half-awake dream world, has not damaged race relations or lowered white peoples concepts of coloured people ... Stepin Fetchit is no Uncle Tom role ... I am an original looking man to start with and I try to look as dumb as I can when I'm acting. I look as if I'm always trying to get out of something, but you can see that I have a soul and that I'm thinking fast[106].

Again in 1971, Stepin Fetchit was quoted in *Film Quarterly* as defending his screen portrayals. In an interview conducted with Joseph McBride, Fetchit stated:

I was the first Negro militant. But I was a militant for God and country and not controlled by foreign interests. I was the first black man to have a universal audience. When people saw me and Will Rogers together like brothers, that said something to them. I elevated the Negro. I was the first Negro to gain full American citizenship ... I defied white supremacy and proved in defying it that I could be associated with. There was no white man's ideas of making a Negro Hollywood motion picture star, a millionaire Negro entertainer. ...

They've made the character part of Stepin Fetchit stand for being lazy and stupid and being a white man's fool. I never did that, but they're all so prejudiced now that they just can't understand. Maybe because they don't really know what it was like then[107].

As he attempted to convince others, he was obviously attempting to convince himself, using the argument of 'what it was like then'. But in his real life he had become the buffoon he had perfected on the screen and stage. The *Afro-American* (Baltimore) remained unconvinced, in the end. 'Stepin Fetchit will always remain the shiftless, inarticulate, lazy bones ... Step is really the Step you see on the screen. He is typed for life'[108].

Memoirs of **WILL ROGERS** in **JUDGE PRIEST** with **STEPIN FETCHIT**

Fig. 6. Will Rogers and Stepin Fetchit as 'brothers' in *Judge Priest* (1934).
[Courtesy of the John Ford Collection, the Lilly Library, Indiana University.]

Ford and Zanuck

It is noteworthy that as late as 1946 Fetchit was still being recruited to appear on the screen in uncomplimentary roles by Hollywood motion picture studio executives. For example, in a letter to Darryl Zanuck from John Ford, Ford stated, 'I am offering as a suggestion the name of Stepin Fetchit, the coloured actor. If we can get him for Buttons I think we would have a great character to introduce to the public again as bellboy, porter, night clerk, waiter, bootblack, bartender and chambermaid at the hotel. His primary function, of course, is to prepare the easy chair that the Marshall sits in when the stagecoach arrives as per our discussion'[109]. Darryl Zanuck in response to John Ford wrote, 'No one has laughed louder at Stepin Fetchit than I have, but to put him on the screen at this time would I am afraid raise terrible objections from the coloured people. Walter White, when he addressed us on the problem of coloured people, singled out Stepin Fetchit, as I recall, as an example of the humiliation of the coloured race. Stepin Fetchit always portrays the lazy, stupid, halfwit, and this is the thing that the coloured people are furious about. In view of this do you think we should take the chance'[110]? Apparently by the late 1940s,

motion picture producers were becoming more concerned with the objections African Americans raised regarding their screen portrayals.

The black press after the 1940s reported only occasionally on his acting appearances. In the 1950s it was reported that he was scheduled to portray Satchel Paige, a famous African American baseball player of the American league[111]. It is not certain as to whether this film project ever materialized. In 1952 when Fetchit was cast in *Bend of the River*, *Ebony* magazine reported that:

Fetchit sports a full head of hair instead of the former clean-head appearance, and gone are the head-scratching sequences which highlighted his earlier picture performances. Often under attack by Negroes for his Uncle Tom roles, Fetchit insists that he has never done anything on the screen to hurt the Negro. Movie people are moving cautiously with any roles assigned to Fetchit to avoid any trouble from Negro groups which are waging war on screen stereotypes[112].

This article provoked a response from one critic who in a letter to the editor of this magazine stated:

Fig. 7. John Ford engineers Stepin Fetchit's return to the screen as Judge Priest's (Charles Winninger's servant in *The Sun Shines Bright* (1953).
[Courtesy of the John Ford Collection, the Lilly Library, Indiana University.]

Everyone of us was very sorry to see a magazine as great as yours print an article on Stepin Fetchit. We have seen him in movies and we do not classify him as a Negro comedian but rather as a parasitical fool.

We thought the day was coming when we would see Negroes in intelligent roles in movies, television and radio, but instead Hollywood has taken a backward step in reviving this 'comedian' Fetchit.

How in the world can a man such as Fetchit have the nerve to meet another Negro face to face? ... We have had 14 years of peace with Fetchit out of roles in movies. Let's have 1,400 years more[113].

Other screen appearances in the later years include: *Miracle in Harlem* (1947), *The Sun Shines Bright* (1953), *Amazing Grace* (1974) and *Won Ton Ton The Dog Who Saved Hollywood* (1976). His press coverage was negligible.

A problematic image

Fetchit's relationship with the African American press fluctuated. In the early years, Fetchit was himself an arm of the black press. He served as a correspondent who provided entertainment news on African American involvement in vaudeville and on stage, and his columns echoed the concerns of the black press for positive images both on and off the screen. However, later in his career when he became consumed by his own success, Fetchit failed to live up to his own beliefs and principles that he had articulated in the early phase of his career. As Fetchit became popular for his screen portrayals, the African American press began a vigilant relationship with him, applauding him for his successes, while simultaneously condemning him for his failures. Additionally, the black press assumed an assertively proprietary position, assigning him the role both on and off screen of representing his race. Black reviewers and reporters alike, denounced or praised him for film portrayals and for day-to-day behaviour. African American audiences both responded to the press and used it to voice their own reactions to Fetchit.

During a time when few black actors could penetrate the largely white motion picture industry, those who did, such as Fetchit, were often thrust into the position, willingly or unwillingly, of having to represent all African Americans. These African American actors had to assume this role regardless of the arena they were seeking to enter, and they had to share in the responsibility of presenting the most positive portrayal of the race. This was a heavy burden given the discriminatory practices that were in place and that were founded on the film industry's stereotypical assumptions about African Americans. Fetchit's behaviour both on and off the screen was constantly being watched and reported on by the African American press.

The role of the black press, in serving as a voice to denounce racially unfavourable portrayals, is consistent with their historical tradition. According to Martin Dann, 'Two currents in black intellectual history evident in the black press converge repeatedly: a response to white racism and an assertion of self-determination'[114]. Dann continued, 'Both were inextricably linked and developed almost simultaneously, and both were directed toward the same goal of freedom, equality, and racial pride that had been denied black people'[115]. The African American press, therefore, was fulfilling its historic role.

Although Fetchit, who happened to be an experienced writer, also used the press to express his own views, he could not quite convince African American audiences of the rightness of his position; instead, he seemed to be convincing himself. We will never know if Fetchit was subconsciously ashamed of himself, or if he truly believed he was a pioneer leader, reacting and responding to the climate of his era. In retrospect, we sense that Fetchit's comedy technique of self-demeaning humour ended

by scarring the humorist himself. Stepin Fetchit, it seems, was an imitator who had become his own imitation. He mimicked racist stereotypes and perfected the buffoon character with such skill and genius on the screen that off the screen these caricatures permeated his own behaviour. When examining Stepin Fetchit, it is necessary to explore his career in terms of his relationship with the African American press because the black press provides a more well rounded view of Fetchit by exposing his strengths as well as his weaknesses. He should not be ignored or dismissed in reconstructing black cinema history where without question he remains an intriguing and significant figure.✳

Notes

1. James Baldwin, *The Devil Finds Work* (New York: Dial Press, 1976), 19–20.

2. Donald Bogle, *Toms, Coons, Mulattoes, Mammies, and Bucks: An Interpretive History of Blacks in American Films* (New York: Continuum, 1989), 39–41. It is noteworthy that Lincoln Perry's Death Certificate Provided by the Department of Health Services, State of California, reports that his father (Joseph Perry) and mother (Dora Monroe) were both born in England. The *Negro Digest* added that 'his father was a reader in a cigar rolling factory. A reader, he once explained, is an educated man who reads to cigar makers while they role cigars. His father, who was very educated, read to the cigar makers in Spanish' ('Do You Remember Stepin Fetchit', *Negro Digest* 9 No. 1 (November 1950): 42.

3. Gary Null, *Black Hollywood: The Black Performer in Motion Pictures* (New York: Citadel Press-Carol Publishing Group, 1975), 59.

4. *Ibid.*

5. Donald Bogle, *Toms, Coons, Mulattoes, Mammies & Bucks*, 44.

6. *Ibid.*, 39.

7. *Ibid.*, 44.

8. Lincoln Perry, 'Lincoln Perry Writes', *Chicago Defender*, 4 December 1926, 8.

9. Lincoln Perry, 'Lincoln Perry Writes', *Chicago Defender*, 18 December 1926, 7.

10. Lincoln Perry, 'Lincoln Perry's Letter,' *Chicago Defender*, 2 July 1927, 8.

11. Lincoln Perry, 'Lincoln Perry's Letter', *Chicago Defender*, 13 August 1927, 10.

12. Lincoln Pery, 'Lincoln Perry's Letter', *Chicago Defender*, 27 August 1927, 9.

13. *Ibid.*

14. Lincoln Perry, 'Lincoln Perry's Letter', *Chicago Defender*, 25 February 1928, 9.

15. *Ibid.*

16. *Ibid.*

17. Lincoln Perry, 'Lincoln Perry's Letter', *Chicago Defender*, 5 November 1927, 11.

18. *Ibid.*

19. *Ibid.*

20. 'Race Stars in Play', *Chicago Defender*, 5 November 1927, 11.

21. 'In Old Kentucky', *Chicago Defender*, 28 January 1928, 8.

22. 'Actor Too Proud To Work In Films With Own Race', *Chicago Defender*, 29 December 1928, 11.

23. *Ibid.*

24. Maurice Dancer, '"I Didn't High-Hat Colored Players", Answers Fetchit', *Pittsburgh Courier*, 2 February 1929, 1, Third Section.

25. *Ibid.*

26. Maurice Dancer, 'Manhattan Critic Reviews New All-Colored Talkie', *Pittsburgh Courier*, 9 March 1929, 1.

27. Robert Benchley, 'Hearts In Dixie: The First Real Talking Picture', *Opportunity*, 7 no. 4 (April 1929): 122. Films in which Stepin Fetchit appeared were provided by the *International Dictionary of Films and Filmmakers, Vol. III – Actors and Actresses*, James Vinson, ed. (Chicago: St. James Press, 1986), 227.

28. 'Stepin Fetchit and "Bubbles" Battle For Public', *Afro-American* (Baltimore), 6 July 1929, 9.

29. *Ibid.*

30. 'Says Fetchit Jilted Her; Sues For $100,000', *Afro-American* (Baltimore), 13 July 1929, 8.

31. Donald Bogle, *Toms, Coons, Mulattoes, Mammies & Bucks*, 39.

32. 'Stepin Fetchit At Lando Theatre', *Pittsburgh Courier*, 14 December 1929, 9.

33. 'Fetchit Writing Songs', *Afro-American* (Baltimore), 2 November 1929, 8.

34. 'Stepin Fetchit To Tour Country', *Pittsburgh Courier*, 21 December 1929, 9 Second Section.

35. Stepin Fetchit Is Sure Movies Rule', *Chicago Defender*, 16 December 1933, 8.

36. 'Stepin Fetchit Back In: Famed "Laziest" Comic Off Lot For 13 Years', *Chicago Defender*, 28 July 1951, 34.

37. Fay M. Jackson, 'Hollywood Personalities: Stepin Fetchit', *Afro-American* (Baltimore), 23 December 1933, 19 and 'Stepin Fetchit's Work Wins Him New Contract With Fox', *Chicago Defender*, 21 April 1934, 9.

38. 'Step Holds Out For Kitchen and Line of Girls', *Afro-American* (Baltimore), 4 November 1939, 14.

39. 'Movie Comic Entertains Friends', *Chicago Defender*, 5 September 1936, 9.

40. Sylvester Russell, 'Sylvester Russell's Review', *Pittsburgh Courier*, 27 July 1929, 3, Second Section.

41. Ruby Berkley Goodwin, 'When Stepin Fetchit Stepped Into Fame', *Afro-American* (Baltimore), 6 July 1929, 11.

42. 'Stepin Fetchit on Screen Pleases Regal Movie Fans', *Chicago Defender*, 24 August 1929, 8.

43. *Ibid.*

44. 'Stepin Fetchit in Big Time at Regal Nov. 2', *Chicago Defender*, 19 October 1929, 10.

45. 'Stepin Fetchit in Salute Tops Big Week at Regal', *Chicago Defender*, 7 December 1929, 10.

46. 'Stepin Stays Up Late To Get Sleepy', *Pittsburgh Courier*, 18 January 1930, 16.

47. 'Sans The Footlights', *Chicago Defender*, 14 November 1931, 8.

48. 'Stepin Fetchit Gets Big Contract With Columbia', *Pittsburgh Courier*, 25 January 1930, 16.

49. '"Stepin" Failed to "Fetchit", So Now He's Out In The Cold Again', *Pittsburgh Courier*, 8 February 1930, 16.

50. 'Fetchit Out, Muse In', *Afro-American* (Baltimore), 22 February 1930, 9.

51. 'Tells Stepin Fetchit Why He Fell Down', *Chicago Defender*, 19 July 1930, 8.

52. 'Can't Keep A Good Man Down' – Stepin Fetchit, *Pittsburgh Courier*, 22 February 1930, 16.

53. 'Stepin Fetchit's Lazy Drawl Big Hit In Chi.', *Pittsburgh Courier*, 10 May 1930, 10.

54. *Ibid.*

55. *Ibid.*

56. 'Fetchit Balks When Salary Is Withheld', *Afro-American* (Baltimore), 7 June 1930, 8.

57. 'Fetchit In Good Graces', *Afro-American* (Baltimore), 13 September 1930, 8.

58. 'Son Born to Mrs. Fetchit in New York', *Chicago Defender*, 20 September 1930, 7.

59. 'Going Backstage With The Scribe', *Chicago Defender*, 13 December 1930, 6.

60. 'In Hot Water', *Chicago Defender*, 8 November 1930, 6.

61. 'Troubles Come Fast for Film Funny Man: Stepin Fetchit Faces Two Suits on the West Coast', *Afro-American* (Baltimore), 15 November 1930, 9.

62. *Ibid. The Southerner* was also known as *The Prodigal* (1931).

63. 'Stepin Fetchit Preaches A X-Mas Sermon to Actors', *Afro-American* (Baltimore), 27 December 1930, 8.

64. 'Fetchit Blames "Friends" For Marital Rifts', *Chicago Defender*, 9 May 1931, 9 and 'A Happy Family, We'll Say', *Chicago Defender*, 7 February 1931, 22.

65. 'Movie Comedian Expects God to Help Him Keep His Wife', *Afro-American* (Baltimore), 16 May 1931, 9.

66. 'Stepin Fetchit's Wife Enters Divorce Suit: Says Brutality Replaces Comic Roles In Home', *Chicago Defender*, 29 August 1931, 7.

67. Frankye M. Whitlock, 'Fetchit' and Muse in Near Fist Battle', *Chicago Defender*, 5 September 1931, 7.

68. 'Stepin Fetchit Will Play Cafe in September', *Chicago Defender*, 29 August 1931, 7.

69. 'Say Stepin Fetchit To Produce Own Film', *Chicago Defender*, 19 September 1931, 6.

70. 'Stepin Fetchit Is Star in This Film' *Chicago Defender*, 18 November 1933, 9.

71. 'Stepin Fetchit, Lazy in Speech, Is Rather Smart', *Chicago Defender*, 25 February 1933, 9.

72. Ralph Matthews, 'Looking At the Stars', *Afro-American* (Baltimore), 20 May 1933, 10.

73. 'Can Lazy-Bones Stepin Fetchit Come Back'?, *Afro-American* (Baltimore), 3 February 1934, 21.

74. 'Lost! One Film Star; Name, Stepin Fetchit: Studio Searches for Ace After Waiting Week to Start Picture', *Chicago Defender*, 21 October 1933, 9.

75. Harry Levette, 'Gossip of the Movie Lots', *Afro-American* (Baltimore), 2 September 1933, 19.

76. 'Is Stepin Fetchit the Equal of Bert Williams? Lionel Barrymore says Yes; Eddie Cantor, No', *Chicago Defender*, 10 March 1934, 8.

77. *New York Times Film Reviews 1932–1938* Vol. 2 (New York Times & Arno Press: 1970), 1033.

78. *Variety Film Reviews 1934–1937* Vol. 5 (New York: Garland Publishing, 1983).

79. 'Defends Fetchit in Role Played in Carolina', *Afro-American*, (Baltimore), 7 July 1934, 8.

80. 'Stepin Fetchit is Hero of Regal's Picture', *Chicago Defender*, 19 May 1934, 8.

81. 'Stepin Fetchit', *Afro-American*, (Baltimore), 10 March 1934, 6.

82. 'Fetchit Fetches $1,404 Back Rent', *Afro-American* (Baltimore), 3 March 1934, 7.

83. 'Why Can't Stepin Fetchit Keep Himself Out of Trouble'? *Afro-American* (Baltimore), 21 December 1935, 9.

84. 'Stepin Fetchit Denies Story of Attack On Two', *Chicago Defender*, 23 November 1935, 13 and "Stepin Fetchit Wins In Court and Is Freed', *Chicago Defender*, 4 January 1936, 8.

85. James H. Purdy, Jr., 'My Real Following is White, Says Step', *Afro-American* (Baltimore), 30 April 1938, 11.

86. *Ibid.*

87. 'Step Fetchit At Park Sunday in On the Avenue Film Revue', *Chicago Defender*, 15 May 1937, 12.

88. 'Step Fetchit Finds Encores Too Taxing', *Afro-American* (Baltimore), 21 March 1936, 11.

89. 'Fetchit in a Hurry For Once – He Elopes', *Afro-American* (Baltimore), 16 October 1937, 1.

90. 'Step, Wife Argue On Baby's Name', *Afro-American* (Baltimore), 18 June 1938, 10.

91. '$25,000 Suit Against Stepin Withdrawn', *Afro-American* (Baltimore), 9 March 1938, 10.

92. 'Stepin Fetchit Freed After Steak Fight', *Chicago Defender*, 22 April 1939, 13.

93. 'Failure to Pay $92 Duty Costs S. Fetchit $469', *Afro-American* (Baltimore), 13 July 1940, 13.

94. 'Stepin Fetchit's Mind Not on Debt, Gets Sock on Jaw', *Afro-American* (Baltimore), 2 March 1940, 14.

95. 'Attachment', *Afro-American* (Baltimore), 9 March 1940, 13.

96. 'Stepin Fetchit Loses in Non-Showup Act: Ace Comic Now Faces Bankruptcy', *Afro-American* (Baltimore), 6 September 1941, 13.

97. 'Stepin Fetchit Back In: *Famed* "Laziest" Comic Off Lot For 13 Years', *Chicago Defender*, 28 July 1951, 34.

98. 'They Exaggerated My Trouble', *Chicago Defender*, 25 November 1939, 11.

99. Stepin Fetchit 'An Open Letter To Stepin Fetchit', *Chicago Defender*, 14 May 1938, 8.

100. Harry Levette, 'Gossip of the Movie Lots', *Afro-American* (Baltimore), 2 September 1933, 19.

101. *Ibid.*

102. 'Stepin Fetchit and Girl Taken in Hotel Raid', *Afro-American* (Baltimore), 17 July 1943, 1.

103. 'Camera Catches Fetchit As He Checks Out of Chicago Prison', *Afro-American* (Baltimore) 23 October 1943, 8.

104. 'Fetchit "Stand-in" Myth Falls Down Under Probe', *Afro-American* (Baltimore), 23 October 1943, 8.

105. E.B. Rea, 'Encores and Echoes', *Afro-American* (Baltimore), 14 August 1943, 10.

106. 'Stepin Fetchit: Lincoln Perry Says He's No Uncle Tom; Feels He Has Helped Race Relations', *Afro-American* (Baltimore) 26 May 1945, 5.

107. Joseph McBride, 'Stepin Fetchit Talks Back', *Film Quarterly*, 24 no. 4 (Summer 1971): 22.

108. Fay M. Jackson, 'Movies Want Only "Uncle Tom" and "Mammy" Types', *Afro-American* (Baltimore), 12 October 1935, 8.

109. Letter-From John Ford of Twentieth Century-Fox Film Corporation to Darryl Zanuck, 4 February 1946, John Ford Manuscripts, Manuscripts Department, Lilly Library, Indiana University, Bloomington, Indiana.

110. Letter-From Darryl Zanuck, Twentieth Century-Fox Film Corporation to John Ford, 5 February 1946, John Ford Manuscripts, Manuscripts Department, Lilly Library, Indiana University, Bloomington, Indiana.

111. 'Fetchit To Do Movie on Paige', *Chicago Defender*, 28 March 1953, "Stepin Fetchit May Get The Title Role', *Chicago Defender*, 29 September 1951, 23, and 'The Satchel Paige Story Hollywood's Next Mixed Film', *Chicago Defender*, 29 October 1949, 27.

112. 'Stepin Fetchit Comes Back: Comedian Of Yesteryear Returns To Hollywood In New Western Movie', *Ebony* 7 no. 4 (February 1952): 64–65.

113. 'Letters to the Editor', *Ebony* 7 no. 10 (August 1952): 8.

114. Martin E. Dann, ed. *The Black Press (1827–1890): The Quest for National Identity* (New York: Capricorn Books, 1971), 12.

115. *Ibid.*

Film History, Volume 6, pp. 522–534, 1994. Copyright © John Libbey & Company
ISSN: 0892-2160. Printed in Great Britain

Enemies, a love story: Von Stroheim, women, and World War I

Lucy Fischer

He's going to make you *hate him* even if it takes a *million dollars* of our money to do it!
– Poster, *Foolish Wives*, Universal Jewel

In recent years, feminist film criticism has focused relentlessly on such issues as voyeurism, fetishism, rape and romance as applied to numerous classic texts. Privileged among these have been the thrillers and melodramas of such male directors as: Alfred Hitchcock, Josef von Sternberg, D.W. Griffith, Max Ophuls, Michael Powell, Orson Welles and Brian De Palma, to name but a few[1]. Surprisingly, given the narrative thrust of his *oeuvre*, the early films of Erich von Stroheim have been largely ignored. For, in the movies which he directed or enacted, von Stroheim was cast as a womanizing foreign officer-aristocrat who mercilessly persecuted and exploited American women. Hence, sexual politics was at the heart of his dramas, functioning as the axis around which his *persona* – 'The Man You Love to Hate' – evolved. Curiously, contemporary Anglo-American feminist critics have seemed exempt from this spectatorial loathing – from this ambivalent and consuming passion[2].

This essay will attempt to redress this gap through an analysis of a selection of Stroheim texts from the period around World War I (1916–1921). In addition to discussing certain theoretical questions raised by his work, it will try to place his portrayal of woman within the context of the social history of the era (a period that has received far less attention in Film Studies than World War II). Several topics will inform this examination: (1) the ascendancy of the middle class American 'New Woman' and the rise of females in the workplace; (2) the decline of Victorian sexual mores; (3) the growing instability of traditional marriage; (4) the presence of American women abroad during World War I. Furthermore, the entire focus of Stroheim's films on European/American relations will be viewed within the framework of the simultaneous debates on isolationism *vs* internationalism. Significantly, this political tension is played out as a conflict over the body of woman.

Borrowing John Berger's paradigm in *Ways Of Seeing*, this essay will be divided into two parts. Section I: 'The Surveyor' will concentrate on von

Lucy Fischer is the author of *Shot/Countershot: Film Tradition and Women's Cinema* (1989) and the editor of an anthology of articles on *Imitation of Life* (1991). She is Director of the Film Studies Program at the University of Pittsburgh. Correspondence c/o Department of English, 526 Cathedral of Learning, University of Pittsburgh, Pittsburgh, PA 15260, USA.

Fig. 1. The Man with the Monocle: von Stroheim as Count
Karamzin in *Foolish Wives* (1922).
[All photos courtesy of Richard Koszarski.]

Stroheim's persona; Section II: 'The Surveyed' will
consider the early twentieth century woman – the
object of his fictional and directorial gaze.

The surveyor

Voyeurism, seduction, and rape

> [T]here is but one sexuality, one libido – and it
> is masculine.
> – Jean Baudrillard[3]

The trademark prop identified with von Stroheim is
his monocle, an object that announces his character's
scopophilic regimens and pleasures. As early as John
Emerson's *The Social Secretary* (1916) von Stroheim
adopts it to portray Adam Buzzard, a gossip columnist in pursuit of licentious stories. As an intertitle tells
us: 'No clandestine affair is ever safe from [his]
prying eyes'. Hence, throughout the film, we see him

peering through bushes, monitoring the sexual liaison
of a wealthy young man and his mother's female
assistant. Ultimately, Buzzard's voyeurism is re-
couped when his investigation allows him to warn
the family matriarch of a shady Count's designs on
her unsuspecting daughter.

   In later films, however, von Stroheim would *be*
that Count – as though to borrow from the protagonists who populated the films in which he acted. In
Alan Holubar's *The Heart of Humanity* (1918), he
plays a German officer during World War I. When,
in the midst of battle, he is attracted to a Red Cross
nurse, he removes his monocle and stares at her with
erotic concentration. But, it is in the films which von
Stroheim authored that a discourse of voyeurism is
most aggressively articulated. In *Blind Husbands*
(1919), he plays Lieutenant von Steuben, a man
who 'loves wine, women and song'. In his initial
appearance, he arrives at the Tyrolean Alps by

Fig. 2. In *Blind Husbands* (1919), the Husband (Sam DeGrasse, extreme right) ignores his Wife (Francelia Billington, lower left), who is the object of the Other Man's (von Stroheim's) attentions. They are accompanied by the Mountain Guide (T.H. Gibson-Gowland) and the Honeymooners (Valerie Germonprez, Jack Perrin).

coach, accompanied by an American couple, Dr. and Mrs. Armstrong. We see von Steuben adjust his monocle, then view Margaret Armstrong's legs – marking him the master of the male gaze. If husbands are blind, seducers are not.

In *Foolish Wives* (1922) the focus on vision is more extensive. In the beginning of the film von Stroheim's character, Count Vladislaw Sergius Karamzin, is visited by the counterfeiter, Ventucci, and his adult, retarded daughter. Shots of the Count looking are intercut with camera pans up the girl's body, tracing the illicit path of his vision. His desire seems equally registered in the lens netting which sensually blurs the image. But the main axis of the Count's optical desire is Mrs. Helen Hughes, the wife of an American diplomat who has been dispatched to Monte Carlo. The Count first notices her on the porch of a hotel, where she reclines on a

chaise longue, reading a book. Shot/countershot editing alternates an image of her legs with a close-up of the Count peering. She responds by pulling her dress down over her shins. The final and most audacious instance of voyeurism occurs when the scheming Count purposely 'loses' himself and Mrs. Hughes in a storm and sequesters them in the cabin of the witch-like, Mother Garoupe. When Mrs. Hughes removes her wet clothes, she modestly banishes the Count to the other side of the room, where he apparently complies by sitting with his back turned. He then surreptitiously produces a mirror and gazes at her through a lecherous 'rear-view'. An image renders both his face and her body reflected in the glass – the former overwhelming the latter in scale and focus. (For S.J. Perelman, this was as 'near a sample of voyeurism ... as any ever reported by Wilhelm Stekel'[4]. (Significantly, in an earlier scene

Mr. Hughes mocked Karamzin's affectation of a monocle, noting that at least his *own* eyes were 'pretty good yet'. While he meant this on an ocular level, it applies to a moral one as well.

For, it is clear that the trajectory of von Stroheim's voyeurism moves toward conventional notions of 'perversion' – exemplified in his quasipediphilic fascination with a child-woman and in his sadistic sexual victimization of Mrs. Hughes (a penchant slyly suggested in his sporting a whip, pistol and patent leather boots). Such a characterization strongly opposes the sentimental tenor of the era – still tinged by a Victorian etherealization of romance and of the feminine. (It was, after all, the era of Mary Pickford's ascendancy.) It is interesting that von Stroheim's fascination with monocular vision even transgressed Hollywood production codes. As he once stated (with characteristic relish): 'there is a great prejudice against allowing actors to wear glasses, because of the halations that take place when the light strikes the edges ... *I am very fond of these halations on highly polished surfaces*' (emphasis added)[5].

One of the reasons that von Stroheim's voyeurism seems nefarious is that it is associated with other more concrete violations of the female body – seduction and rape. In one of his most vicious roles (as the German officer, Erich von Eberhard in *The Heart of Humanity*), he traps Nanette (Dorothy Phillips), a Red Cross Nurse, in a room and attempts to defile her. He breaks down the door (as a metaphor for her body), then tears her clothes, and murders the infant she clutches to her breast (when its cry upsets his sexual thrall). The sheer depravity of his act is accentuated by his lascivious grin and by his obsessive shifting of his monocle.

By the time of *Blind Husbands* and *Foolish Wives*, the von Stroheim villain is more of a 'lounge lizard' than a rapist – though sometimes his behaviour crosses the line. (An advertisement for *Foolish Wives* calls him 'the swaggerest villain that ever lied his way into a pretty woman's heart'[6]). In *Blind Husbands*, von Steuben employs flattery in hopes of winning the sexual and monetary favours of Margaret Armstrong. But, on one occasion, his actions veer toward physical assault. He surprises Margaret one morning when she is half-dressed and, in the course of making advances, grabs her. In *Foolish Wives*, Karamzin's actions are more decadent and pernicious. When he tricks Helen Hughes into staying the night at the cabin (which seems set in Transylvania), he approaches her bed (like Dracula) as though to ravish her while she is dazed. Like Nosferatu, his plan is ultimately foiled by the entrance of a priest. (Significantly, a review of the film called him a 'super-he vamp'[7].) Karamzin later attempts a debasement of Ventucci's sleeping daughter – only to be deterred by her father who awakens, kills him, and stuffs his body into the sewer. In *The Social Secretary*, von Stroheim's character was named *Buzzard* and his gossip column deemed '*carrion copy*'. Extending this theme, *Foolish Wives* leaves Karamzin as rotting flesh – a scavenger's meal.

The European: An Officer and a Gentleman

> Until now when we have started to talk about the uniqueness of America we have almost always ended by comparing ourselves to Europe. Toward her we have felt all the attractions and repulsions of Oedipus.
> – Daniel Boorstin[8]

If von Stroheim's monocle signalled voyeurism, it might also have registered cultured, blue-blooded, *Europeanism* and this, too, was part of his *persona*. In a sense, then, he was the quintessential, masculine 'Other' to the American consciousness. During his early career, due to hostilities between the United States and Germany, his Continental image was associated particularly with the Teutonic – a fact that played on his Austrian heritage. In *For France* (1917), directed by Wesley Ruggles, he appears as a Prussian officer; and in *Hearts of the World* (1918), directed by D.W. Griffith, he is cast as a 'Hun'[9]. In *The Heart of Humanity*, however, von Stroheim stars as the loathsome von Eberhard – 'scion of the Prussian military autocracy'. Likewise, in Alan Crosland's *The Unbeliever* (1918), von Stroheim depicts Lieutenant Kurt von Schnieditz, an evil German officer who murders Belgian women and children[10]. In *The Hun Within* (1918), directed by Christy Cabanne, he enacts the role of a German spy who tries to enlist German-Americans in sabotage. Finally, in *Blind Husbands*, the character of von Steuben is, culturally, Prussian (if literally Austrian).

Even von Stroheim's depiction as a twisted rapist drew on specific characterizations of that period. As Susan Brownmiller has noted, the German military was charged with having perpetrated brutal assaults on women, beginning with its invasion of Belgium in 1914[11]. She quotes J.H. Morgan, a law professor of the era, who wrote that: 'Outrages upon the honour of women by German soldiers have been ... frequent'[12]. Once asserted, such heinous acts functioned as potent tools of political persuasion. As Brownmiller observes: 'In the hands of skilled Allied manipulators, rape was successfully launched in world opinion ... as a *characteristic German crime*, evidence of the "depraved Boche" penchant for warfare by atrocity ... Neutral America was the chief target of the propaganda technicians from both sides of the fence ... "The Rape of the Hun" became an instant byword in this country'[13]. Such portrayals appeared not only in epic and melodramatic texts but in comedies as well. In Charlie Chaplin's *Soldier Arms* (1918), a scene occurs in which a Belgian woman (befriended by The Tramp) is threatened by a Prussian officer.

Interestingly, in the European cinema of the period, the enemy was sometimes represented as a potential lover rather than as a mere brute. In *Maudite soit la guerre* (a French film of 1914), a German man (studying aviation in Belgium before the war) falls in love with a local woman. When the international conflagration erupts, he must return to Germany and ends up having to fight against her brother also his good friend. The tone of the film is decidedly pacifist and, when the two men die, the Belgian woman mourns both deaths equally. In another film from France, *Alsace* (1915), a Frenchman (living in German territory) falls in love with a woman of Prussian heritage. Though they marry, their national and political differences eventually surface and lead to a tragic end.

In America, however, the national enemy was generally positioned as the cinematic villain, and von Stroheim's billing drew upon this theme. As Harold D. Lasswell notes: 'So great are the psychological resistances to war in modern nations that every war must appear to be a war of defence against a menacing ... aggressor. *There must be no ambiguity about whom the public is to hate*' (emphasis added)[14]. There was, certainly, no ambivalence in the voice of the reviewer for *The Evening Mail* who, in 1919 saw *Blind Husbands* as: 'an expose of the Teutonic character'. He saw von

Steuben as an 'Officer of the Hun forces "invalided" to the Tyrolean alps after the war, [who] preys upon all womankind and proves to be a victim of the moral leprosy common to officers who served under the double eagle'[15].

Clearly, in this era, von Stroheim's monstrous image was conceived as serving a *didactic* purpose for the American male. As von Stroheim recalled in 1941, his 'job was to arouse hate so that [they] ... would get so stirred up [they] would be ready to go over and gouge out the stomach of the first German soldier he saw'[16]. This is precisely how Robert Yost imagined audience response in 1919:

'Things reached a point where ordinarily sane men, after witnessing von Stroheim with his arrogant Prussian ways and his German clothes would go home and melt up the baby buggy, fashion it into a trench knife and go downtown to join the marines'[17].

While von Stroheim clearly profited financially from his loathsome image, it is not so obvious what he gained psychologically from the audience's rabid antipathy. It seems only certain that he savoured it with an enthusiasm bordering on masochism: 'I have played [these roles] myself to be sure ... [to] draw out the maximum amount of hate'[18]. Perhaps, he was really The Man Who Loved To Be Hated.

By the time of *Foolish Wives* (some three years after the war ended), von Stroheim's aristocrat had become the Russian Count Karamzin – a more neutral European figure who might even have won initial audience sympathy as an apparent refugee from the controversial Soviet revolution. Implicit in von Stroheim's depiction as a European (for an American audience) was his imperial and cosmopolitan bearing. His characters appealed to the egalitarian American's retrograde fascination with titled nobility, an element that lured the films' naive heroines (and, perhaps, some viewers) into his protagonists' romantic traps. When Karamzin wishes to impress Mrs. Hughes, he pays a hotel bellboy to page him, emphasizing the word 'Count'. (Interestingly, von Stroheim seemed subject to the same deviousness as his alter-egos). While he represented himself as 'Count Erich Oswald Hans Carl Maria Stroheim von Nordenwall' – the son of a count and

Fig. 3. The quintessential European: von Stroheim, as Count Karamzin in *Foolish Wives*, seems a perfect gentleman as he courts Mrs. Hughes (Miss Dupont).

of a baroness – Richard Koszarski states that he was really the child 'of a Jewish dry-goods merchant'[19].

But it is von Stroheim's sexual sophistication that is most compelling – with its aura of decadence and dandyism[20]. Again, such eroticism was part of America's image of a jaded Europe, which as Cushing Strout has observed, had come to represent both a 'playground' and 'a school of instruction through amusement'[21]. Hence, it is no accident that we find Dr. and Mrs. Armstrong vacationing in the Alps or that the Hughes are stationed in the resort town of Monte Carlo. It is within this atmosphere that von Stroheim's suavely degenerate Don Juans operate – with their smirking leers, with their lip-licking wickedness, with their sensual drags on oversized cigarettes, with their feminized manicures and sprays of cologne, with their lesbian companions and questionable *ménages-à-trois*, with their associations with witches, hunchbacks, 'simpletons' and the like. It is precisely this ambience that led certain critics to

view his film as especially European. A *Variety* reviewer calls *Foolish Wives* 'revolting ... from an American standpoint'. He notes that it was probably 'produced with a view to distribution possibilities in other countries as well; certain European countries ... where the weakness of the American woman ... will be taken for granted as the usual thing'[22]. As Frederick James Smith writes in *Motion Picture Classic*, von Stroheim's films are: 'not for the provincial or the prude. Von Stroheim has taken the one real theme of life – sex – and played upon it with Continental discernment and, let us say, abandon'[23]. Among the Continental imports to which Smith may have been referring were French films like *Un coup de feu dans la nuit* (1916) and *La scandale* (1918) – which both concerned wives' infidelities. The sensational tone of von Stroheim's films led some conservative groups (like the Daughters of the American Revolution and the Women's Vigilant Committee) to call for their censorship[24]. *Foolish*

Wives was banned in Ohio, and a reviewer for the *Albany Knickerbocker Press* claimed that censors 'should have the right to bar such a photo drama in its entirety'[25]. It was deemed by *Photoplay* as an 'insult to every American'[26] (Curtiss, 133) as well as a 'gruesome, morbid, unhealthy tale ... unfit for the family to see'[27]. The *Variety* reviewer felt that the film was especially offensive because of von Stroheim's national roots: 'If written by an American, it would be pretty rough, but when stuff like this is handed out by a foreigner (von Stroheim is an Austrian), it's aggravating'[28].

The surveyed

If von Stroheim's fictional victims were, primarily, American women, how were their off-screen counterparts positioned within a social historical frame? A review of the films in question suggests the configurations of that placement.

Working girls and new women

> The habit and the taste for freedom, adventure, and economic independence is becoming generated among millions of women who once merely trod the ancient beaten paths, and we must not be so foolish as to suppose that they can suddenly renounce those habits and tastes at the threshold of marriage.
> – Havelock Ellis[29]

The Social Secretary concerns an attractive young woman named Mayne (Norma Talmadge) who is employed in a clerical capacity. The premise of the narrative is that problems ensue when a beautiful woman enters the work force. In Mayne's first job, she is romantically pursued and harassed by her boss, an official of the New York Purity League. The second post for which she applies advertises for a *homely* secretary (since the employer has had a series of comely young women quit to get married). In order to secure the position, Mayne masquerades as a frump. Given what we have learned about sexual abuse, *The Social Secretary* seems way ahead of its time.

Clearly, the film reveals certain tensions about females in the work place during an era in which woman's position was radically changing[30]. As Sara M. Evans states, in this period: 'growing numbers of working women in blue-collar, clerical and service occupations ... reshaped the parameters of female experience. By 1890, 19 per cent of women over sixteen years old were in the labour force'[31]. Their economic autonomy led to a measure of personal freedom as they lived independently as 'bachelor girls'[32]. As Evans notes, '[t]he flapper, so identified with the 1920s, was already a powerful image by 1913'[33]. Similarly, Robert L. Daniel has commented how, in this era, 'the public print explored birth control, prostitution, divorce and sexual morals on an unprecedented scale. "Victorianism" became an epithet'[34]. The collapse of conventional morality is registered in *The Social Secretary* through anxieties concerning Mayne's sexual liberty and being.

In other films associated with von Stroheim we see intimations of the 'New Woman' – the middle-class female who moved beyond the cult of domesticity into the realm of employment or volunteer service. In *The Heart of Humanity*, Nanette is a rural French Canadian who marries her sweetheart on the eve of World War I. When fighting breaks out and her husband enlists, she remains home and bears their first child. As the war progresses, however, she becomes dissatisfied with her passive position – particularly when she learns that European children have been wounded and orphaned. As the intertitles proclaim: 'Louder and louder came the cry of the baby voices from afar. The great motherly heart of Nanette awoke'. Hence, she volunteers as a Red Cross nurse and is assigned to the front lines. It is here that she is assaulted by Erich von Eberhard and goes temporarily insane.

While Nanette does not literally conform to the prototype of the urban New Woman, there are suggestions of that figure in Nanette's depiction. According to Evans, one of the major professions that the New Woman selected was nursing[35]. Furthermore, those that did not seek employment often did volunteer work with such organizations as the National American Woman Suffrage Association, the Women's Christian Temperance Union and the settlement house movement. But *The Heart of Humanity* also reflects the specific actions of women in World War I. According to Dorothy and Carl J. Schneider, of the 25,000 American women who volunteered on the European front, some 10,000 nurses and 4,610 female relief workers were sent by the American Red Cross[36]. In particular, many of these volunteers were concerned with the plight of children. In 1915, Mary Roberts Rinehart wrote *Kings Queens and Pawns* from the perspective of An American Woman at the Front – describing those she had seen running soup kitchens or staffing hospitals. Hence, despite Nanette's Canadian nationality, her experience draws on the practices of women in the United States – her primary viewing audience[37].

In von Stroheim's own films, we are more so-

Fig. 4. A trade advertisement for *Foolish Wives.*

guilt [and] evil'[40]. It is within this context that we find Margaret Armstrong and Helen Hughes – credulous women fascinated and repulsed by the European male's nobility and intriguing *savoir faire*. Significantly, a poster for *Foolish Wives*, featuring von Stroheim, addresses this theme. It predicts that '[w]omen [will] watch this heart-breaker in wonder' and will be taught 'things they never dreamed of'[41]. An ad promises that 'he's going to fascinate your women patrons

lidly within the realm of the upper-middle-class. The fact that *Blind Husbands* and *Foolish Wives* are set in Europe is indicative of the fact that such travel had become common, if not *de rigeur* in leisured, bourgeois circles. As Strout notes, 'Despite the narrow limitations of the orthodox Grand Tour, Americans displayed a broa[d] zest in going to Europe ... By the early twentieth century there were already familiar signs of an American invasion'[38]. Interestingly, an advertisement for *Foolish Wives* proposes it as an ersatz *trip*: 'Fling wide the doors on a life of luxury, self-indulgence, beauty, wealth, power ... You've read about it ... Dreamed about it ... Hoped some day to see it ... Here it is more real than a personal visit could reveal ... Monte Carlo, the hidden dramas of passion – intrigue'[39].

Despite their growing sophistication, Americans were often viewed as 'innocents abroad', and, for them, 'the Old World was a dark one, evocative of

with his maddening knowledge of their true motives.' While the ad lauds von Stroheim's urbanity, other sources feared it. The *Albany Knickerbocker Press* warned of the film's 'psychological effect' 'upon thoughtless young women'[42].

In *Blind Husbands* and *Foolish Wives*, the American matron's gullibility, however, leaves her unprepared for the European male's sinister connivances – which seek to put her in a compromising position. Again, this vision of duplicity taps contemporary stereotypes of the Teutonic. As a commentator of the period stated: '[o]ne of the most subtle tendencies of the German character is the hypocritical lie, which appears under the guise of naive sincerity'[43]. Hence, the importance of such an image as Karamzin mugging for the camera and shedding crocodile tears as he tricks his maid, Maruschka (Dale Fuller), into surrendering her life savings.

While Margaret Armstrong and Helen Hughes are not shown to work outside the home, employment is never ruled out as a possibility for them on the homefront. In fact, as Robert L. Daniel, has noted many traditional married women had experienced prior independent lives: 'the New Woman wanted to sample both marriage and a career ... Completing school, she secured a job and left home for an apartment of her own. She met and dated males who were unknown to her family, but in the end she quit her job, married one of these men, and submerged herself in home and family'[44].

While the issue of career is elided from *Blind Husbands* and *Foolish Wives*, the spirit of the New Woman 'returns' around questions of marriage and sexual politics. For both Mrs. Armstrong and Mrs. Hughes are dissatisfied with matrimony and have allowed themselves to explore its alternatives – however tentatively. It is important to recall that, in this era, women who 'once had married for economic security, now ... were to marry for love' – a fact which placed greater demands on the matrimonial bond[45]. Furthermore, as Ethel Maud Colquhoun notes, many marriages of this period dissolved after the first decade because 'other men offer[ed] [women] the homage and consideration which they no longer receive[d] from their husbands'[46]. Finally, the 'word divorce no longer suggest[ed] social ostracism'[47]. Given this framework, it is not surprising that a review of *Blind Husbands* reports that von Stroheim has tackled 'a problem all too frequent in American married life'[48]. Interestingly, around the time of the film's release a syndicated national column announced a contest which inquired: 'What Makes an Ideal Husband'?. The promotional copy in *The Cumberland Evening Times* read as follows:

> What do you think? The *Evening Times* has asked a number of charming women to name the points they think an ideal husband should possess ... What is the most important characteristics a husband should possess? Write your opinion in 200 words and mail it to the Woman's page editor. The best opinions will be published[49].

The newspaper also printed a response from one Helen Worthing, who stated that: 'The one quality in [the] love of a man for a woman that the wife most appreciates in her husband is a deep romantic tenderness. The rock on which most marriages split is the failure of the husband to continue to be the lover'[50]. No better precis of *Blind Husbands* (or *Foolish Wives*) could be written.

Women of the teens and twenties were also beginning to have a sense of their own erotic potential through learning of the work of European 'sexologists' like Havelock Ellis[51]. For him, traditional marriage was based on inequality: 'the sovereign husband resembles the Sovereign State'[52]. Furthermore, he felt that matrimony stifled woman's sexual desires: 'the marriage order ... [has] led to the indirect result of banning pleasure in women, or at all events in wives'[53]. Finally, Ellis validated woman's wish for more emotional consideration in marriage – though he viewed the issue in essentialist terms: 'The desire of women for courtship is not a thing by itself ... It is naturally intertwined – and to a much greater degree than the corresponding desire in men with her deepest personal, family and social instincts'[54]. Consonant with the thoughts of Helen Worthing, he even suggested that 'it is often the lover more than the husband that the modern woman needs'[55]. Ellis concludes that 'the marriage question to-day is much less the wife-problem than the husband-problem'[56].

It is within this framework (of the 'husband-problem') that we might understand the marital discontent and romantic curiosity of Mrs. Armstrong and Mrs. Hughes. An opening title of *Blind Husbands* blames the male for forgetting his 'wooing skills', for leaving his woman available to the 'other man'. In an early scene, as the couple breakfasts in the hotel dining room, Dr. Armstrong reads a newspaper and disregards his wife. When he ignores her again one evening, she compares her situation to that of affectionate newlyweds honeymooning at the same resort. It is into this vacuum that the calculatingly debonair von Steuben enters (asking her 'How can one love alone'?). In his first encounter with Margaret, he gallantly offers her a stool and a blanket for relaxing on the hotel veranda (courtly acts he manages to invest with lust). He later asks her to go away with him and she does not dismiss him out of hand. As Richard Koszarski has noted: 'That Margaret stops even to consider the attentions of von Steuben was a daring break with tradition'[57]. Significantly, the narrative annihilates von Steuben for his affront. As Thomas Quinn Curtiss remarks: 'In Europe

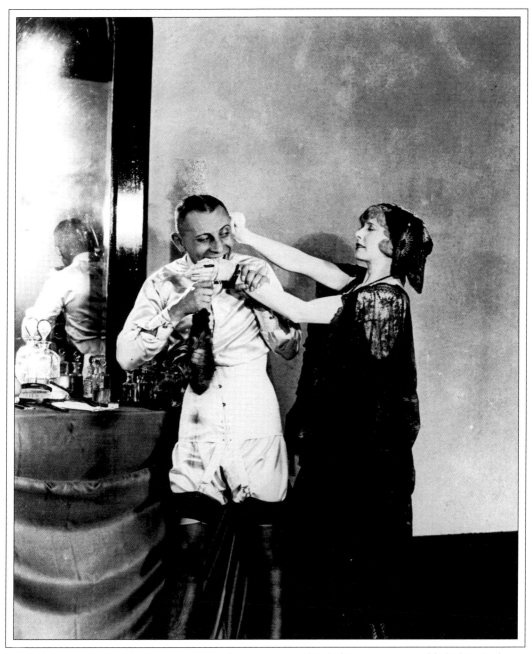

Fig. 5. A figure of decadence, von Stroheim also represents a kind of passion presumably lacking in the American male. This scene from *Foolish Wives* with Mae Busch was cut from the finished film.

it was thought that the official Puritanism of the producers required von Steuben to pay with his life for having attempted to seduce a married American woman'[58]. Ultimately, the figure of von Steuben is employed to teach American men an emotional lesson – that modern women need 'love' (as von

Eberhard was utilized to teach men the need for patriotism and courage). As von Stroheim once stated (giving his films a pretentiously pedagogical rationale): 'If I can cause the blind husbands who go to my picture to see the light, to be more considerate, more companionable, more chivalrous toward their wives I will have accomplished a great good'[59].

In *Foolish Wives*, Karamzin, again, represents the passion allegedly lacking in the American male – as evidenced by the Count's residence in the Villa *Amorosa*. As one of his female cohorts makes clear, he is successful with American wives because they are generally lonely – wedded to workaholic males. In Mr. Hughes' absence, Karamzin is continually solicitous of Helen: discussing her book, kissing her hand, sending her flowers, flattering her. ('I hope Mr. Hughes' business affairs will detain him indefinitely'.) Clearly, Karamzin thinks that Mr. Hughes is a fool. 'Husbands are stupid', he remarks; 'With them a woman won is a woman secure'. When Mr. Hughes becomes annoyed at Karamzin's omnipresence, his wife retorts, rebelliously: 'Please, Andrew, don't try to choose my friends for me – remember – I'm free – white and twenty one'. Interestingly, in the original six-hour version of *Foolish Wives* there was a subplot involving Mr. Hughes' *own* 'amorous temptations', but it was excised from the film to reduce its running time. This motif, of course, resonates with the assumptions of the era that conceived men as 'instinctively polygamous'[60].

But, if von Stroheim's films present unconventional aspects of the New Woman, they also reinforce traditional roles. In *Blind Husbands*, Dr. Armstrong is an obstetrician and it is when he leaves to deliver a baby that von Steuben pursues his wife. There is a sense that if Margaret, herself, had fulfilled her maternal mission, she would not have been in moral jeopardy. (Similarly, in *The Heart of Humanity*, had Nanette remained home with her *own* child, she would not have fallen into von Eberhard's clutches.) In the release print of *Foolish Wives*, this message was even more explicit. In the three and one half hour version that premiered in New York City, Mrs. Hughes gives premature birth to a baby after her traumatic rescue from Karamzin's burning villa. (Curiously, neither she nor the audience seemed previously aware of her pregnancy.) It is at this moment that she is reconciled with her husband, who reads to her a passage from her book about 'a foolish wife who found in her own husband the nobility she had sought for in a counterfeit'. Hence, her return to the marital fold coincides precisely with her ascension to maternity – and is, thereby, secured by it. Significantly, in this era, even 'Feminists of all

persuasions ... agreed that the chief fulfillment of a woman's life was motherhood'[62]. With maternity, Helen Hughes becomes a 'natural woman' – no longer 'counterfeit' herself.

Interestingly, von Stroheim used a birth metaphor to describe his annoyance with the excision of this and other sequences from *Foolish Wives*. He told *New York Tribune* columnist Hariette Underhill that the version she had seen was only 'the skeleton of [his] dead child'.

Citizens of the world

> The greatest things that remain to be done must be done with the whole world for stage and in cooperation with the wide and universal forces of mankind ...
> – Woodrow Wilson[63]

With the exception of *The Social Secretary*, all of the films examined portray Americans[64] abroad – a significant issue for the period between 1918 and 1921. (Even *The Social Secretary* includes the despicable character of a foreign count.) Significantly, it was during this era that the United States struggled with questions of isolationism *vs* internationalism around American involvement in World War I and participation in the League of Nations. As Woodrow Wilson told his constituency: 'We are provincials no longer'[65]. According to Strout, many conservatives opposed to such global ventures imagined the United States 'as a virtuous innocent victimized by a wily, guilty Europe caught dealing from the bottom of the deck'[66]. Clearly, parallels to von Stroheim's *persona* are apparent in this representation of the shady Continental preying on the trustful American naif.

Hence, one might read his films as parables of America's foray into world citizenship. But while, on the surface, works like *The Heart of Humanity* or *Hearts of the World* present a patriotic justification of internationalism, they also record fears of its cost. Significantly, these misgivings are recorded primarily on the female body – in the attempted rapes of Nanette and The Girl (Lillian Gish)[67]. In *Blind Husbands* and *Foolish Wives* the danger persists, but outside the military context – in the elegant landscape of a tourist's and diplomat's Europe. Again, it is mainly woman who stands in for the endangered Motherland: Mrs. Armstrong and Mrs. Hughes. (Here, I am reminded of a contemporary Barbara

Kruger photograph depicting a woman's face, which bears the caption: 'Your body is a battlefield'.)

While the European male (von Schnieditz, von Eberhard, von Steuben, or Karamzin) slyly ravages the American female, her man proves inadequate to the onslaught – as evidenced by Mr. Hughes awkwardness as a husband and as an attache. (As a reviewer for *Moving Picture World* noted: 'The American diplomat was made into a bowing, scraping jackass ... [and] the entire play was a studied and flippant slam at all things American[68].) But a more interesting (though peripheral) figure is the American soldier whom Mrs. Hughes encounters repeatedly in the hotel and thinks rude for not retrieving her dropped book. As she later discovers (when his cape slips off), he is armless – an amputated victim of the war. It is this image of symbolic castration and impotence[69] that finally moves her and makes her regret her hasty valorization of the debonair European at the expense of the mundane American – of the 'counterfeit' for the 'real'. The reviewer for *Moving Picture World* felt that von Stroheim's 'cheap sneering at the supposed bad manners of American marines could better have been omitted'. He concluded: 'The [film's] final flag waving couldn't save it'[70].

Hence, the works associated with von Stroheim tell a tale of modernity and lost innocence on both a public and personal register. Within that scenario, von Stroheim is an American enemy on two battlefields: that of world politics and that of heterosexual relations. As a couple in Monte Carlo says of Karamzin in *Foolish Wives*, his reputation is truly *'International'*.*

Notes

A shorter version of this paper was delivered at the XVth IAMHIST Conference on 'Film and World War I' in Amsterdam (5–11 July 1993). The conference was sponsored by the Netherlands Filmmuseum and the University of Amsterdam.

1. See: Laura Mulvey, 'Visual Pleasure and Narrative Cinema', in *Visual and Other Pleasures* (Bloomington and Indianapolis: Indiana University Press, 1989) 14–26; Linda Williams, 'When the Woman Looks' in Mary Ann Doane, Patricia Mellencamp, Linda Williams, eds., *Re-Vision: Essays in Feminist Film Criticism* (Frederick, MD: The American Film Institute, 1984) 83–99; Lucy Fischer, *Shot/Countershot: Film Tradition and Women's Cinema* (Princeton: Princeton University Press, 1989) 89–110; Tania Modleski, *The Women Who Knew Too Much: Hitchcock and Feminist Theory* (New York and London: Methuen, 1988).
2. While little attention has been given, recently, to von Stroheim, Miriam Hansen has considered in depth audience reaction to Rudolph Valentino – who was adored by many, but (like von Stroheim) hated by others. See Hansen, *Babel & Babylon: Spectatorship in American Silent Film* (Cambridge, MA: Harvard University Press, 1991) 243–268.
3. Jean Baudrillard, *Seduction* (New York: St. Martin's Press, 1979), 6.
4. S.J. Perlman, *The Most of S. J. Perlman* (New York: Simon and Schuster, 1958), 596.
5. Thomas Quinn Curtiss, *Von Stroheim* (New York: Farrar, Straus and Giroux, 1971), 132.
6. Herman Weinberg, *Stroheim: A Pictorial Record of his Nine Films* (New York: Dover, 1975), 371.
7. 'The Banishment of the She-Vamp ...', *Norringstown News* 1 May 1920).
8. Daniel Boorstin, *America and the Image of Europe: Reflections on American Thought* (New York: Meridian, 1960), 11.
9. According to Peter Noble, the Prussian aspect of what developed into the von Stroheim stereotype began with his work on John Emerson's *Old Heidelberg* (1915). He was the 'Supervisor of Military Details' and an actor in the role of a Prussian officer.
10. Lawrence Suid, 'The Marines in World War One Films', paper delivered at the XVth International IAMHIST Conference on 'Film and World War I', Amsterdam, 5–11 July 1993.
11. Susan Brownmiller, *Against Our Will: Men, Women and Rape* (New York: Bantam, 1975), 34.
12. *Ibid.*, 36.
13. *Ibid.*, 37–38.
14. Harold D. Lasswell, *Propaganda Technique in World War I* (Cambridge, MA: MIT Press, 1927) 47.
15. *'Blind Husbands'*, *The Evening Mail* (25 October 1919).
16. Robert Dana, 'Von Stroheim Finds His Face Doesn't Fit the War', *New York Herald Tribune* (2 February 1941).
17. Robert Yost, 'Gosh How They Hate Him'! *Photoplay* (December 1919) 80, 82, 123.
18. Jane Dixon, 'Ugh! The Most Hated Man in the World', *Evening Telegram* (11 December 1919).

19. Yost, 80; Celia Brynn, 'An Hour With a Villain', *Picture Play* (November, 1919) 60–61; Richard Koszarski, *An Evening's Entertainment: The Age of the Silent Feature Picture, 1915–1928* (New York: Scribner's, 1990), 235.

20. Perlman, 595.

21. Cushing Strout, *The American Image of the Old War* (New York: Harper & Row, 1963), 111, 109.

22. Bell, '*Foolish Wives*', *Variety* (20 January 1922).

23. Frederick James Smith, 'The Celluloid Critic', *Motion Picture Classic* (April 1922).

24. Weinberg, 35.

25. '*Foolish Wives*', *Albany Knickerbocker Press* (12 March 1922).

26. Curtiss, 133.

27. '*Foolish Wives*', *Photoplay* (March 1922).

28. Bell, *Variety*.

29. Havelock Ellis, *Little Essays of Love and Virtue* (New York: Doran, 1921, 1922), 93.

30. For a good discussion of the working woman on film during the teens and twenties, see Sumiko Higashi, *Virgins, Vamps, and Flappers: The American Silent Movie Heroine* (Montreal: Eden Press, 1978).

31. Sara M. Evans, *Born for Liberty: A History of Women in America* (New York: The Free Press, 1989), 164.

32. *Ibid.*, 169.

33. *Ibid.*, 169.

34. Robert L. Daniel, *American Women in the 20th Century: The Festival of Life* (New York: Harcourt Brace Jovanovich, 1987) 21.

35. Evans, 147.

36. Dorothy and Carl J. Schneider, *Into the Breach: American Women Overseas in World War I* (New York: Viking, 1991), 287, 289.

37. Mary Roberts Rinehart, *Kings Queens and Pawns: An American Woman at the Front* (New York: Doran, 1915).

38. Strout, 110.

39. Weinberg, 37.

40. Strout, 127.

41. Weinberg, 37.

42. '*Foolish Wives*', *Albany Knickerbocker*.

43. Lasswell, 79.

44. Daniel, 23.

45. Lois W. Banner, *Women in Modern America: A Brief History* (New York: Harcourt Brace Jovanovich, 1974), 117–118.

46. Ethel Maud Colquhoun, *The Vocation of Woman* (London: Macmillan, 1913), 86–87.

47. *Ibid.*, 88.

48. '*Blind Husbands*', *Variety* (5 December 1919).

49. 'What Makes an Ideal Husband'? *Cumberland Evening Times* (29 October 1919).

50. *Ibid.*

51. Evans, 171.

52. Ellis, 86–87.

53. *Ibid.*, 106–107.

54. *Ibid.*, 107.

55. *Ibid.*, 101.

56. *Ibid.*, 75.

57. Richard Koszarski, *The Man You Love to Hate* (New York: Oxford University Press, 1983), 42.

58. Curtiss, 103–104.

59. Dixon.

60. Colquhoun, 84–85.

61. Weinberg, 40; Koszarski, *The Man You Love to Hate*, 80.

62. Banner, 119.

63. Boorstin, 20.

64. Nanette is a North American (from Canada, not the United States).

65. Boorstin, 20.

66. Strout, 167.

67. The Girl is a character in Griffith's *Hearts of the World* (1918). She is assaulted by the character of von Strohm.

68. 'A Million! A Million'! *Moving Picture World* (January 21, 1922).

69. Interestingly, Sumiko Higashi finds the American husband in von Stroheim's films 'curiously asexual', 186.

70. 'A Million'! *Moving Picture World*.

Book Reviews

Hollywood's overseas campaign. The North Atlantic Movie Trade, 1920–1950.Ian Jarvie, Cambridge University Press, NY, 1992, 473 pp. ISBN 0-521-41566-7.

an Jarvie's study of the motion picture trade among Canada, the United Kingdom and the United States may well be the first *diplomatic* history of the film industry. It is diplomatic not so much in terms of its style or tact but in terms of its focus and methodology. Jarvie examines the diplomacy involved in the international trade in motion pictures. He constructs his diplomatic history out of a vast array of primary documents – both published and unpublished – generated by the United States Department of Commerce and State Department, the Hays Office, the British Board of Trade, and other governmental and quasi-governmental bodies. These official documents are supplemented with speeches and debates in British Parliament, the papers and letter of individuals working in the film industry or in trade offices, and materials found in various public archives, ranging from the Canadian Film Archives and the British Imperial War Museum to the National Archives (USA) and the libraries of American Presidents Hoover, Roosevelt, and Truman. If nothing else, Jarvie's book is a *tour de force* of first-rate primary research.

Using this material, Jarvie reconstructs the role of Joseph Kennedy, US Ambassador to Great Britain during World War II, in negotiating dollar exchange and remittance agreements on behalf of American film companies. His research reveals the hidden agenda of Harold Wilson, then president of the British Board of Trade, in the 1948 negotiations; at that time, Wilson sought to shift the lion's share of profits in the first-feature or 'A' picture market from American to British product by reclassifying all British films, regardless of their quality, as first features or 'A' pictures on all double bills, thus relegating many quality American films to 'B' picture status and revenues when they played alongside British product. John Grierson emerges as a savant, whose understanding of the structure and practices of the American film industry, enabled him to put Canadian filmmaking on the map. Thus Grierson concentrated the efforts of the National Film Board of Canada on documentaries rather than on fiction films, for which the domestic market had been cornered by Hollywood.

One of the chief strengths of the book lies in its

methodology – or, more exactly, its point of view. Much as a successful diplomat must understand the perspective and needs of the foreign representatives with whom he or she deals, so Jarvie adopts the guise of the diplomat in the organization of his book. He looks at the phenomenon of 'North Atlantic Movie Trade' from a series of different national perspectives, beginning with a Canadian viewpoint of trade with the US (and Great Britain), then shifting to a British understanding of trade with Hollywood,

Hollywood's Overseas Campaign

THE NORTH ATLANTIC MOVIE TRADE, 1920–1950

IAN JARVIE

dominance of American films in overseas markets, specifically in Canada and Great Britain. Jarvie suggests that the primary reason for American success is economic; it is due to the structure of the American film industry, the marketing strategy adopted by that industry, its capitalization, the vast supply of films it could provide, its success in distributing them, and the assistance not only of the US government but also of the industry's own trade organization, the Motion Picture Producers and Distributors of America (the

and finally presenting an American take on doing business with (primarily) Britain. Previous histories of national cinemas have tended to consider them in a vacuum or in terms of an adversary relationship with a dominant Other, such as the US. Adopting a suitably modernist approach (resembling that of Welles in *Citizen Kane* 1941), Jarvie's successive collage of different and often opposed points of view results in a portrait of international economic relationships that acquires a cumulative force. The nature of these relationships emerges gradually and indirectly (almost 'maieutically', to borrow an adjective Annette Michelson uses to describe Vertov's editing strategies) over the course of the book as a consequence of the process of juxtaposition rather than being presented directly and didactically.

The stated goal of the book is to explain the

MPPDA), later known as the Motion Picture Association of America (the MPAA).

A graduate of the London School of Economics, Jarvie tends to foreground economic issues over all others. Though he generalizes about the content of Hollywood films and their potential appeal to Canadian and British audiences, he does not examine individual films in terms of the specific values which audiences might find in them. And though he repeatedly talks about audiences in Canada and Britain and their passion for American films, he provides no specifics. He decries the omission of the desires of British audiences from the various discourses by British government officials on film quota legislation, but provides no research or data which might confirm the existence, make-up and interests of this audience. Though technology, in the form of sound (but not colour), plays something of a role in Jarvie's account, technological determination remains a minor factor. The coming of sound enabled overseas producers to provide their audiences with films in which their native language – or (in the case of English) dialect – was spoken, thus undermining, albeit briefly, Hollywood's hegemony.

In other words, the problem with Jarvie's argument is that it assumes an audience which prefers American films to its own cinema, but it fails to explore this assumption in depth and gives little textual evidence to support it. Of course, it is extremely difficult to talk about audiences and audience taste and/or preference. As a result, Jarvie sidesteps this issue and, instead, grounds his thesis in data which is more easily documented and proven. Yet Jarvie's assumptions about audience preferences hang over the argument like a cloud. He presumes that audiences are drawn to American films because those films are more populist; they convey values that are supposedly attractive to Canadians and Britains – values which their own cinemas do not readily provide them. Thus Hollywood films espouse an ideology of egalitarianism, capitalism and individualism. Canadians identified with Hollywood's 'social' vision, in part, because they shared a common experience in nation building on the American continent; in this respect, at least, Canadians had more in common with Americans than they did with Britains.

British cinema, according to Jarvie, was 'too West End' for mass tastes. The vast majority of films tended to reflect the tastes and concerns not of the British empire or of the United Kingdom (England, Scotland, Wales and Northern Ireland) but of a single city – London – and of a single district within that city – the West End. British producers, on the other hand, tended to view American films as a threat both to British culture and to traditional social structures. American films promoted 'an ideology different from the paternalistic form of democracy developed in Britain'. Slapstick comedies ridiculed authority; thesis dramas portrayed businessmen and politicians in a bad light.

American egalitarianism undermined class structure. 'There was no place for deference and respect to those set over us; ... the British ruling élites ... were correct to fear the American product, because it portrayed a successful society that rejected

deference'. In 1918, the United Kingdom had extended the vote to all adult males and, in 1928, women were enfranchised. American films raised concerns among the 'ruling elites' that these newly-enfranchised masses would fall victim to 'manipulation by the mass media'. American mass culture threatened to undermine the élitist culture of the upper classes.

As the creation of lower class Jews, Hollywood realized the American dream both on screen and off. Both characters and movie stars relived the Horatio Alger plot line in which an average person's virtues and energies were rewarded by success. At the same time, in Hollywood films (and in the movie palaces where they were seen), elegance is transformed into a mass commodity that could be purchased by anyone for the modest price of a movie ticket. Made for a multi-ethnic mass (the American population), Hollywood films fared better around the world than did British films, which were made for a much less diverse audience.

To some extent, the discourse surrounding the movie trade is grounded as much in issues of nation as in those of class. Within this discourse, American films are seen to espouse American ideals, to present an American vision of social, political and economic relations, and to encourage audiences to think the way Americans do. Hollywood films threaten to Americanize the world. In resisting this form of cultural colonialism, champions of Canadian and British cinema adopt the language of nationalism.

During the debates over the 1927 quota act (the Cinematographic Films Bill), Sir Philip Cunliffe-Lister noted that 'the cinema is today the most universal means through which national ideas and national atmosphere can be spread, and, even if those be intangible things, surely they are among the most important influences in civilization'. For this reason, Britain must not permit foreigners to dominate the media. But beneath this nationalism lay an imperialist subtext. British cinema must be protected if the British empire is to be preserved. Jarvie repeatedly reads these debates in terms of a reactionary, élitist agenda. Those defending the imposition of quotas speak on behalf of special interest groups within the industry rather than on behalf of the average moviegoer.

Hollywood's domination of Canadian and British screens was, indeed, genuinely monstrous. In

Canada, where only a handful of films were produced, roughly 98 per cent of all films screened were American (during the 1922–28 period). During this same period, Hollywood's market share was roughly 95 per cent in Britain and 99 per cent in the Colonies and Dominions. The bulk of Jarvie's book seeks to explain this success and the reactions of the Canadian and British film industry to it.

The argument found in traditional histories is that Hollywood took advantage of the disruption in film trade caused by the outbreak of World War I to improve its position in foreign markets. This explanation remains more or less accurate. In *Exporting Entertainment*, Kristin Thompson dates the American campaign to improve its overseas market to December, 1916, citing a State Department memo instructing consuls to provide the film industry with information about foreign markets. But she also notes that American penetration of the British market began years before the outbreak of war. By 1911, US films accounted for 60–70 per cent of all imports.

The formula for Hollywood's success, however, lay more in its business practices and trade strategy than in accidents of war. American firms established film exchanges throughout the world. These exchanges were staffed by industry representatives who not only sold films but analysed changes in the overseas markets and reported these changes back to their superiors in the United States. With one or two exceptions, British producers failed to set up overseas sales offices and rarely engaged in an analysis of overseas markets.

More importantly, Hollywood enlisted the US Department of Commerce and the State Department to gather data related to motion picture production, distribution and exhibition around the world. In 1926, the Department of Commerce established a Motion Picture Division, which was charged with providing information to the film industry on the overseas movie trade. Jarvie reprints several government memos enlisting the cooperation of commercial attachés and consuls in furthering the interests of the American film industry abroad.

Unlike Britain, which formed no comprehensive trade strategy, American films established a trade organization that worked in tandem with government agencies and that represented the industry's interests abroad. This trade organization was the

MPPDA, headed by Will Hays. In a fascinating and novel argument, Jarvie insists that though the chief function of the MPPDA or Hays Office, involved industry self-censorship, it also served a more economically significant purpose – to promote overseas trade.

Starting in 1922, Hays slowly put together an umbrella organization that would cohere the various interests of the American studios. As part of its duties, the MPPDA established uniform contracts within the industry, standardizing a crucial area of its business practices. It also served to channel the data gathered by US government agencies abroad back to film executives in New York and Hollywood. In his dealings with foreign governments, Hays functioned as if he were a state official, serving as a goodwill ambassador for the film industry, lobbying foreign governments to eliminate restrictions on American films, and negotiating trade agreements.

Though Jarvie acknowledges the need to restrict American imports in order to ensure the survival of the British film industry, he regards certain aspects of the quota legislation as unnecessarily biased. For example, he refers to the British Cinematograph Films Act as 'the major piece of anti-American film legislation in the world'. And he suggests that the blockage of remittances to US producers was unfair. 'On what theory of international trade', he asks, 'was a government [British] entitled to treat the export earnings of the industry of another nation as funds somehow misappropriated or diverted, and hence ripe to be sequestered and used to build up their own competing industry'?

One of Jarvie's best points is that American films had a positive effect in Britain, that created an audience for all sorts of motion pictures, including British product. He argues that 'British films owed their existence to … the exhibition industry created by the American product. Thus there was an art of British film, not despite the power of the US majors, but because of it'.

The average reader – as well as the economically obtuse film scholar like myself – will find topics such as quotas, triple quota credits, dollar balance and remittances, blocked balances, product spread, and ad valorem duty rather difficult to fathom. Jarvie tends to assume some familiarity on the part of his audience with complex economic terminology; as a result, the specifics of the economics of the movie trade are not always clear.

The book's greatest virtue is also its greatest flaw: its richness of detail and its attempt to reconstruct, blow by blow, the various debates over quota legislation subject the reader to a certain excess of information and occasional tedium. Jarvie's study strives to be the final word on the subject – and it succeeds in this endeavour. But much as the advocates of film quotas ignored the desires of movie audiences, Jarvie does not always think of his own.

Earlier versions of sections of Jarvie's book were initially published in *Film History* as 'Dollars and Ideology: Will Hays' Economic Foreign Policy', vol. 2, No. 3, and 'The Postwar Economic Foreign Policy of the American Film Industry', vol 4, No. 4. *Hollywood's Overseas Campaign* was winner, in the business category, of the 1993 Kraszna-Krausz Award for Books on the Moving Image.✻

John Belton

Correspondence

Dear Editors,

In the *Film History* issue devoted to exhibition (vol. 6, no. 2), Robert Sklar asserts in the introduction to his essay, 'Hub of the System: New York's Strand Theater and the Paramount Case', that some current historians have neglected the implications of exhibition when discussing the Hollywood studio system. I do not disagree with his assertation that exhibition 'has yet to receive *detailed* scholarly attention' (emphasis mine). However, Sklar then provides a footnote that states: 'The *Paramount* case does not appear in the index of David Bordwell, Janet Staiger and Kristin Thompson, *The Classical Hollywood Cinema: Film Style and Mode of Production to 1960...*'.

While the statement is literally true, the implication is not. The term 'divorcement' does occur in the index, and several pages of text are devoted to discussing the case's implication for shifting modes of exhibition, distribution and production. Moreover, throughout the book, exhibition is introduced when it is a pertinent factor ot the questions we are addressing. I respectfully request that this correction be noted by readers of *Film History*.

Sklar should be pleased that in Thomas Schatz's forthcoming volume on the 1940s for the Scribner's American film series, Schatz discusses the implications of the anitrust case at length, and I contribute a forty-page chapter on exhibition and audiences. So some of this detailed scholarly attention is already being accomplished by the individuals Sklar believes should be doing the work.

Yours sincerely,

Janet Staiger

Back issues of Film History – volumes 1-5 (1987-93)

Volume 1, Number 1, 1987

'We Can't Get Much Spinach': The Organization and Implementation of the Fleischer Animation Strike, by Harvey Deneroff

Jack London and the Movies, by Robert S. Birchard

A World Across from Broadway: The Shuberts and the Movies, by Kevin Lewis

G.W. Pabst in Hollywood, by Jan-Christopher Horak

'No Problems. They Liked What They Saw on the Screen': An Interview with Joseph Ruttenberg, by Richard and Diane Koszarski

Volume 1, Number 2, 1987

The Western, 1909-1914: A Cast of Villains, by Peter Stanfield

Hungry Hearts: A Hollywood Social Problem Film of the 1920s, by Kevin Brownlow

National Film and Video Storage Survey Report and Results, by Stephen Gong

French and British Influences in Porter's American Fireman, by Martin Sopocy

Commercial Propaganda in the Silent Film: A Case Study of A Mormon Maid, by Richard Alan Nelson

A World Across from Broadway (II): Filmography of the World Film Corporation, 1913-1922, by Kevin Lewis

Volume 1, Number 3, 1987

United States of American vs. Motion Picture Patents Company and others: Brief for the United States

Volume 1, Number 4, 1987

Between Reform and Regulation: The Struggle Over Film Censorship in Progressive America, 1909-1922, by Nancy Rosenbloom

Marriage – The Ideal and the Reel: or, The Cinematic Marriage Manual, by Lisa L. Rudman

The Hand That Rocks The Cradle: An Introduction, by Kay Sloan

The Hand That Rocks The Cradle: The Original Continuity, by Lois Weber and Phillips Smalley

The Production of George Stoney's Film All My Babies: A Midwife's Own Story, by Lynne Jackson

Review – Before Hollywood: Turn-of-the-Century Film From American Archives, by Robert S. Birchard

Volume 2, Number 1, 1988

The Armat-Jenkins Dispute and the Museums, by H. Mark Gosser

The Moving Picture World of W. Stephen Bush, by Richard L. Stromgren

The Black Action Film: The End of the Patiently Enduring Black Hero, by Mark A. Reid

Early Home Cinema and the Edison Home Projecting Kinetoscope, by Ben Singer

The Great Northern Film Company: Nordisk Film in the American Motion Picture Market, by Ron Mottram

$NR = MC^2$: Rossellini, Neo-Realism, and Croce, by Tag Gallagher

Volume 2, Number 2, 1988

Life After Divorce: The Corporate Strategy of Paramount Pictures Corporation in the 1950s, by Timothy R. White

Labor Power and Organization in the Early U.S. Motion Picture Industry, by Michael C. Nielsen

Include Me Out: Samuel Goldwyn and Joe Godsol, by Kevin Lewis and Arnold Lewis

Cabiria, an Incomplete Masterpiece: The Quest for the Original 1914 Version, by Paolo Cherchi Usai

From Edendale to E.H. Allen: An Interview with Jack White, by David N. Bruskin

Volume 2, Number 3, 1988

The Making (and Unmaking) of Pull My Daisy, by Blaine Allan

Dollars and Ideology: Will Hays' Economic Foreign Policy, 1922-1945, by Ian Jarvie

Cel Animation: Mass Production and Marginalization in the Animated Film Industry, by David Callahan

The Key Animation Patents, Bray-Hurd

Professional Results with Amateur Ease: The Formation of Amateur Filmmaking Aesthetics, 1923-1940, by Patricia R. Zimmermann

In the Morning, by Erich von Stroheim

Volume 2, Number 4, 1988

The Spectre of Joan of Arc: Textual Variations in the Key Prints of Carl Dreyer's Film, by Tony Pipolo

Orson Welles, George Schaefer and It's All True: A 'Cursed' Production, by Richard B. Jewell

Iwasaki and the Occupied Screen, by Erik Barnouw

The Development of Cinemascope, by Herbert E. Bragg

The Films of Mabel Normand, by Betty Fussell

Four Tributes: Jean Mitry, Jay Leyda, George Pratt and Jacques Ledoux, by William Gilcher, Elena Pinto Simon, Herbert Reynolds and William K. Everson

Volume 3, Number 1, 1989

The First Moving Picture in Arizona – or Was It? The Tragic Tale of C.L. White's Marvelous Projectoscope Show in Arizona and New Mexico Territories, 1897-1898, by George C. Hall

The Edison – Biograph Patent Litigation of 1901-1907, by Martin Sopocy

Film History: Index to Volume 6

FILM HISTORY

Back issue and subscription order form

PLEASE SUPPLY:

.... Subscription(s) to *Film History*
at Institutional/Private rate (please specify)
Surface/Air Mail (please specify)

.... Back issues of the following volumes/issues

....
....

I enclose payment of £/US$ ....
Please send me a Pro-forma invoice for: £/US$ ....

Please debit my Access/Master Card/Visa/
American Express/Diner's Club credit card:
Account no..Expiry..........

Name ....
Address ....
....
....
.... Zip/Postcode ....

Signature ....Date ....
(This form may be photocopied)

SUBSCRIPTION RATES & BACK ISSUE PRICES

Institutional Subscription rates:
All countries (except N. America)
Surface mail £70   Air mail £80
N. America
Surface mail US$126   Air mail US$144
*Private Subscription rates (subscribers warrant that
copies are for their PERSONAL use only):*
All countries (except N. America)
Surface mail £30   Air mail £40
N. America
Surface mail US$54   Air mail US$72
Back issues: All issues available – Volumes 1 to 4:
£5/US$10 each number; Volume 5 on: £10/US$20.

JOHN LIBBEY & COMPANY LTD,
13 Smiths Yard, Summerley Street,
London SW18 4HR, UK.
Tel: 081-947 2777 – Fax: 081-947 2664

FILM HISTORY

An International Journal

Aims and Scope

The subject of Film History is the historical development of the motion picture, and the social, technological and economic context in which this has occurred. Its areas of interest range from the technical and entrepreneurial innovations of early and precinema experiments, through all aspects of the production, distribution, exhibition and reception of commercial and non-commercial motion pictures.

In addition to original research in these areas, the journal will survey the paper and film holdings of archives and libraries world-wide, publish selected examples of primary documentation (such as early film scenarios) and report on current publications, exhibitions, conferences and research in progress. Many future issues will be devoted to comprehensive studies of single themes.

Instructions to Authors

Manuscripts will be accepted with the understanding that their content is unpublished and is not being submitted for publication elsewhere. If any part of the paper has been previously published, or is to be published elsewhere, the author must include this information at the time of submittal. Manuscripts should be sent to the Editor-in-Chief:

Richard Koszarski
American Museum of the Moving Image
36–01 35th Avenue
Astoria, New York, NY 11106, USA

excepting for submissions to thematic issues directed by one of the Associate Editors.

The publishers will do everything possible to ensure prompt publication, therefore it is required that each submitted manuscript be in complete form. Please take the time to check all references, figures, tables and text for errors before submission.

Form: Please wherever possible submit manuscripts on diskette – IBM format (preferably)